Individual Conduct and Social Norms

Individual Conduct and Social Norms

A Utilitarian Account of Social Union and the Rule of Law

Rolf E. Sartorius
University of Minnesota

Dickenson Publishing Company, Inc.
Encino, California and Belmont, California

ISBN-0-8221-0148-3
Library of Congress Catalog Card Number: 74-27744

Printed in the United States of America
Printing (last digit): 9 8 7 6 5 4 3 2 1

To my parents, wife, and children,
without whose encouragement and understanding
this book would never have been written

Contents

The Dickenson
Series in Philosophy

Philosophy, said Aristotle, begins in wonder—wonder at the phenomenon of self-awareness, wonder at the infinitude of time, wonder that there should be anything at all. Wonder in turn gives rise to a kind of natural puzzlement: How can mind and body interact? How is it possible that there can be free will in a world governed by natural laws? How can moral judgments be shown to be true?

Philosophical perplexity about such things is a familiar and unavoidable phenomenon. College students who have experienced it and taken it seriously are, in a way, philosophers already, well before they come in contact with the theories and arguments of specialists. The good philosophy teacher, therefore, will not present his subject as some esoteric discipline unrelated to ordinary interests. Instead he will appeal directly to the concerns that already agitate the student, the same concerns that agitated Socrates and his companions and serious thinkers ever since.

It is impossible to be a good teacher of philosophy, however, without being a genuine philosopher oneself. Authors in the Dickenson Series in Philosophy are no exceptions to this rule. In many cases their textbooks are original studies of problems and systems of philosophy, with their own views boldly expressed and defended with argument. Their books are at once contributions to philosophy itself and models of original thinking to emulate and criticize.

That equally competent philosophers often disagree with one another is a fact to be exploited, not concealed. Dickenson anthologies bring together essays by authors of widely differing outlook. This diversity is compounded by juxtaposition, wherever possible, of classical essays with leading contemporary materials. The student who is shopping for a world outlook of his own has a large and representative selection to choose among, and the chronological arrangements, as well as the editor's introduction, can often give him a sense of historical development. Some Dickenson anthologies treat a single group of interconnected problems. Others are broader, dealing with a whole branch of philosophy, or representative problems from various branches of philosophy. In both types of collections, essays with opposed views on precisely the same questions are included to illustrate the argumentative give and take which is the lifeblood of philosophy.

Joel Feinberg
Series Editor

Acknowledgments

My intellectual debt to others is too enormous to begin to document here. I would, however, like to express my special appreciation to those who were kind enough to give me their most helpful critical comments on the first draft of this book: Norman Dahl, Joel Feinberg, Barry Hoffmaster, and Thomas Kearns.

I am most grateful to the American Council of Learned Societies for a fellowship during my sabbatical year 1972-73 when this book was written. Support from the Graduate School of the University of Minnesota is also gratefully acknowledged.

Chapter 4 contains portions of my "Individual Conduct and Social Norms: A Utilitarian Account," originally published in *Ethics*, Vol. 82, No. 3, April, 1972, © 1972 by the University of Chicago.

Chapter 5 contains portions of my "Utilitarianism and Obligation," which originally appeared in the *Journal of Philosophy*, Vol. LXVI, No. 3, February 13, 1969.

Chapter 8 incorporates my essay "The Enforcement of Morality," which is reprinted here by permission of The Yale Law Journal Company and Fred B. Rothman & Company from *The Yale Law Journal*, Vol. 81, No. 5, April, 1972, pp. 891-910.

Chapter 10 contains portions of my article "The Justification of the Judicial Decision," originally published in *Ethics*, Vol. 78, No. 3, April, 1968, © 1968 by the University of Chicago; as well as portions of my "Social Policy and Judicial Legislation, originally published in the *American Philosophical Quarterly*, Vol. 8, No. 2, April, 1971.

I am grateful to the editors of the above journals for their permission to reprint the material indicated above.

1   *Introduction*

Utilitarianism in its classical form—as advocated by Jeremy Bentham and, I believe, John Stuart Mill—is the ethical theory according to which the rightness or wrongness of a particular act depends solely upon the goodness or badness of the consequences of that act. It is this moral theory, act-utilitarianism, that I shall elaborate upon and defend in the present essay. I shall not attempt to defend it against all or even most of the many serious criticisms that have been leveled against it, but only against a closely knit family of objections all of which relate to its supposed inability to account for the possibility and desirability of general social norms. For what has been claimed is that a stable social order depends for its existence upon the widespread acceptance of rules and principles which prohibit the individual agent from entering into the very sorts of deliberations which utilitarianism seemingly demands of him. If men are to successfully associate with one another as moral agents under the rule of law, it has been argued, they must, to at least some degree, abdicate the freedom of individual judgment which is associated with the employment of the act-utilitarian principle. "Life would be chaotic," writes Richard Brandt, "if people tried to observe . . . a straight directive to do the most possible good."[1] In a recent paper, Jeffrie Murphy has put the objection this way:

> [I]f one is going to decide each case solely upon its merits as one sees them, then there is no sense to the notion of social rule or the rule of law as a social decision procedure. And it is this realization, I think, which is at the heart of the belief that there is such a thing as political obligation—a prima facie obligation to obey the law as such.[2]

[1]Brandt, "Merits," 58. (*Note:* Complete bibliographical information for all source notes can be found in the Reference Bibliography at the end of this book, pp 219-226.)
[2]Murphy, "Obligation," 44-45.

The view here is not that promises, for instance, must always be kept, come what may, or that the law must always be obeyed, whatever the consequences—but rather that a viable social organization depends upon certain kinds of acts predictably occurring with a degree of regularity which simply could not exist in a situation where each individual felt free to decide how to act in particular circumstances simply upon the basis of an estimation of what the likely consequences of his act would be. The predictable regularities in human behavior upon which a stable social union depends, it is argued, are rooted in the acceptance of general rules and principles which at least sometimes bar the individual agent from acting upon the basis of a direct utilitarian calculation. To put it another way, the claim is that the members of a community must be able to rely upon their fellows fulfilling their social *obligations*. The contention is that such obligations are based upon the acceptance of general social norms of a sort which can have no place in an act-utilitarian ethic. For the act-utilitarian, it has been claimed, social rules can have the status only of rules of thumb—rough guides to action which are totally devoid of the prescriptive force which characterizes a rule of obligation.

It is here in the notion of obligation, and the related concept of a social norm, that the conceptual fulcrum of the present work is to be found. For to speak of an individual's social obligations is to speak of what may be legitimately expected of him by the members of a community to which he belongs, and in virtue of his status within which he has the norm dependent obligations that he has. The philosophical perplexity in general, and the problem for the utilitarian in particular, is to account for the bonds of social union in terms of the shared expectations generated by the general acceptance of moral, political, and legal norms within a community.

I agree, in other words, with the contention that social community in general, and political association in particular, depend upon the existence of shared social norms and accepted social decision procedures which admittedly do, in a manner which remains to be specified, bar direct appeals to utility on the part of the individual agent. The problem is to show that such norms and procedures, far from being inconsistent with the individualistic moral principle of act-utilitarianism, can in fact be understood as being based upon it.

Although the position defended in this essay is avowedly utilitarian, it is my intent to elaborate a general structural account of the relationship between individual conduct and social norms which will hold interest even for those who are unable to accept a utilitarian ethic. For in most general terms what I seek to show is that one can consistently hold to an individualistic moral principle of a kind which bases the rightness or wrongness of any given act solely upon that act satisfying certain criteria which are to be applied by the agent, while at the same time, and on the basis of the very same criteria, one can support social norms which prohibit the application of those criteria in determining the morality of particular acts. In adopting such a general perspective, I am not only committing myself to the view that one single account can span the diversity of social norms associated with the notions of moral, political, and legal obligation; I am also urging that many of the apparently independent concerns of moral, political, and legal philosophy are in fact one: To explain the bonds of social union.

Utilitarianism is a theory of moral reform, and my chief concern shall be to elaborate its prescriptive implications with respect to certain primary features of a moral social order under the rule of law. Given the nature of the general problem sketched above, though, it should be clear that much of the analysis will of necessity revolve around Kantian questions of the form: "How, within an act-utilitarian framework, could such and such be possible?" Also, on occasion, I shall be intent upon providing a description of social practices and institutions as they in fact are. Concern with these three types of questions, the prescriptive, the Kantian, and the descriptive, may naturally merge—as indeed it does both in my discussion of promissory obligation and in my account of the rule of law. In both instances, what is at issue is the possibility of providing an act-utilitarian rationale for the salient features of familiar practices which do and should play a central role in our social lives.

The book, in brief, is organized as follows:

Chapter 2 presents the theoretical framework within which my account of social union and the rule of law proceeds. Various forms of utilitarianism are discussed, and my reasons for choosing to adopt and elaborate upon act-utilitarianism are indicated. The concept of utility is developed in terms of the notion of preference, and my position with respect to the important problem of interpersonal utility comparisons is then sketched. Whose utility counts, and when, as well as how it is to be taken into account, is also dealt with. Finally, the metaethical status of act-utilitarianism is treated, especially with respect to what have been called "our considered moral judgments."

Chapter 3 is a brief excursus into the theory of definition necessitated in large part by the extremely curious things that have been claimed for and about definitions of such terms as 'legal system' and 'valid law', terms which obviously must play a considerable role in any account of the rule of law, including my own. The putative moral relevance of definitions of such terms is shown to be spurious, and real definition as an analytic tool is rejected as being worthless, if not in general, at least within the confines of the present enterprise. What takes the place of appeals to the notions of analyticity and necessary truth in my own account is then described.

Chapter 4 turns to the theoretical core of my overall argument. An act-utilitarian account of social norms as more than rules of thumb or summary rules is developed in full generality, and the role which such conventional rules can play as reasons for action within an act-utilitarian framework is then explained. My chief concern here is to illuminate in the broadest possible terms the manner in which, and the reasons why, an act-utilitarian can support social norms which bar direct appeals to utility while retaining the freedom to deviate from them on direct utilitarian grounds. Since I believe that such rules provide the foundation for the reciprocal expectations upon which a stable social order depends, most of the remainder of the book is devoted to exploring the implications of this general account with respect to different kinds of social rules and principles, particularly those of obligation—moral, political, and legal.

Chapter 5 contains an account of social obligation in general, and moral obligation in particular, with primary attention being given to promissory obligation, both because of its intrinsic importance, and because of its role in contractual theories of political obligation. Coupled with the previous chapter, Chapter 5 is meant to complete the general structural analysis of the relationship between individual conduct and social norms which many critics of act-utilitarianism have claimed this theory is unable to provide.

Chapter 6 applies the foregoing general account to political obligation, including questions concerning the nature and justification of civil disobedience. It is argued that both classical and contemporary political philosophy share the same mistaken perspective on the character of the citizen's obligation to obey the law; viz., that government rests either upon the effective wielding of coercive force or expertise by those in power, or else upon the general recognition by citizens of a mutual obligation to obey the law as such. Within the framework of the general theory developed in Chapters 4 and 5, another alternative is developed and defended, one which permits the moral autonomy which would be denied by the acknowledgment of a moral obligation to obey the law as such to be retained by the individual citizen without implying either that government is virtually infallible or that it is a bare power organ. Majority rule as a favored form of social decision procedure from a utilitarian point of view is also discussed.

Chapter 7 is concerned with what many have taken to be the most fundamental principles of a moral social order: those of justice, both distributive and retributive. Here again we encounter the view that there are principles of social union which require a subordination of considerations of utility, and thus the all too ready conclusion that the act-utilitarian is incapable of accounting for one of the most significant dimensions of our social experience. John Rawls's is the theory of distributive justice examined and found to be wanting, both intrinsically and as a basis for a sound objection to utilitarianism. A positive account of principles of distribution is then sketched. Retributive justice is next considered, and an attempt is made to show that act-utilitarianism does no violence to those aspects of our notions of moral responsibility and desert which are worth saving.

Chapter 8 also deals with various aspects of the fundamental structure of a just society; as with the previous chapter, again at the level of basic moral rules and principles as well as central features of the design of political and legal institutions. Institutional guarantees of the opportunity to compete for favored economic and social positions are briefly discussed, as are traditional liberal ideals concerning political freedom. The bulk of the chapter, though, is devoted to a discussion of personal liberty as the freedom from interference with self-regarding conduct. It is here that I consider Mill's view that the members of a moral social order would recognize an absolute prohibition on the enforcement of social norms which have as their aim the protection of individuals against themselves. Not only do I seek to refute the charge that Mill's anti-paternalism is inconsistent with his act-utilitarianism; I also seek to show that Mill was well aware of the general line of argument which this essay seeks to develop, one which has broad implications concerning the possible justification for the kinds of principles established by the Bill of Rights as well as the more specific issues which emerge from a consideration of the current heated controversy concerning the enforcement of morality through the vehicle of the criminal law.

Chapter 9 begins with a number of questions concerning the rule of law, surely the primary means of achieving social order in a pluralistic advanced industrial society such as our own. What is the rule of law? What are the conditions necessary for its effective maintenance? What are the moral implications of having achieved it? My own answers to these questions emerge in large part in response to Lon Fuller's views concerning what he has called "the internal morality of law" and the nature of adjudication as a distinctive form of social decision procedure, the very sorts of things of which we have seen it claimed that the act-utilitarian can make no sense. Especially in the concluding section of this chapter, I argue that the act-utilitarian can, as he must, make good sense indeed of the rule of law.

Chapter 10 is directed to a central question raised but left unanswered by the argument of the preceding chapter: What is the role of extra-legal standards, particularly moral ones, in the justification of judicial decisions made within the framework of a constitutional democracy which has adopted the ideal of the rule of law? This issue is dealt with as just one aspect of the general problem of characterizing the institutional role and responsibility of the judiciary in terms of the decisional standards appropriate for the justification and criticism of judicial decisions. Once again, the general theory developed in Chapters 4 and 5, now extended to account for the relationship between individual conduct and social norms where the norms in question are constitutive of the judicial role, provides the basis for my argument. In terms of it, I seek to reconcile two persistent but apparently incompatible jurisprudential theses: (1) The responsibility of the judge within a constitutional democracy is to apply the law rather than make it; in all cases he is confined by his role to the task of discovering the correct decision to which the litigants are entitled as a matter of legal right; (2) In at least some cases, the law which the judge is bound to apply will not determine a uniquely correct decision; in such cases the judge must exercise personal discretion and choose among extra-legal principles—perhaps the act-utilitarian principle itself—as a basis for decision. At this point his role has become that, not of an adjudicator, but of a legislator of social policy.

In conclusion, Chapter 11 attempts to tie together the various pieces of my overall account of social union and the rule of law. In particular, I am concerned here to relate my discussion of the institutional role and responsibility of the courts in applying the law to my discussion of the citizen's obligation of obedience to law.

The Appendix reprints in its entirety Section 12 of Book IV, Part XI of Mill's *Principles of Political Economy*. Although the present essay is far from historical in character, my considerable sympathy with what I take to be the chief themes in the writings of Mill and Hume on matters of normative ethics and political theory should be evident. Late into the writing of the first draft of this essay, I read Mill's *Principles* for the first time. While the bulk of that book is now of little interest to other than economic historians, my reasons for believing that this section is well worth reprinting will be clear to those who have followed my own argument concerning the relationship between individual conduct and social norms.

Chapters 1, 2, 4, and 5 thus contain the main argument; Chapter 2 being a methodological digression which can be passed over without loss of continuity. Chapters 6-8 are relatively independent treatments of issues which will be of greatest interest to those whose chief concern is with political philosophy. Chapters 9 and 10, which are in turn independent of 6-8, speak to (some of) the concerns of the philosopher of law.

2 *Utilitarianism*

The present chapter contains a brief sketch of the theory of utilitarian ethics upon which my account of individual conduct and social norms is based. Although in some instances arguments are either lacking or merely hinted at, and in others questions are raised without being answered, I have in the main sought to indicate my views on the most important of the controversial issues which exist within the framework of a general utilitarian position. No attempt is made to acknowledge, let alone to meet, the bewildering variety of objections which have been made to utilitarianism. Although I believe that most of them are without foundation, it would be impossible to give careful consideration to them all within the compass of a single work. What I do seek to do within the scope of the entire essay is to elaborate upon and answer one closely related family of objections to utilitarianism in general, and to act-utilitarianism in particular.

1. Sources of the Theory's Appeal

The chief source of appeal for any normative theory should be its consonance with our considered moral judgments—a matter discussed below in Section 8. But two other sources of the persistent appeal of utilitarianism should, at the outset of a work such as this, at least be mentioned. Although far from profound, in combination they provide very strong reasons for taking seriously the defense of utilitarianism against putative objections.

Firstly: although there may be no necessary truths in moral philosophy (or anywhere else, for that matter), the utilitarian dictum that one is to do that which is likely to have the best consequences does have the ring of the obvious. What more, and what less, could morality reasonably demand of the conscientious moral agent than that he seek to promote the good? And what

9

more reasonable conception of the good could one have than the utilitarian one: that that (and that alone) which is good is that which is conducive to the happiness of sentient creatures? For what else could be of value, and to whom could it be of value, without its being of utilitarian value?

Secondly, there is the appeal, both at the theoretical and at the practical level, of the structural simplicity of a utilitarian ethic. For, regardless of the form of utilitarianism adopted, any utilitarian theory is ultimately concerned only with the maximization of a single moral value. Although some non-utilitarian theories, such as ethical egoism, may share it, this feature of utilitarianism is notably lacking in the kinds of theories usually considered as serious alternatives to a utilitarian position. The consequences of this are much more serious than is often admitted. A theory (like W.D. Ross's[1]) which postulates a number of independent prima facie duties—such as to tell the truth, keep promises, avoid needless suffering, and promote justice—must acknowledge the possibility of such duties coming into conflict. For example, to prevent an injustice from being done, I may have to break a sincere promise, or tell a lie. How are such conflicts to be resolved? By doing that which has the best utilitarian consequences when there is a conflict among prima facie duties, and otherwise (where there is no conflict) doing one's duty? But if among one's prima facie duties is a duty of general benevolence, then the theory is covertly utilitarian, for no case could possibly arise where it was obligatory to do something which was not likely to have the best consequences. For any case which was apparently of this sort would present a conflict of duties, one between the duty of general benevolence and some other prima facie duty, and in cases of this kind, by hypothesis, one is to do that which will have the best consequences. On the other hand, if a deontological theory denies any place to a duty of benevolence, it is wildly implausible on its face, and still left with the original problem of conflicts among those duties that it does recognize. And if it does recognize a prima facie duty of benevolence, but does not permit it to take priority over other duties in cases of conflict, it is again left with the original problem. To answer, as Ross does, that one is to *intuit* which of one's conflicting prima facie duties is one's actual duty is to provide no solution at all, either in theory or in practice. The serious deontologist must recognize that he has no theory as an alternative to utilitarianism until he has given a structural account of the relations amongst

[1]W. D. Ross, *The Right and the Good.*

the prima facie duties which he posits which would make possible the assigning of relative weights and priorities amongst them. The magnitude of the difficulty is testified to by the conspicuous absence of attempts to come to grips with it.[2]

To illustrate by way of the problem of civil disobedience, which will be discussed at greater length in Chapter 6: many writers still hold to some version of the view that the citizen can be taken (under certain conditions) to have given his tacit consent to some form of social decision procedure (for example, majority rule), this putting him under a prima facie obligation to obey any duly enacted law. Good liberals that they are, though, they also maintain that this obligation of obedience to law may sometimes be outweighed by other moral considerations. In particular, an act of civil disobedience calculated to bring about the legislative repeal of a racially discriminatory law, say, might be justified in terms of a duty to prevent injustice. What we are urged to consider is that a moral price has been paid in such a case because it is a moral obligation that has been, and had to be, overridden. Disobedience to law is a serious matter, and the existence of an obligation to obey the law puts the burden of proof upon the civil disobedient to justify his act by showing that countervailing moral considerations of sufficient weight actually exist.[3]

But just how is such justification to take place? How is one to compare the obligation to obey the law (which is at bottom a promissory obligation if it is taken to rest upon tacit consent), and the supposedly independent obligation to eliminate injustice? What could possibly be meant here by "weighing things up" if it is explicitly denied that there is a fundamental dimension of value in terms of which such different values are to be compared? As Sidgwick realized long ago,[4] this is not simply a problem for the deontologist, to be dealt with in due course as the science of morals advances; it is a conclusive objection to his "theory." For without a solution to this problem, the deontologist does not have a theory, but simply an unsystematized set of anti-utilitarian intuitions.

2. *Forms of Utilitarianism*

While critics of utilitarianism may be charged with having failed to put their objections in terms of a comprehensive alternative account, it may be complained that utilitarianism has

---

[2]But see Nozick, "Moral Complications."
[3]One of the more sophisticated expressions of this view is to be found in Waltzer, *Obligations.*
[4]Sidgwick, *Methods,* 406.

recently been shown to be faced with a genuine embarrassment of such theoretical riches. For not only has there been controversy concerning the historical question of just what form of the utilitarian principle Mill accepted;[5] it has seemed that there are almost as many forms of utilitarianism worthy of serious consideration as there are serious philosophers with express utilitarian sympathies. And, as might be expected, deep and often difficult questions have consequently been raised as to whether or not supposedly different forms of utilitarianism are really theoretically distinguishable after all.[6] Although the extensive literature on this problem cannot be reviewed here, I shall attempt to clarify some fundamental distinctions amongst various forms of utilitarianism, and to indicate the reasons why I have chosen to elaborate upon the theory in its classical form. As theories of objective right, three quite different principles may be distinguished as follows:

Act-Utilitarianism (AU): Act X is right if and only if the doing of X would have consequences at least as good as the consequences of performing any alternative act open to the agent.

Rule-Utilitarianism (RU): Act X is right if and only if the doing of X is in accord with a set of moral rules the general acceptance of which would have consequences at least as good as the general acceptance of any alternative set of rules.[7]

Utilitarian Generalization (UG): Act X is right if and only if it is a kind of act everyone's doing which under similar circumstances would have consequences at least as good as the consequences of everyone's performing any alternative act.

While according to AU it is always open to the agent to consider the likely consequences of any particular act, both RU and UG are explicitly designed to prohibit just this. While the justification of an act on AU grounds requires a demonstration that the consequences of performing *that act* are best; both RU and UG require the process of justification to proceed in a two-step manner. For RU, an act is in the first instance justified by showing that it is in conformity with a set of moral rules; further moral questions are to be answered by justifying the set of rules

[5]See J. O. Urmson, "Interpretation"; this paper, as well as many of the others referred to in this chapter, is reprinted in Gorovitz, *Mill.* Most recently, it has been argued that Bentham was not a utilitarian at all. See Lyons, *Interest.* My reasons for rejecting Lyons's novel reinterpretation of Bentham are stated in my "Review" of his book.

[6]The definitive work here is Lyons, *Forms and Limits.*

[7]Different versions of rule-utilitarianism may be obtained by substituting different expressions for 'general acceptance'. See for instance Brandt's carefully worked out notion of the *currency* of a set of moral rules in his "Merits."

in terms of the consequences of *their* adoption. Similarly for UG: An act in the first instance is justified by indicating that it is of a certain kind; further moral perplexities are to be resolved by justifying the general performance of *that kind* of act in terms of the associated consequences. As both RU and UG prohibit a direct appeal to consequences in the justification of the performance of an act, while AU permits this and only this, some acts which are justified on AU grounds will not be justified in terms of either RU or UG, and vice versa.

But do RU and UG really differ from one another? Indeed, might not the answer to the question "What would happen if everyone did that?"—the question which UG implicitly asks—be taken as the basis for an answer to the question, "What set of rules is it the general adoption of which would have the best consequences?"—the question which RU asks? It is here that one must exercise caution. If one speaks of *invariant conformity* to a set of rules, rather than of *general adoption* or *acceptance of* those rules, then RU and UG are indeed indistinguishable. For the consequences of everyone's always acting in manner K are surely identical with the consequences of everyone's invariably following the rule "Do K!" But the formulation of RU which has been presented above does not imply invariant conformity to the rules in question; understood rather in terms of the notion of general acceptance, it is meant to reflect the fact that the general acceptance of and conformity to social rules is typically accompanied by a significant number of instances of nonconformity. So RU and UG are seen to differ, in that with respect to any given standard of conduct the former asks us to consider the consequences of general but not universal conformity, while the latter asks us to consider the consequences of absolute conformity. With respect to at least some kinds of acts, this difference is surely a significant one.

There are, it seems, three closely related objections to AU which have inclined those with initial utilitarian sympathies to abandon it in favor of either RU or UG.

In the first place, it has been claimed that a specific act—of murder, promise-breaking, or what have you—might maximize utility and yet be wrong, or—as in the case of casting a non-crucial vote at some inconvenience in a democratic election —that some act which failed to maximize utility might be one's duty. Such unacceptable implications of AU may be avoided, it has been contended, by applying utilitarian considerations at a level which precludes the possibility of individuals applying the utilitarian test directly to particular acts.

Secondly, it has been claimed that even if there are no genuine counter examples to AU of the above sort, the situation in which each individual felt free to judge the morality of each act solely in terms of its consequences would be one of absolute social chaos. This objection is meant to call our attention to familiar human failings with respect to moral judgment, especially where one's own interests are involved. While it concedes that correct application of the act-utilitarian principle yields plausible judgments of objective right, it contends that attempts to apply the theory would so often lead to mistaken judgments about what really did have the best consequences that the theory, in practice, would be self-defeating.

The third objection is perhaps the most interesting. Like the first objection, it assumes the correct application of the act-utilitarian principle; like the second objection, it implies that the consequences of the adoption of AU—from a utilitarian standpoint itself—would be undesirable. Its basic contention is that there are valuable social practices which are to be understood in terms of constitutive moral rules which bar participants from deciding whether they will conform to the rules on direct utilitarian grounds. Such practices, it is argued, would not be possible within a society of act-utilitarians, and the good consequences of having them would thus be lost.

The differences amongst these three related objections may best be seen by considering how they would be brought to bear on the same kind of act: let us take promise-keeping as our example.

The first objection might run as follows: There are instances in which some slight net advantage would accrue from the breaking of a sincerely made promise, perhaps a suddenly realized advantage to the promiser himself tipping the scales, according to AU, in favor of nonfulfillment. But promissory obligations are not to be taken so lightly; "it had the best consequences" is not an acceptable reason for breaking a promise. [8]

The second objection would suggest that the adoption of AU, which would encourage people as a matter of course to consider breaking their promises, would result in many people thinking that they were maximizing utility by breaking their promises when in fact they were not. The discretion which AU would grant to promisers would be so often abused that not only would many wrongful acts of promise-breaking be performed, but the beneficial results of the practice would in large part be lost

[8] See W. D. Ross, *The Right and the Good*, 35, and Rawls, "Two Concepts."

because of the general erosion which would take place in people's confidence that promises will usually be kept.[9]

The third objection would hold that the practice of promise-keeping would be a virtual impossibility in a community within which it was common knowledge that all or most individuals were rational act-utilitarians. A sincerely made promise permits the promisee to tie down the future in advance more securely than he could otherwise do only because it warrants an expectation that the promiser will feel himself bound to keep his promise in a manner which precludes his deciding how to act solely upon the basis of what will have the best consequences. If A and B are rational act-utilitarians, A will have no particular reason to keep his promise to B to do X unless he believes that B expects him to do X *because he has promised to do so.* But B, being a rational act-utilitarian, and knowing that A is one, too, will only expect A to act so as to produce the best consequences. But this expectation he would have had of A regardless of whether A had promised to do X, and A will understand this. Thus A will have no reason to do X that he wouldn't have had if he hadn't promised to do it; his promise to B, in other words, could make no difference. The desirable consequences of being able to tie down the future in advance due to the knowledge that conventional practices concerning the making and keeping of promises are being generally adhered to would be lost amongst a society of act-utilitarians.[10]

On the face of it, both RU and UG, whatever their other merits or demerits, seem capable of meeting all three of these objections, for each would bar direct appeals to utility in the assessment of the morality of particular acts. But as is often the case with philosophical problems, the obvious, upon investigation, has proved to be anything but the case. Thanks in large part to the results of the detailed analysis contained in David Lyons' recent *Forms and Limits of Utilitarianism*, it must be concluded that there are inescapable difficulties of the most general kind with both RU and UG.

The basic objection to both RU and UG is simply this: neither permits consideration of the fact that the effects, and thus the morality, of specific acts often depend upon the way in which other people are acting. As they totally ignore this crucial dimension of human choice and action, they have unacceptable implications in a wide variety of cases. They both demand moral

[9]Nozick, "Moral Complications," 6-7, stresses this general type of consideration, although he does not apply it specifically to the case of promise-keeping.
[10]See Rawls, "Two Concepts," and Hodgson, *Consequences.*

idealism of the wrong sort, each requiring that one act on the basis of a consideration of hypothetical situations which may very well—indeed, typically do—fail to obtain.

Consider first rule-utilitarianism. In order to avoid moral conservatism of the very worst sort, the rule-utilitarian surely must avoid appealing of necessity to the moral rules which are in fact current in the society of which the agent (to whom the theory is directed) is a member. That members of a community might usually appeal to some shared social norms in justification of their acts surely cuts no normative ice—their norms, and thus the acts validated by them, might be grossly immoral. So it is in terms of some *ideal* set of rules—those the adoption of which *would* have the best consequences—that the rule-utilitarian must formulate his theory. But suppose, as is surely most often the case, that while doing X is what would be in conformity to the ideal set of moral rules, other people are not acting in the manner in which they would be if those rules were generally accepted, and *their so acting is a necessary condition for my doing X having good consequences.* Can it seriously be said that I ought to do X? Although some have claimed that the ideal set of moral rules would contain provisions which would permit one to consider how other people were acting, it is far from clear what form such provisions would take, and even less clear what a set of rules containing them would require.[11]

The difficulty with utilitarian generalization is essentially the same. UG bases the morality of any specific act upon a consideration of what the consequences would be of everyone's performing *similar* acts under *similar* circumstances. But when are acts and circumstances relevantly similar? In particular, in describing and distinguishing acts for the purpose of the application of UG, is it permissible to include a specification of the way in which others are behaving or are likely to behave? If the answer is in the affirmative, it may be demonstrated that UG is theoretically indistinguishable from AU.[12] If in the negative, the result is that UG, like RU, precludes a consideration of the fact that there are many acts the consequences, and thus the morality, of which depend upon the way in which other people are behaving—in particular, upon whether or not they are performing acts of the same kind. This—the proverbial straw that broke the camel's back—is of sufficient weight to force the rejection of

[11]See Brandt, "Merits"; Harrod, "Utilitarianism Revised"; Harrison, "Utilitarianism."

[12]Lyons, *Forms and Limits,* Chapter 3.

UG as worthy of serious consideration as a moral theory, let alone a utilitarian one.

Although the above objections strike me as conclusive, I would like to mention a second quite general objection to both RU and UG which has not been generally noticed. Any careful formulation of AU must be deliberately framed so as to take account of the fact that there might be more than one act which maximizes utility; what is required by the theory is not necessarily the performance of some unique utility-maximizing act, but simply the performance of one which is optimal in this respect. Do not the formulations of RU and UG require similar qualifications? Given the possibility of quite complex relations among the members of a set of moral rules, is it not clear that quite different sets of rules could have equally good consequences if generally adopted? Similarly, might there not be a number of quite different ways of everyone's acting in some particular set of circumstances all of which would maximize utility?

The formulations of RU and UG presented above were deliberately phrased so as to permit of just these possibilities. But consider the implications. To the extent to which alternative sets of utility-maximizing rules are conceivable, RU is indeterminate with respect to what it requires. To which set of ideal moral rules am I to conform my conduct according to RU? One may not respond, as one may in the analogous case of equally utile acts under AU, that it doesn't matter which. For suppose I found myself a member of a society in which there was general acceptance of a set of utility-maximizing rules, A; surely it is not the rule-utilitarian's intention that I be permitted to act in the manner dictated by a quite different set of rules, B, which *would* be equally optimific *were* they adopted. One can imagine adding some kind of a rider to RU to handle this kind of case, but what is one to do with the typical—if not universal—case where no set of utility-maximizing rules has found general acceptance, and one can conceive of a number of different possibilities? Although the clear intent of the rule-utilitarian must be to achieve convergence on some one set of moral rules amongst the members of a given community, it is not clear how the adoption of his principle could help to bring this about.

Similar remarks apply to UG. Different kinds of acts might be equally optimific, *if* everyone performed them; typically, no one kind of utility-maximizing act is being generally performed under given circumstances; and whether or not everyone's performing a given kind of act would be optimific must frequently depend upon what *other* kinds of act everyone was performing.

Unless one believes that there is some unique moral world which is the best of all possible worlds from a utilitarian point of view, it must be concluded that the thought experiments upon the performance of which the application of both RU and UG depend demand the impossible.

I choose, therefore, to return to act-utilitarianism as the only form of utilitarianism worth further exploring. As the sequel will show, I believe that the objections to it in terms of its putative inability to account for the role of social rules barring direct appeals to utility can be met, and that whatever is necessary for social union by way of shared social norms can quite consistently be generated within an act-utilitarian framework. Once this has been shown, perhaps the difficulties with RU and UG will not be lamented, but rather welcomed. For one form of plausible utilitarian ethics is surely enough.

3. *Act-Utilitarianism*

As formulated above, act-utilitarianism is the moral theory based upon the following principle: An act is right if and only if the consequences of performing it are at least as good as the consequences associated with the performance of any alternative act open to the agent.

Put as it is in terms of the actual consequences of the performance of an act, this is a principle of *objective* rightness; it operates most reliably only with the benefit of hindsight. But there is also good sense to be made of saying of someone that "he did the right thing," even though what he did in fact had bad consequences which would have been avoided had he chosen to do something else. For if he had good reason to believe that what he did would have the best consequences, he did all that could reasonably be demanded of him. Men are not infallible in their predictions about the future in general, or in their estimates of the likely consequences of their acts in particular.

If we wish to capture this notion of "doing the right thing," we may define a notion of *subjective* rightness as follows: An act is subjectively right if and only if the agent does it in the belief that it is objectively right (in the sense of having the best consequences). Whether or not the belief that an act is right (in either sense) is a *reasonable* belief is, of course, a different story.

While the notion of subjective rightness implies something about the agent's beliefs and motives (the expression 'acting *in the belief that'* was intended to capture this), neither the objective nor the subjective rightness of an act implies anything directly about the praiseworthiness or blameworthiness of the agent. For the act-utilitarian, praising and blaming, rewarding and punishing, and so on, are acts which like any other acts are to be evaluated in terms of their actual or intended consequences.

While these distinctions are elementary, and have been explicitly made by a number of writers,[13] they are so often overlooked by critics of utilitarianism that I believe it worth mentioning them here. There will be much more to be said about praise and blame, especially legal and social sanctions, in what follows.

It has frequently been complained that act-utilitarianism places intolerable demands upon the moral agent. One all too often is simply in no position to know what the consequences of one's acts will be, it has been said, and yet one would have to know just this sort of thing in order to know that one was acting rightly. A theory which implies the impossibility of so important a thing as moral knowledge, it is implied, is unacceptable.

Although the points are again elementary, three comments are in order: Firstly, except in a strict philosophical sense which is surely not relevant here, we know very well what the consequences of our acts will be in many significant instances. Secondly, even where there is substantial uncertainty, we may have reasonable beliefs as to which consequences are more likely than not, and the utilitarian asks us to do no more than act accordingly. Finally, the fact of the matter is that in some situations one is in no position to know what is the right thing to do, and yet one must do something. A failure to acknowledge this universal feature of the human situation by suggesting the possibility of moral certainty is to court not only moral, but psychological, confusion.

4.   *Whose Utility Counts, and How?*

Whatever may be the precise characterization given to the concept of utility (see Section 6 below), the questions of whose utility counts, and how it is to be taken into account, are far from unproblematic.

Leaving aside the question of whether or not creatures other than human beings are to be viewed as moral agents, the classical utilitarians were surely correct in insisting that it is the

[13]See for example Smart, *Outline.*

consequences of an act as they affect *any sentient being* that are relevant in the application of the utilitarian formula. The moral indignation we feel at, and the resources we feel justified in expending to prevent, the infliction of avoidable suffering upon animals is sufficient testimony to this. But aside from the fact that recognizing this compounds the difficult enough problem of interpersonal utility comparisons (see below, Section 7),[14] we may be left somewhat ill at ease by its implications. For if utilitarianism compels us to prevent the inhumane slaughtering of domestic animals, for instance, might it not equally well compel us to stop slaughtering them altogether? And if we *are* justified in the humane killing of some sentient creatures, such as domestic animals, why not others, such as human beings?

Must the consistent utilitarian make the hard choice between vegetarianism and generalized euthanasia? I think not. For while any acceptable construction of the concept of utility will force us to recognize the relevance of the consequences of our acts for creatures other than human beings, there still remains a crucial and relevant difference between human beings and most, if not all, other sentient creatures. It has to do with the intellectual capacity to conceptualize the past and the future, an ability upon which the possibility of rational thought and action in large part depends. For although my faithful pet dog may share with me certain basic biological *needs* for food, sex, and shelter from a harsh environment, and, like me, acquire *desires* as conditioned responses to external stimuli,[15] I have no reason to believe that he experiences *regret* over the turn of past events, or becomes preoccupied with what the future may hold, experiencing *disappointment* when it fails to fulfill his *expectations*. To the considerable extent that human thought and action are concerned with more than the immediate moment, in other words, dimensions of happiness and unhappiness are opened up which are largely unknown to other creatures. Perhaps this distinction will explain how it is that the utilitarian may recognize that sentient beings other than human beings count, without being forced to conclude that they count for as much. Although tempted, I shall not explore here what I believe are the obvious implications of this distinction, within a utilitarian framework, with respect to the controversial issue of nonmedical abortions.

[14]As Sidgwick realized (*Methods*, 414).
[15]Brandt explicitly treats desires as conditioned responses in his "Rational Desires."

What cannot be avoided, though, is the discussion of a quite general problem which has a direct bearing upon current controversies concerning population control. For whatever may be understood by utility, it is far from clear just what is to be understood by "the greatest good of the greatest number" as between, for instance, the following states of affairs, where each cell represents, say, one person, and the number in any cell represents the utility value of that state of affairs for that person:

I	II	III		IV			V	
3	2	2	2	1	1	1	2	
3	2	2	2	1	1	1	2	
3	6	2	2	1	1	1	6	3.3

Let us assume that the status quo is represented by I; that II represents some redistribution of whatever it is that produces the utility levels in I; and that III, IV, and V are states of affairs where new members have been added to the status quo population of I. Will the act-utilitarian remain content with the status quo, or will he seek to change it in favor of II, III, IV, or V? And if he will seek to change it, *how* will he seek to change it, and *why?*

The sum total satisfaction levels in I through V respectively are: 9, 10, 12, 9, and 13.3. If it is simply the *greatest good* that is to be produced, V (and then III, II, and I and IV indifferently, in that order) is to be preferred.

If it is the preferences of the *greatest number* of the status quo population that are to be consulted, it is to be expected that any proposal for change would be defeated two to one, but that if a change were imposed, the majority would be indifferent between II, III, and V, any one of which would be preferred by each to IV.

Surely the utilitarian does not intend to consult the selfish interests of the greatest number in this manner; he would not, for instance, view VI as preferable to VII.

VI	VII
100	99
100	99
100	1,000

On the other hand, exclusive concern with simply the greatest sum total of satisfactions would seem to have equally unacceptable implications; III, for instance, achieves a happier state of affairs than I only by increasing population size at the cost of a drop in the average level of happiness; more dramatically so with IV, which on the greatest happiness criterion would have to be viewed as indifferent to I.

What one wants to say here is that although the utilitarian may have an obligation to maximize the happiness of those who exist as members of the status quo population, there are no moral grounds for claiming that he has an obligation to the as yet unborn to bring them into existence, so that they may be happy.

To make people happy; not to make happy people. How might one capture this? The notion of the *greatest average* (net per capita) *happiness* would seem to do quite well. Calculated in this manner, II and V are indifferent, and preferable to I, III, and IV in that order. But this solution, adopted by many recent authors wishing to avoid embarrassing implications for utilitarianism on matters of population control, is not without its difficulties. For consider the following:

VIII	IX	X		
10	20	0	31	31
10	20	0	31	31
10	20	0	31	31

The average happiness of those in the status quo population, VIII, is 10; and this could be doubled by moving to IX. But our present interpretation of the utilitarian principle would force us to prefer X to both. For although the satisfaction level of the three original members is there reduced to 0, the level of average happiness is raised to 20.66 due to the quite happy condition of the six new members of the population. Surely we have no obligations to the as yet unborn of this sort either.

Sidgwick, who was unfortunately not bothered by the notion that the utilitarian is under an obligation to increase population where this will increase happiness, proposed a maximization formula which would give X an even greater edge over VIII and IX. For his suggestion was that one maximize the product obtained by multiplying the average happiness by the number of individuals in the population.[16] Calculated in this manner, VIII, IX, and X would have values of 30, 60, and 123.96, respectively.

A too hasty reaction here might be to simply return to the notion that the utilitarian principle is to be interpreted so as to

[16]Sidgwick, *Methods*, 415.

demand the maximization of the sum total of happiness, but with the restriction that its range of application is to be limited to those presently living. But this will certainly not do. As the growing realization of what men have done to their natural environment has made all too clear, we do have obligations to the members of future generations. And consider the question of whether or not an individual ought to bear children if he knows that he will pass on to them a congenital defect which will make their lives miserable.[17]

There is, I believe, a consistant way out which permits one to eliminate the apparent asymmetry between the two things that we want to say: (1) We have no obligation to *increase* the population size because those as yet unborn would be happy (to whatever degree) were they alive; (2) We do have an obligation to prevent the avoidable unhappiness of the yet unborn, and this may extend to the moral necessity of taking steps to *decrease* the population size of future generations. The way out is due to Jan Narveson.[18] As I interpret it here, it constitutes a construction of the principle that one is to act so as to maximize the average happiness of sentient creatures.[19]

It all turns on a simple point concerning the logic of quantified statements. A universally quantified statement of the form $(x) (Gx \supset Hx)$ is logically equivalent to one of the form $(x) (-Gx \lor Hx)$, and can only be falsified by an existential statement of the form $(\exists x) (Gx \& -Hx)$. If there are no G's, the universal statement is trivially true. The act-utilitarian principle that one is to maximize the sum total of happiness might, then, be put as follows: For any person, p, and any set of individuals, s, *if* the members of s are sentient creatures, p is to maximize utility within s. In notational form: $(p) (s) (Ss \supset Max_{p,U,s})$. But this is equivalent to $(p)(s)(-Ss \lor Max_{p,U,s})$, and may only be falsified by $(\exists p)(\exists s)(Ss \& -Max_{p,U,s})$. So if the act-utilitarian principle is interpreted as a logical conditional, it imposes an obligation on any person which he can fail to meet only by acting in a manner which brings about a state of affairs where *there exists* some set of sentient creatures within which he has failed to maximize utility. If I perform an act today which has as a consequence the existence of some totally miserable creature at a later date, I have breached my duty as a utilitarian. For there then exists, in the relevant, tenseless, sense, some set of persons

---

[17]The example is from Narveson, "Utilitarianism."

[18]Narveson, "Utilitarianism."

[19]From a reading of his *Morality and Utility,* I am not sure that Narveson would go along with *this.*

within which I have failed to maximize utility; i.e., the set of all persons who exist at that later date, the happiness of which would have been greater had it not included the unfortunate member for which I am responsible. On the other hand, if I fail to act today in a manner which would have as a predictable consequence the existence of some very happy person at a future date, there is no obligation, at least toward him,[20] that I could have breached. For by my act of abstinence I have seen to it that no existential statement of the appropriate form could be true.

The act-utilitarian principle as I shall understand it, then, demands simply the maximization of the net per capita happiness of all sentient creatures—existing creatures, past, present, and future.

So interpreted, the theory gives no direct consideration to the manner in which the total happiness is distributed. It would thus give a preference to II over I, and be indifferent as between I, XI, and XII.

I	II	XI	XII
3	2	0	6
3	2	0	3
3	6	9	0

Many, of course, would argue that altering I so as to bring about II would be to work an injustice upon the two individuals in I who sustain a loss in the exchange. Likewise, some would contend that considerations of justice, other things being equal, favor the equitable distribution in I over the unequal distributions of the same quantum of happiness in XI and XII. A consideration of such objections must be deferred until Chapter 7.

5. Suspect Utilities

According to the act-utilitarian principle, the rightness or wrongness of an act depends solely upon the utilities associated with the consequences of the performance of that act. All satisfactions and dissatisfactions, for whomever and however they may come about, are to be taken into account, and accorded equal weight. Neither the rich nor the poor, the wise nor the foolish, the virtuous nor the wicked, are to have their interests count for any more, or any less, than those of others. In spite of

[20]Although I might, for independent reasons, have an obligation to others to bear it.

its seeming egalitarianism, it is this very feature of utilitarianism which may be understood as lying at the basis of many of the objections which have been made to the theory. Especially by those who would conjoin other, independent, moral principles to a principle of general benevolence, it has been argued that although the utility of an act may often count, the consideration of certain sorts of consequences in calculating its utility ought, as a matter of moral principle, to be ruled out. Partly because viewing matters in this way permits one to bring unity to what is apparently an otherwise heterogeneous set of objections, it will perhaps be of some value to enumerate here the varied members of this class of "suspect" utilities.

Perhaps most noteworthy is John Rawls's claim that the advantages which accrue to the beneficiaries of an unjust social practice are to be accorded no weight whatsoever when it comes to assessing the overall moral merits of that practice.[21] Considerations of distributive justice, he has argued, are of absolute weight with respect to considerations of utility. Slavery, for instance, which is unjust for a variety of reasons, could not, morally, be defended by claiming that the benefits for slaveholders and other freemen which it produces outweigh the disadvantages to slaves. Rawls's argument will be discussed at length in Chapter 7.

In a similar manner, it has been claimed that there is a moral duty of fair play which is also absolute with respect to considerations of utility.[22] If I have voluntarily accepted the benefits which result from others having done their share in a just cooperative social practice, it is argued, then I have a duty (of fair play) to do my share when it comes my turn. This duty is one which I cannot seek to avoid by claiming that the best consequences will follow from doing otherwise. Although other kinds of moral reasons may outweigh a duty of fair play, utilitarian considerations as such are ruled out. I shall turn to an examination of this argument, often presented as an explanation of the citizen's obligation to obey the law, in Chapter 7.

The notion of moral desert is often taken to imply that neither are all pleasures good nor are all displeasures bad. The good man deserves to be happy in reward for his virtue, and the wicked man deserves to suffer for his wrongs. The satisfactions of the undeserving are, on this view, of positive disvalue.[23] This position, which would weight utilitarian considerations not

[21]See Rawls, "Justice as Fairness," as well as his *Theory of Justice.*
[22]Rawls, *Theory of Justice.*
[23]Kant is perhaps the most extreme proponent of this view.

simply according to their intrinsic magnitudes, but as a function in part of the moral worthiness of their recipients, will be dealt with in Chapter 7 in the context of a general discussion of retributive justice. It is there that I shall also discuss the familiar charge that the act-utilitarian would under certain circumstances be committed to the grave injustice of punishing the innocent.

Finally, there is a problem which is internal to utilitarianism itself. It is a familiar fact that people (including utilitarians) are happy in their belief that what they feel ought to be the case is the case, and experience displeasure when they have cause to believe that wrong is being done. Of what weight is the utilitarian to give to such satisfactions and dissatisfactions when they accompany *non-utilitarian* moral views? Is the utilitarian social reformer to desist from criticism of what he views as a morally intolerable status quo because his appeals for reform will create great displeasure amongst the members of a predominantly non-utilitarian community? What has struck many as the only reasonable alternative for the utilitarian to adopt—to discount such predictable consequences of action entirely[24]—seems no more satisfactory a solution. I shall discuss this problem in connection with Mill's libertarian principle in Chapter 8.

These four varieties of "suspect" utilities have been lumped together here for more than heuristic purposes. For although I shall seek to defend act-utilitarianism against each of the objections which they imply, I shall concede that they each contain a grain—indeed, a large grain and the same grain—of truth. For what they all in most general terms imply is that certain kinds of considerations of consequences ought to be accorded a status in some sense subordinate to that of others. While they all of course imply much more than this, with this much I can agree. The sequel will attempt to demonstrate the manner in which the act-utilitarian can consistently support and participate in social practices which do in fact result in certain kinds of utilitarian considerations receiving a heightened, and others a subordinate, status.

6. *The Concept of Utility*

Bentham, and sometimes Mill, understood the concept of utility in terms of that of happiness, this in turn being equated with the presence of pleasure and the absence of pain. Such an

---

[24]Hart, *Law, Liberty, and Morality*, 46-47.

explicitly sensationalistic approach has seemed too subjective for scientific purposes to a number of later writers, especially in economics and psychology, and the tendency nowadays is to speak in terms of the more behavioristic notion of preference. As used by the modern utility theorist, the concept of preference has been stripped of all mentalistic connotations, for a numerical utility scale describing an individual's "preferences" is nothing more than a numerical representation, unique only up to a linear transformation,[25] of his choices and what is implied by them according to the canons of rational decision.[26]

Without wishing to deny the obvious—that we do sometimes have sensations of pleasure and pain—something like the utility theorist's concept of preference seems to me the most appropriate for our present purposes. This is chiefly because it is neutral between such notions as that of need, desire, and happiness, each of which sometimes, but none of which always, seems the most natural vehicle for expressing that which the utilitarian is concerned to maximize. Although often we are able to associate specific states with an individual's preferences—biological needs, sensations of pleasure or pain—at those times when we cannot, the concept of preference has enough substance to it to bear the sense of the notion of maximizing utility. For the preference ordering imputed to an individual is based upon his choice behavior; to maximize an individual's utility level is simply to bring about that state of affairs which he would choose to have obtain, or has indeed already chosen to have obtain, amongst the states of affairs possible under the circumstances of action.

To the age-old charge that utilitarianism is uncritically hedonistic, debasing all human values to the level of brute pleasures, the answer must thus be this: It is no more and no less hedonistic than are men's actual preferences at any given stage of human development. But to the degree that it is hedonistic, pushpin is to be distinguished from poetry, if at all, only to the extent that men choose to engage in one of these activities rather than the other. Although numerical representations of strengths of preferences may be possible, there is no room in the concept of preference, any more than there is within a sensationalistic concept of pleasure, for both qualitative and quantitative distinctions.[27]

[25]X is a linear transformation of Y if and only if X = aY + b, where a and b are constants.

[26]For example, that strict preferences be transitive.

[27]Mill, of course, tried to make just such a distinction in Chapter II of his *Utilitarianism*. For an argument that it is in principle defensible, see Dahl, "Mill's Hedonism."

The concept of utility, then, is tied directly to the actual needs and desires of individuals as they are experienced by them and revealed in their choice behavior. It is thus that the utilitarian may guard against the claims of the moral zealot; that an individual may be a very poor judge of his own interests, and may thus justifiably be "forced to be free," as Rousseau expressed it and Plato implied. But although the utilitarian is committed to equating value with utility as revealed in an individual's choice behavior, the stable preference patterns revealed are not identical with any particular set of choices, so that an individual's choice in any given instance may consistently be said to fail to represent what he really prefers. There is thus some room for the notion that an individual may be mistaken about his own interests, a point the implications of which will be explored in the context of my discussion of Mill's anti-paternalism in Chapter 8.

7. *Interpersonal Utility Comparisons*

The act-utilitarian principle, as it calls for maximizing utility over all individuals affected by an act, clearly requires that one in principle be able to make sense out of interpersonal comparisons of utility. If an act may be justified because the disadvantages it creates for Smith are outweighed by the advantages it implies for Jones, there must be some common scale of value upon which the preferences of each may be measured and compared. But the individual preference orderings established by the choice behavior of each, even including choices amongst lotteries, are unique only up to a linear transformation, and thus the same numerical values on Jones's scale cannot be taken to represent the same absolute intensities of pleasure, satisfaction, or what have you, as the same numerical values on Smith's scale. The choice of both the zero point and the unit of measurement in each scale is arbitrary; interpersonal comparisons of utility based upon preference orderings constructed solely upon the basis of choice behavior are empirically meaningless.

Taken merely as a characterization of the logical status of the utility assignments made within interval scales based solely upon choice behavior, the claim that interpersonal comparisons of utility are meaningless is unobjectionable.[28] But a much stronger claim has frequently been made; that an interpersonal utility calculus is in principle impossible, and that interpersonal

[28]See Luce and Raiffa, *Games and Decisions*, Chapter 2.

comparisons of utility, on whatever basis, are meaningless. Lionel Robbins, for instance, who is often cited in the literature of welfare economics as the authority upon whom such denials rely, wrote:

> There is no means of testing the magnitude of A's satisfactions as compared with B's. If we tested the state of their bloodstreams, this would be a test of blood, not satisfaction. Introspection does not enable A to measure what is going on in B's mind, nor B to measure what is going on in A's. There is no way of comparing the satisfactions of two different people.[29]

As has often been noted, the kind of argument which Robbins employs seems to rest upon a refusal to countenance anything but direct introspection as evidence for the existence of mental states. But since we cannot introspect the mental states of others, the argument would seem to imply a complete and total skepticism about the existence of other minds, not just doubts about the meaningfulness of interpersonal utility comparisons.[30] To the extent to which we are justified in believing that other minds do exist, and that other people experience mental states similar to our own, are we not also justified in making interpersonal comparisons of strengths of desire, levels of satisfaction, and intensities of pleasures (pains)?

We of course do make judgments of comparative welfare all the time, and it is not only utilitarianism, but any moral theory which incorporates even a limited principle of benevolence, that must assume that in doing so we are not involved in a fundamental conceptual error. For in spite of the apparent misconceptions of some welfare economists, the principle of Pareto optimality surely will not take us very far. At least sometimes, the benefits to some must outweigh the losses to others.[31]

Robbins's comment that testing people's blood streams would be testing blood and not satisfaction levels almost makes the relevant point of reply by so completely missing it. For well established correlations between physiochemical states and levels of satisfaction are just the sort of thing upon which the choice of a nonarbitrary zero point and unit of measurement for an interpersonal utility calculus could in principle be based. Our knowledge

---

[29]Robbins, *Essay*, 140.

[30]As has been pointed out by a number of writers, including Little, *Critique*; Harsanyi, "Cardinal Welfare"; Waldner, "Empirical Meaningfulness."

[31]The Pareto principle takes a changed distribution to constitute an advance in the general welfare when *and only when* each concerned individual would either prefer or be indifferent to the change, and at least one person strictly prefers it.

of the relevant psychological and physiological laws is at present admittedly primitive. But do we not already have a common sense theory—backed up at some points by hard empirical data—which connects strength of preference with a number of independent factors? Sex, gross physical characteristics, intelligence, religious affiliation, social background, level of wealth, willingness to expend physical or intellectual energy, choice latency and probability, verbal and nonverbal expressions of attitude, biological needs and the levels at which they are satisfied—these and other factors have quite rightly been mentioned by various writers as linked with degrees of preference.[32]

Indeed, given enough such information about two individuals, it seems that we could with considerable confidence identify at least one state of affairs for each which could be taken to be of equivalent interpersonal value. Given a personal calculus for each, this alone is enough to set up an interpersonal calculus between them by means of the appropriate mathematical transformations; likewise for any number of individuals as long as at least one such interpersonal equivalence can be established for each pair.[33] And if further seemingly plausible assumptions may be made, it would even appear to be possible to establish a nonarbitrary zero point for the interpersonal calculus.[34]

Further technical considerations need not detain us here, although it might be mentioned that methods are available for constructing finite sensory orders which should be of use in establishing individual preference orderings and which do not employ the prevalent method of forced choice amongst probability mixtures of states of affairs. Due to Nelson Goodman, these methods have the advantage of treating the relation of indifference realistically—as intransitive—and of requiring only judgments of indifference to construct individual orderings with constant j.n.d. (just noticeable difference) functions.[35] Although it is an open question whether or not j.n.d.'s may be intersubjectively equated as measuring intersubjectively equal

[32]See the papers by Harsanyi and Waldner as well as McNaughton, "Metrical Concept."

[33]McNaughton, "Metrical Concept," 180.

[34]Find three states of affairs, A, B, and C, such that:
A is preferred to B, and B to C, and A + C is indifferent to B.
We can then take B = O if we may assume that the value (A + B) is equal to the value (A) + the value (B). For another method which makes a similar assumption, see Thurstone and Jones, "Rational Origin."

[35]Goodman, *Structure of Appearance*, Chapters IX and X.

increments (or decrements) in value, if they could be they would provide a most natural unit of measurement for an interpersonal utility calculus.[36] And if not the j.n.d. itself, perhaps some function of it could be shown to be appropriate by establishing the kinds of empirical equivalences discussed in the previous paragraph.[37]

There are, it thus seems to me, no good grounds for believing that interpersonal utility comparisons of the sort which we frequently make cannot be given a firm conceptual foundation and, eventually perhaps, an experimental one. Being as any acceptable moral theory must provide a place for a principle of benevolence based upon interpersonal comparisons of welfare, it is surely no complaint against utilitarianism that the theoretical foundation for such judgments is not presently available in completed form. For this is a case in which the moral philosopher has good grounds for believing that developments in other disciplines—notably psychology and measurement theory —will eventually provide the needed supplements to his own efforts. And as Chapter 7 will suggest, the lack of experimental procedures for constructing interpersonal utility calculi is of no great consequence to utilitarian theory either, for there are good grounds for claiming that it would not be worth the cost of constructing such calculi for the purposes of practical decision-making even if we were able to do so.

In sum, the problem of interpersonal utility comparisons is not the basis for any serious objection to utilitarian theory; would that the deontologist were able to say the same with respect to the problem of assigning relative weights to and priorities amongst his bewildering variety of independent prima facie duties.

8. *The Justification of Moral Theories*

As the present essay is in large part concerned with the elaboration and defense of act-utilitarianism, some general comments on the justification of moral theories are in order.

Any given rational adult, at any particular time, could have elicited from him a great number of judgments of objective right, some at least accompanied by reasons at various levels of generality. Now it would of course be folly to believe that all

[36]See Armstrong, "Utility"; Luce and Raiffa, *Games and Decisions*, 346-348.

[37]See Galanter, "Axiomatic and Experimental Study."

such judgments of right with accompanying reasons would fall consistently into line with some one plausible moral theory. We are simply too fallible a species to be able to expect that; our moral judgments, like our judgments of other sorts, to some degree inevitably being the product of bias, myth, irrational inference, and mistaken conceptions of fact. But with such initial moral beliefs one must at least begin, for otherwise one would have no touchstone whatsoever for the critical assessment of moral theory. Any moral theory of any interest, though, will force one to reconsider these beliefs in the light of principle, and will demand that one consider the implications of the theory for actual and hypothetical cases previously unenvisioned. But while revisions, perhaps on a large scale, are to be expected in one's initial judgments, there will be considered judgments—initial or otherwise—that will be held on to, come what may by way of principle. It is upon the basis of these that initial formulations of theory may themselves undergo revision. This process of mutual adjustment between general principles and particular judgments is to proceed until principles have been identified which achieve a maximal degree of coherence with the considered moral judgments which at any given time provide the bedrock for the justification of theory. And of course what constitutes a satisfactory fit today may not do so tomorrow; we can grow out of our sincere moral convictions just as easily as, and sometimes more quickly than, our best pair of shoes. But as the saying goes, "if the shoe fits wear it"—one can do no better than seek a principled basis for those moral convictions that one has, although just as the shoe may shape the foot, so may the convictions be formed by an appealing theory.

The formative influence which an appealing set of general principles may have upon our particular judgments is not only natural but rational, one of the aims of moral philosophy being simply that of bringing the general and the particular consistently into line with one another. Thus there is considerable room for changes to be made in initial judgments on the basis of theory; this is especially so when the theory explains why we came to hold them in the first place—in so explaining them, the theory may explain them away.[38]

It is thus that a moral theory with genuine initial plausibility is not likely to be abandoned in the light of isolated putative counter examples; the counter examples will only be seen as necessitating an abandonment of the theory when there is an

[38]Rawls, *Theory of Justice*, 48.

alternative theory to take its place.[39] But there are of course limits to this; dramatic technological or social changes, for instance, might bring to light varied and numerous implications of hitherto accepted principles that one simply could not, as a matter of considered moral judgment, accept. In such a case, it surely would be rational to abandon the theory even if one had yet to discover something better to take its place. Although one may expect any theory that one is capable of formulating to be mistaken in part, enough mistaken parts must force rejection of the whole. If it is replied that the moral vacuum that a rejection of previously accepted principles would create were no alternative theory to take their place is in some way a conceptual or psychological impossibility, the correct response seems to me to point out that the sad fact is that many persons appear to exist in just such a vacuum with little difficulty throughout their entire lives.[40]

Act-utilitarianism has come to seem to me to have such great initial plausibility so as to be virtually immune from being discredited by means of isolated counter examples—the unprincipled potshots of those moral "philosophers" who are either unwilling or unable to defend alternative theories of their own. The present essay is in large part concerned with developing an act-utilitarian response to those systematic objections to which, at one time, it seemed to me to be most vulnerable: those having to do with its putative inability to account for the undeniably significant role which shared social norms play in our moral lives.

I would also make a concerted effort to examine critically any serious alternative theories were any available. But, to my mind, none are, the best developed alternatives to act-utilitarianism being either other forms of utilitarianism or incomplete fragments of more comprehensive theories the remainders of which their proponents have not yet revealed. My reasons for rejecting other forms of utilitarianism, notably RU and UG, have already been given. In Chapter 7 I shall examine that fragment of a moral theory which I believe constitutes the most serious challenge to utilitarianism to yet be raised: John Rawls's theory of distributive justice, presented by him as just one component of a comprehensive contractarian theory of moral right.

---

[39]Rawls, *Theory of Justice*, 52.
[40]My account here owes much to Rawls, *Theory of Justice*, and to Scheffler, "Justification."

My defense and elaboration of act-utilitarianism must necessarily rely heavily upon empirical considerations. Where others have sought to explain certain kinds of considered moral judgments on the basis of a plurality of independent moral principles, I shall have to base those judgments—to the extent that upon consideration I agree with them—upon a single moral principle the implications of which are borne in large part by empirically contingent features of our physical and social environment. That a variety of significant moral judgments of some generality are accorded only a contingent status will be unsettling to some. To others I hope it will strike a note of genuine fidelity to the nature of man's actual situation as a moral being. For to suggest that our moral judgments would and should be different in a world which lacked certain salient empirical features of our own is, it seems to me, to suggest the obvious.

The prescriptive principle of AU, then, in conjunction with broadly empirical considerations, is the basis upon which my account shall proceed. As does Rawls,[41] I deny any privileged status to definitions of moral terms, my analysis throughout deliberately avoiding any appeal to the notion of analytic or necessary truth. But more on this in the following chapter.

Finally: It is often said that a moral theory must meet the requirement of universalizability; that the principles which it contains must be ones to which all men could comply without absurdity or morally unacceptable results. This demand, whether it be viewed as prescriptive or in some sense analytic of the notion of a moral theory, is surely a plausible one. Likewise the requirement of publicity: A moral theory is not to depend for its appeal upon being kept as a closely guarded secret amongst those who subscribe to it; its public acknowledgment must not be self-defeating. I mention these requirements in conclusion here because much of what I shall have to say about social norms and the rule of law is directed to the contention, already outlined, that the known acceptance of and general compliance with the act-utilitarian principle would have grave consequences in terms of the utilitarian's theory of value itself, let alone in terms of competing moral views.

[41]Rawls, *Theory of Justice*, 51.

3　　*Definition*

Questions about the nature of definition may run as deep as, and are indeed often tantamount to, questions about the nature of philosophy itself. The theory of definition is thus a complex and sometimes highly technical subject. Although there are exceptions, notably G.E. Moore[1] and more recently H.L.A. Hart,[2] most writers in social philosophy seem to believe that general inquiries concerning definitional analysis are best left to epistemologists and metaphysicians. Leaving aside issues concerning the division of philosophical labors, and admitting that a comprehensive treatment of the theory of definition would demand a book unto itself, it seems to me that certain questions about the nature and status of definitions of such terms as 'law' and 'obligation' could be avoided in the present work only if I were willing to pay the price of incomprehensibility or equivocation at crucial points. I am not. Thus the present chapter is devoted to an explanation of the position I have adopted on what I believe are the most central issues concerning definition for the purposes of the present account of social union and the rule of law.

1. Real Definition

In contrast to a mere stipulation or express convention as to the meaning which a given expression is to be understood to have in the context of a given inquiry—a *nominal definition*—a *real definition* of a word is taken to be based upon and to reflect its pre-analytic meaning. Although different accounts of real definition have relied on different theories of meaning—ranging

---

[1]Moore, *Principia Ethica.*
[2]Hart, *Concept of Law*, Chapter 1; "Definition and Theory"; "Theory and Definition."

from the notion of non-mentalistic Platonic universals to Lockean Mental concepts to linguistic meanings in use—they all seek to identify the necessary and sufficient conditions for the correct application of the expression under analysis. For instance, if 'bachelor' in one of its senses means, and is thus to be defined as, 'unmarried male adult', then it is *necessary* that a bachelor be male, that he be an adult, and that he has never been married; and that one is an unmarried male adult is *sufficient* for one's being a bachelor.

The notion of necessary and sufficient conditions is in turn to be understood in terms of the concept of *entailment;* B is a necessary condition for A, and A is a sufficient condition for B, just in case A *entails* B. And A entails B if and only if it is *not possible* that A be the case and B not be the case. Although not a matter of *logical* necessity (that is, being true in virtue of its logical form), it is not possible that one be a bachelor without being an unmarried male adult; thus being the former entails being the latter.

A real definition, then, supports the strongest of all possible statements; it permits one to say, "This must be so; it could not conceivably be otherwise." To one who fails to assent to such a claim, there is little more that can be said; he must be viewed as failing to understand the language or appropriate concepts. The *definitional stop* has been put to the discussion.

As a move in philosophical arguments, the definitional stop has been frequently employed by moral, political, and legal philosophers. To incur an *obligation,* it has been claimed, is—must be—to have a reason for action.[3] One who has made *a promise* may not justify failing to keep it on direct utilitarian grounds; to attempt to do so would be to show that one does not understand what it means to make a promise.[4] *A valid law* is a legal rule; *a rule* unlike a command, permits a consideration by the addressee of its purposes in the course of its application; thus judges, in applying the law, must have discretion.[5]

I would need to permit few such moves in order to undercut entirely the possibility of providing an act-utilitarian account of obligation, social union, and the rule of law. As the sequel shall show, I will countenance none of them, arguing that they all represent normative principles disguised as definitions.[6] But I must indicate why I reject real definition as an analytic tool in

[3]Searle, "'Ought' From 'Is.'"
[4]Rawls, "Two Concepts."
[5]Gottlieb, *Logic of Choice,* 116.
[6]This way of putting matters is due to Hart, "Theory and Definition."

social philosophy; demonstrate that so doing is not to compromise any significant moral issues; and explain the status of the analyses that will be presented of such concepts as law and obligation.

2. *Clusters and Families of Conditions*

The most general difficulty with the idea of real definition is simply this: It relies upon the notion of nonlogical entailment, which is totally obscure. Extensional equivalences may hold as a matter of contingent fact, and their identification may support statements about necessary and sufficient conditions which can be explicated within the framework of truth functional logic. For example, A is a necessary condition for B if and only if, whenever B is true, A is true. But real definition, we have seen, employs a notion of necessity much stronger than this, one which, if it can be understood at all, must be understood in terms of nonlogical necessary truth. But what kind of evidence could one conceivably have which would permit one to distinguish, amongst those things that are in fact the case, those that could be, and those that couldn't be, otherwise? This, Quine's question, has yet to be satisfactorily answered.[7]

A second general objection is this: Sameness of meaning (intensional equivalence, synonymy) is understood to imply sameness of denotation (extensional equivalence). Thus if the latter is unreasonable as a criterion of definitional adequacy, so is the former. But in fact it seems that some of the best known definitional analyses which philosophers have been able to produce do not satisfy the extensional criterion, thus suggesting that neither extensional nor intensional equivalence is required of an acceptable definition. What a reasonable criterion of definitional adequacy for constructional systems may be is a long and difficult story which fortunately need not detain us here.[8]

Thirdly, there are the general strictures against the philosophical essentialism underlying the notion of real definition found in the writings of (the later) Wittgenstein. In his *Philosophical Investigations,* the following challenge is laid down to those who would request a real definition specifying the essential and common attributes of *games*—necessary and sufficient conditions for the correct use of the word 'game':

[7]Quine, "Two Dogmas."
[8]Goodman, *Structure of Appearance,* Chapter 1; Quine, "Ontological Reduction."

> Consider . . . the proceedings that we call "games". I
> mean board-games, card-games, ball-games, Olympic games,
> and so on. What is common to them all?—Don't say: "There
> *must* be something common or they would not be called
> 'games'"—but *look and see* whether there is anything common
> to all.—For if you look at them you will not see something that
> is common to *all*, but similarities, relationships, and a whole
> series of them at that. . . . Look for example at board-games,
> with their multifarious relationships. Now pass to card-games;
> here you find many correspondences with the first group, but
> many common features drop out, and others appear. When
> we pass next to ball-games, much that is common is retained,
> but much is lost.—Are they all 'amusing'? Compare chess with
> noughts and crosses. Or is there always winning and losing, or
> competition between players? Think of patience. In ball-
> games there is winning and losing; but when a child throws his
> ball at the wall and catches it again, this feature has
> disappeared. Look at the parts played by skill and luck; and at
> the difference between skill in chess and skill in tennis. Think
> now of games like ring-a-ring-a-roses; here is the element of
> amusement, but how many other characteristic features have
> disappeared! And we can go through the many, many other
> groups of games in the same way; can see how similarities crop
> up and disappear.
>
> And the result of this examination is: we see a compli-
> cated network of similarities overlapping and criss-crossing;
> sometimes overall similarities, sometimes similarities of detail.
>
> I can think of no better expression to characterize these
> similarities than "family resemblances"; for the various
> resemblances between members of a family . . . overlap and
> criss-cross in the same way.—And I shall say: 'games' form a
> family.[9]

Some commentators have taken Wittgenstein to be claiming
that the notion of family resemblance is applicable to all general
terms (in natural languages).[10] Be that as it may, it is clear that
where his argument applies, it—like the second objection considered above—provides grounds for rejecting analyses in terms
of extensional as well as intensional equivalence. If the varied
applications of a term are related by nothing stronger than
family resemblances amongst its denotata, in other words, there
is no sense in which one can describe necessary and sufficient
conditions for its correct application.

Two further objections to real definition are each related to
one of the above. To Quine's contention that it is impossible to
distinguish the necessarily true from the contingently true is a
point due to Carl Hempel: What many writers have taken to be

[9]Wittgenstein, *Philosophical Investigations*, Sections 66 and 67.
[10]For example, Bambrough, "Universals."

analytic statements have the embarrassing consequence of logically implying clearly contingent statements when taken in conjunction.[11] To Wittgenstein's characterization of the relations amongst the things denoted by the same general term is related the claim that the general terms in a natural language have an "open texture" which permits extensions of their uses which would be impossible if their meaning could be specified in terms of necessary and sufficient conditions.[12]

Each of the above objections is fully general in character, and casts suspicion upon appeals to the notions of analyticity and necessary truth (and thus real definition) in any philosophical context. But while I find each one of them to some degree convincing, and view their cumulative effect as all but conclusive, I shall not directly rely upon them here. For there seems to me to be a further consideration which supplies sufficient enough grounds for rejecting real definition as a tool of analysis in the present context, but which falls short of claiming that (a) there are no necessary truths at all, or that (b) no sense can be made out of the notion of nonlogical necessary truth.

It may be that the notion of real definition can be made sense of, and some terms may be susceptible to analysis in terms of necessary and sufficient conditions (such as 'brother'$_{=df}$ 'male sibling'). But there may also be other terms such that few, if any, of the conditions associated with them (that is, satisfied in the standard or paradigm cases of their correct application) are individually necessary for their correct use, and those, if any, which are necessary may not be jointly sufficient. Such terms, in other words, may represent what Hilary Putnam has aptly labeled "cluster concepts":

> Suppose one makes a list of the attributes P_1, P_2, . . . that go to make up a normal man. One can raise successively the questions "Could there be a man without P_1?" "Could there be a man without P_2?" and so on. The answer in each case might be "Yes," and yet it seems absurd that the word 'man' has no meaning at all . . . the meaning in such a case is given by a cluster of properties. To abandon a large number of these properties, or what is tantamount to the same thing, to radically change the extension of the term 'man', would be felt as an arbitrary change in its meaning. On the other hand, if most of the properties in the cluster are present in any single case, then . . . we should be inclined to say that what we had to deal with was a man.[13]

[11]Hempel, "Logical Appraisal."
[12]Hart, *Concept of Law*, Chapter 7; Waismann, "Verifiability."
[13]Putnam, "The Analytic and the Synthetic," 378.

Many writers, including Putnam himself, have seen little if any difference between this notion of clusters, and Wittgenstein's notion of families, of conditions.[14] There are indeed close similarities between them: Either writer can be interpreted so as to leave room for some terms to be definable by the specification of necessary and sufficient conditions;[15] and likely candidates for one characterization are likely candidates for the other. But there is yet a crucial difference between them, as may be seen by the fact that it may be possible to describe a standard case of a cluster concept which can serve as a paradigm for any other typical exemplar of the concept; this cannot be the case with a family resemblance concept. A paradigm case of a board game, such as chess, for instance, cannot serve as a paradigm for the quite different kind of game of which baseball is an instance. This captures the point of Wittgenstein's notion of family resemblance; different exemplars of the same concept may be equally paradigmatic and yet share no common defining characteristics; there simply is no single set of features definitive of what it is to be a paradigm. Putnam's notion of a cluster concept, on the other hand, is explained in terms of the status of the conditions associated with the paradigm case. Nothing whatsoever in his account implies that a cluster concept is a family resemblance concept or vice versa.[16]

Although I shall not seek to demonstrate here what I have argued at length elsewhere,[17] I shall proceed on the assumption that the key concepts which enter into my account of social union and the rule of law are cluster concepts in Putnam's sense. Thus the definitional stop will not be recognized as an acceptable move in the context of my overall argument.

3. *Definitions and Moral Judgments*

If such terms as 'legal system', 'valid law', and 'obligation' cannot be pinned down by the specification of necessary and sufficient conditions for their correct application, what is the status of those moral principles which contain them? If my

[14]Putnam, "The Analytic and the Synthetic"; Pitcher, *Wittgenstein*, 221.

[15]Scriven, "Definitions," 105-106, treats 'lemon' as representing a cluster concept and, at page 124, adopts the view that some terms can, and others can't, have real definitions provided for them.

[16]A given concept could be both if it split off into two subconcepts where there was such a thing as *the* paradigm for each, but where the subconcepts themselves were linked only by family resemblances.

[17]See Sartorius, "Concept of Law."

position is that no good sense can be given to the notion of *the* meaning of such terms, am I not also committed to the intolerable view that the moral principles which contain them are wildly indeterminate with respect to what they require? It is questions such as these, I believe, that have provoked the claim that "Immensely important moral issues hinge on how we define 'law.'"[18]

How could a definition be morally important? The argument, which is either implicit or explicit in many controversies concerning the status of international law, runs something like this: There is a moral principle to the effect that, at least under certain conditions, there is a prima facie obligation of obedience to law. There is also a substantial body of rules and principles of international "law." Although they may be honored more often in their breach than in their observance, it would surely be a better world if these rules and principles were more frequently respected. The point is this: Most nations are committed to the principle of fidelity to law. If 'legal system' is defined in such a way as to include international law, then those committed to the principle in question will be committed to recognizing as binding moral obligations those which arise under international law.[19]

Similarly with respect to the definition of 'valid law'. Thus A.L. Goodhart's contention that "Our attitude to administrative law, and especially administrative tribunals, will . . . be affected by our definition of law."[20] And how else is one to explain the great significance which both Hart and Fuller attach to the legal positivists' definitional separation of law and morality—Hart claiming that this is the only way to avoid moral confusion and Fuller contending that such a separation represents the height of moral confusion itself?[21]

The putative moral relevance of definitions of those terms which have key occurrences in our moral principles rests, I believe, upon a radically distorted conception of the plight of the moral decision-maker. For it gives us a picture of a decision-maker who first accepts a general moral principle, then goes out and independently learns the cases to which it is meant to apply, and then, consistently and without question, simply applies it. Something like this may be true of the very young and uncommonly obedient child who "accepts" the principle that one is not

[18]Gellner, "Contemporary Thought," 354.
[19]Such an argument is found, for instance, in Goodhart, "Apology."
[20]Goodhart, "Apology," 298.
[21]Hart, "Positivism"; Fuller, "Positivism and Fidelity."

to pull pussycats' tails, who is often uncertain about what is, and what is not, besides his own Tabby, a pussycat, and who thus asks Mommy, "Is that a pussycat?"—and pulls or fails to tail pull accordingly—whenever he encounters a doubtful case. Normal adult behavior is fortunately not of this nature, for a rational moral agent is expected to appreciate the spirit as well as to know the letter of the moral law. Therefore not only do moral rules have exceptions, but they are always open to reappraisal. More importantly in the present context: Whenever there are border-line cases of the application of a term which has a key occurrence in a moral principle, it is open to question whether or not the borderline cases should constitute exceptions to the rule. The very respects in which a borderline case differs from the standard cases may constitute good reasons for adding it to an already recognized class of exceptions, or, if this is not so, there may still be grounds for making it the first member of a new class of ex-ceptions. Whatever the case, the decisions which we make concerning definitions normally do not have, and certainly never should have, the effect of determining the content of our moral principles.

There is an important insight which is concealed in, and perhaps provides the motivation for, this argument, and this is that the ways in which 'legal system' or 'valid law' are defined may have significant *emotive effects.* Although the relevant attitudes may differ from group to group, the members of a particular socio-economic class, or even a whole society, will often have associated with their conception of law certain well-defined attitudes. The extension of the denotation of the term 'law' to a new class of entities may thus carry along with it an extension of the attitudes in question. In short, a definition of 'legal system' or 'valid law' may be what C.L. Stevenson called a "persuasive definition."[22] This is a simple but important fact the signficance of which has long been recognized by those con-cerned with winning men's political allegiances, and it is one which I by no means seek to deny. Insofar as those who have argued that the answer which is given to the question "What is law?" is morally significant have had this in mind, I thus have no quarrel with them.

4. Explication and Stipulation

Although I have rejected real definition as a mode of analysis, and have argued that no moral significance is to be

[22]Stevenson, "Persuasive Definitions."

attached to this rejection, I do not mean to deny that there are instances in which there is a need for definitions, nor that it is possible to articulate criteria for evaluating them. In claiming that terms such as 'legal system' and 'obligation' represent cluster concepts, I have maintained only that the clear-cut cases of their correct application of which any satisfactory (nonstipulative) definition must take account can be accommodated by any number of alternative definitions which will diverge in their treatment of the borderline cases. In the case of 'legal system', these borderline cases include primitive law, international law, canon law, iniquitous sets of laws serving the thoroughly reprehensible purposes of wicked men, and legal regimes which one might for a variety of reasons describe as being on the verge of collapse. Few if any of the conditions associated with the paradigm cases of the instantiation of a cluster concept can be said to be necessary for its correct application, and there is no extensional basis for choosing amongst competing definitions, all of which handle the paradigm cases but diverge with respect to their treatment of those at the borderline.

But concern with the definition of terms such as 'legal system' often occurs in contexts from which one can elicit, in addition to extensional criteria, pragmatic criteria which provide a basis for a defensible choice amongst possible alternatives. Such definitions, in other words, are often chosen on the basis of their suitability or usefulness in the context of a particular inquiry. A definition of a term such as 'legal system' will not be evaluated in isolation, but only as a part of a broader classificatory schema which itself will be accepted or rejected on the basis of a consideration of its theoretical and heuristic fruitfulness in dealing with a certain set of problems.

Consider, for instance, the anthropologist, who must approach primitive societies with a complex classificatory schema within which law is only one member of an interlocking set of concepts which include religion, custom, positive morality, and magic. Or take the political scientist who is interested in the status of administrative tribunals within modern legal systems. And what of the historian who is interested in tracing the development of the institution of the jury? Is there any reason to suppose that a definition of 'legal system' which would be useful in the description or pursuance of any one of these inquiries would be coextensive with that best suited for any of the others? I think not. Certain institutions found in primitive societies, for instance, will have both analogies and disanalogies with well-developed systems of municipal law. If the features of a primitive society in which the anthropologist is interested—one of which might be the way in which its institutionalized norms have developed over time—have close analogies with systems of modern law, he will have sufficient grounds for classifying them together for the purposes of his inquiry. But the analogies in which the historian is interested may be very different, and if he does not find them in primitive law, he will be justified in defining his terms accordingly. And while for the purposes of the historian it may be useful to be able to speak of "the law" and the "legal institutions" of the Germanic tribes, for instance, the political scientist concerned with the complex relations amongst the various official organs of the modern state may classify as a legal system only an institutional structure within which legislatures, courts, police, etc., are to be found.

Much of this is instructively illustrated by some of the studies which have been made of primitive law. Malinowski's *Crime and Custom in Savage Society* is a classic in the field,[23] while Hoebel and Llewellyn's *The Cheyenne Way* combines the methods of the trained anthropologist with the insights of one of the most important figures in the history of American jurisprudence.[24] Three significant features are found in both of these fascinating studies: (1) A definition of 'legal system' based upon close analogies between primitive and modern law; (2) Arguments to the effect that the acceptability of the definition depends upon its usefulness within the framework of a broader classificatory schema—In particular, the claim that the definition brings together and isolates elements not found in other cultural institutions; and (3) An ever present appreciation of just how much primitive law does in fact differ from modern law, from which is drawn the conclusion, not that primitive law is not *really* law, but that it would simply be a great mistake for the anthropologist to adopt a definition of 'legal system' modeled too closely on the picture presented by a well-developed system of modern municipal law. Let me briefly exhibit each of these three features in turn.

(1) In both studies, the features of a modern legal system found in primitive societies which are taken to constitute the minimal set of conditions individually necessary and jointly sufficient for the application of the term 'legal system' are: (a) The existence of rules of obligation, and (b) the existence of well-defined mechanisms which permit the other than private settlement of conflicting claims made as a matter of felt right on

[23]Malinowski, *Crime and Custom.*
[24]Hoebel and Llewellyn, *The Cheyenne Way.*

the basis of such rules. Hoebel and Llewellyn state that "The material *for* law-stuff is . . . given by the claims, and with the settlements, the raw material *of* law-stuff is produced."[25] For Malinowski,

> 'Civil law,' the positive law governing all the phases of tribal life, consists . . . of a body of binding obligations regarded as a right by one party and acknowledged as a duty by the other, kept in force by a specific mechanism of reciprocity and publicity inherent in the structure of their society.[26]

(2) Malinowski constantly emphasizes his interest in providing a definition of 'legal system' which will distinguish the legal aspect of primitive society from its other normative aspects. The existence of the specific "legal" mechanisms which he discusses in detail "places the *binding obligations* in a special category and sets them apart from other types of customary rules."[27] The minimal definition which he adopts, Malinowski states, will enable him to

> . . . arrive at a satisfactory classification of the norms and rules of a primitive community, at a clear distinction of primitive law from other forms of custom, and at a new, dynamic conception of the social organization of savages.[28]

Speaking of the importance for the development of Cheyenne law of what "in net result, instance by instance, *gets done* about cases of trouble," Hoebel and Llewellyn reveal a similar concern:

> Their crisis-character and their memorability give them a likelihood of setting up lines, patterns, and structures of behavior, *and of setting up anticipable consequences of deviation*, which is, we believe, unrivaled in other phases of culture.[29]

(3) Hoebel and Llewellyn of course realize that the Cheyenne do not have a legal system with a structure—courts, legislature, etc.—anything like that associated with a well-developed system of modern municipal law. But the very fact that they do not minimize these differences makes even more striking the close analogies which they describe between the ways in which Cheyenne law, on the one hand, and Anglo-American common law, on the other hand, have both developed

---

[25]Hoebel and Llewellyn, *The Cheyenne Way*, 283.
[26]Malinowski, *Crime and Custom*, 58.
[27]Malinowski, *Crime and Custom*, 39.
[28]Malinowski, *Crime and Custom*, 15-16.
[29]Hoebel and Llewellyn, *The Cheyenne Way*, 252.

as systems of case law. And as far as Malinowski is concerned, one of the chief obstacles which hindered the development of anthropological theories of primitive law was a tradition of "defining the law in terms of central authority, codes, courts, and constables. . . ."[30]

There are, then, legitimate concerns which call for a definition of 'legal system'. But since the very same features which serve to distinguish one inquiry from another also serve as pragmatic criteria by means of which competing definitions may be evaluated, it is highly unlikely that a definition really suited to the purposes of one field of inquiry will be well suited in other contexts.

Lon Fuller's analysis of what he calls "the internal morality of law," the substance of which will be dealt with in Chapter 9, provides an illuminating philosophical contrast to the anthropological theories discussed above. Fuller quite rightly takes the position that law may be fruitfully viewed as a purposive undertaking to which attach conditions of failure and success. "The morality which makes law possible" is, for Fuller, those procedural requirements which must be followed by those charged with law creation and application if they are to succeed in the enterprise of subjecting human behavior to the governance of general rules. And this *is* Fuller's definition of 'law': The enterprise of subjecting human behavior to the governance of general rules.[31] As Fuller realizes, this definition embraces not only paradigmatic cases of legal systems, but such diverse things as the rules of parliamentary procedure, rules of university governance, the by-laws of social clubs, and the rules which determine the schedule of fines for players in the National Football League. Does this surprisingly broad definition of 'law' vitiate Fuller's account? Of course not. The definition is well chosen for the simple reason that it isolates under the rubric of "the enterprise of subjecting human behavior to the governance of general rules" a group of phenomena about which similar and illuminating things can be said. Insofar as it does so, it heightens our understanding of "law properly so-called"[32] by elucidating the important similarities which it bears to many of those things from which it is typically distinguished by those who seek to define it in terms of necessary and sufficient conditions.

Where, as with the anthropologists mentioned above, the

---

[30]Malinowski, *Crime and Custom*, 14.
[31]Fuller, *Morality of Law*, 122-123.
[32]This phrase is from John Austin, *Province of Jurisprudence*.

definition does not deviate radically from ordinary usage, we may be inclined to describe it as an *explication*.[33] On the other hand, where the deviation from ordinary usage is as great as it is in the case of Fuller, we may prefer to speak of nominal definition or *stipulation*. But in both cases, it is significant to note, the criteria of definitional adequacy are essentially the same. The question is simply whether or not the definition clearly and consistently pulls together a variety of phenomena about which fruitful generalizations can be made. It is in this vein that I seek to distinguish the concept of *obligation* from other prescriptive notions in Chapter 5, and to set off *adjudication* from other forms of decision-making and conflict resolution in Chapter 9.

5. *Natural Necessity*

I have already acknowledged (Chapter 2, Section 8) that what others may treat as independent moral principles will often in my account appear as implications of the act-utilitarian principle as applied to contingent generalizations about man and his natural and social environment. Although such a mode of analysis will yield no necessary truths, there is considerable room for claims the status of which one is tempted to describe as more than merely contingent. Following H.L.A. Hart, we may describe them as statements of "natural necessity."

Let us begin by noting that Hart quite explicitly takes the position that 'legal system' represents a cluster concept. In the sequel to his inaugural address, Hart adopts a stance which he can be viewed as elaborating upon in his later *The Concept of Law*:

> . . . I am not sure that in the case of concepts so complex as that of a legal system we can pick out any characteristics, save the most obvious and uninteresting ones, and say they are necessary. Much of the tiresome logomachy over whether or not international law or primitive law is really law has sprung from the effort to find a considerable set of necessary criteria for the application of the expression "legal system." Whereas I think that all that can be found are a set of criteria of which a few are obviously necessary (e.g., there must be rules) but the rest form a sub-set of criteria of which everything called a legal system satisfies some but only standard or normal cases satisfy all.[34]

---

[33]Current philosophical usage of this term, I believe, goes back to Carnap, *Logical Foundations*, Chapter 1.

[34]Hart, "Theory and Definition," 251-252.

After listing a number of such criteria, Hart concludes that "in the case of a concept so complex . . . we can do no more than identify the conditions present in the standard or paradigm case and consider under what circumstances the removal of any one of these conditions would render the whole pointless or absurd."[35]

The Concept of Law adopts this approach with respect to the natural law theorists' claim that a legal system must necessarily conform to certain substantive moral criteria if it is to qualify as a legal system at all. Of little solace to traditional natural law theorists, Hart's "minimal version" of natural law doctrine is that, given survival as an aim, it is a matter of *natural necessity* that there are certain rules of conduct which any social organization must enforce if it is to remain viable. The natural necessity resides in the fact that there are certain obvious generalizations about man and the nature of the world in which he finds himself which constitute *good reasons* for both law and morals having a specific content. In particular, claims Hart, as long as these generalizations remain true, any viable social organization must provide some minimal protection of persons, property, and promises through a system of mutual forbearances enforced by sanctions, the latter being required "not as the normal motive for obedience, but as a *guarantee* that those who would voluntarily obey shall not be sacrificed to those who would not."[36]

This concept of natural necessity, Hart contends, provides a way of avoiding "certain misleading dichotomies which often obscure the discussion of the characteristics of law."[37] In a passage which I believe is of considerable general significance, he continues:

> We shall no longer have to choose between two unsuitable alternatives which are often taken as exhaustive: on the one hand that of saying that this is required by 'the' meaning of the words 'law' or 'legal system', and on the other that of saying that it is 'just a fact' that most legal systems do provide for sanctions. Neither of these alternatives is satisfactory. . . . For it is a truth of some importance that for the adequate description not only of law but of many other social institutions, a place must be reserved for a third category of statements: those the truth of which is contingent on human beings and the world they live in retaining the salient characteristics which they have.[38]

[35]Hart, "Theory and Definition," 253.
[36]Hart, *Concept of Law*, 193.
[37]Hart, *Concept of Law*, 194.
[38]Hart, *Concept of Law*, 195.

Although Hart's language is novel, and his clarification of the concept an original contribution, the basic idea is not unfamiliar. Consider, for instance, what Hume has to say about the "artificial" but "not arbitrary" character of the laws of justice in the *Treatise*.[39] Or Locke's discussion of the "inconveniences" of the state of nature which are remedied by the institution of government performing the legislative, executive, and judicial functions which for Locke constitutes "the umpirage" of the laws of nature.[40] Indeed, even the approach of Hart's arch antagonist, Lon Fuller, can be interpreted in terms of the notion of natural necessity. For the imperative character of the requirements of the internal morality of law rests to a considerable degree upon contingent features of man and the world within which he seeks to regulate human behavior through systems of general rules.

Much of what follows in my own account is best interpreted in terms of this notion of natural necessity, what counts as good reasons on my view depending directly upon the act-utilitarian principle. In particular, I shall claim that the general necessity for social rules which in some sense bar direct appeals to utility is a "natural" one which reflects certain salient features of the environment in which men must strive to create and maintain the bonds of social union. As Hume, Hart, and, most recently, David Lewis [41] clearly realized, much of morality is in this sense a matter of convention, although the conventions in question may, due to the natural necessity for them, be far from arbitrary.

6. *The Logic of Paradigms*

In addition to explicative and stipulative definitions, and analyses which are to be understood in terms of the notion of natural necessity, my account shall also be based in part upon what I shall call "the logic of paradigms."

In claiming that the concept of a promise, for instance, is a cluster concept, I have maintained that few, if any, of the conditions satisfied in the standard or paradigmatic case of promising are necessary for the making of a promise. But if I am to provide an act-utilitarian account of how it is that most promises ought to be kept—or, at least, of why in most instances a promise to do something gives rise to a (morally) good reason for doing it—I surely must identify those features of promising

[39]Hume, *Human Nature*, Book III, Part II, Section I.
[40]Locke, *Second Treatise*.
[41]Lewis, *Convention*.

which, in conjunction with the utilitarian principle, provide reasons for action. They cannot be necessary features of promising: I have claimed that there might be none. But they both can be and in fact are features to be found amongst those associated with paradigm cases of promising; conditions which, although they cannot be described as necessary, may be described as *necessarily present in paradigm cases of promising.* Lest it be thought that the notion of necessary truth of which such a dim view was taken but a short while ago is being reintroduced at this second order level, let me hasten to add that on my view the notion of a paradigm is itself relative to and defined by the purposes of inquiry.[42] Thus if F is a paradigmatic feature of X for the purposes of a given inquiry, while F′ is not, the situation might be just the reverse in the context of a different inquiry. For instance, the express use of the words 'I promise . . .' might be taken as a necessary feature of a paradigm case of promising by a philosopher-linguist interested in the notion of a performative utterance,[43] while the nature of the expectations created in the promissee by the promissor's utterance of such words might be treated as nonessential. Quite the opposite, we shall see, is the characterization of the paradigm case of promising that the act-utilitarian must consider.[44]

[42]A point seemingly overlooked by Slote in his "Important Criteria."
[43]See J.L. Austin, "Performative Utterances."
[44]In this connection, see Narveson's notion of the "logically normal" case of a kind of action which is prima facie obligatory in his "Promising," 213.

4 Individual Conduct and Social Norms

Preliminary explanations of the problem of individual conduct and social norms, and the basis upon which I shall attempt to solve it, are now completed. A number of promissory notes have already been issued, and the time has come to begin cashing them in. This chapter contains a quite general act-utilitarian account of the conventional norms which render social union possible. Later chapters deal with more specific issues which involve particular kinds of social norms—moral, political, and legal.

1. The Problem Restated

A rule of thumb—or a "summary rule," as John Rawls would call it—is a summary generalization of the kinds of consequences which have been found to accompany the performance of a particular kind of act.[1] "Act X is wrong" is, according to this conception, nothing more nor less than an empirical hypothesis to the effect that acts of kind X typically have bad consequences. It has been claimed, both by critics and by proponents of act-utilitarianism, that this conception of moral rules is the only one which can be consistently held by an act-utilitarian. J.J.C. Smart, for instance, has written that for the act-utilitarian moral rules can have the status only of "mere rules of thumb," and that the act-utilitarian will thus "use them only as rough guides" to action.[2]

---

[1]Rawls, "Two Concepts," 19-24.
[2]Smart, *Outline*, 30; Smart's view remains unchanged in the recently published revised version of this essay contained in Smart and Williams, *Utilitarianism*.

The notion that the individual moral agent is in each instance to attempt to determine what is the right thing to do on direct utilitarian grounds has, we have seen (Introduction; Chapter 2, Section 2), given rise to the following three closely related objections to act-utilitarianism:

(1) Sometimes it is not right to do that which has the best consequences in the instant case. The right action, both the deontologist and the rule-utilitarian would agree, is often what is demanded by moral rules which do not sanction direct appeals to utility.

(2) Each individual deciding each case on its merits would lead to a situation of social chaos. The unreliability of human judgment concerning the future consequences of acts would result in many mistakes being made about what would have the best consequences. The long run effects of choices being based upon specific moral rules barring direct appeals to utility would be more desirable than the results of each case being decided on direct utilitarian grounds, one significant factor in this being that human action would then be much more predictable.

(3) Even assuming the correct application of the act-utilitarian principle, a society of act-utilitarians would lose the enormous benefits which accrue from one's being able to know "that another person will act not for the best, but in a particular way or according to more specific rules."[3] All the advantages of being able to tie down the future in advance on the basis of secure expectations that others will conform their behavior to conventional moral norms which bar direct appeals to utility (for example, those concerning the making and keeping of promises) would be lost.

In response to these objections, I shall seek to indicate *why* it is, and *how* it is possible, that the act-utilitarian can rationally participate in the enforcement of social norms which in at least one familiar sense bar direct appeals to utility, and yet consistently reserve the right to judge the rightness or wrongness of particular acts solely in terms of their consequences. I shall admit, in other words, that the bonds of social union upon which a stable social order depends are based upon the existence of conventional norms which do not countenance direct appeals to utility. But I shall argue that this is no objection to act-utilitarianism, contending that the act-utilitarian, contrary to the prevailing view, can have a conception of social rules as something much more significant than rules of thumb. It is not that I shall deny that moral and legal rules must usually have the status of

[3]Hodgson, *Consequences*, 99.

reliable rules of thumb if they are to be worthy of the act-utilitarian's support. My chief contention is rather that they are grossly misdescribed as having the status *merely* of rules of thumb, for, as will be shown, their character and modes of participation in their support permit them both to provide reasons for action and to redirect human behavior into channels it would not otherwise take in a manner which is impossible for mere summary rules. It is these features which I take to be sufficient grounds for describing them as social *norms*, even though they lack the direct prescriptive force which many would claim is a necessary condition for being a norm or rule at all, a normative import which in my view is enjoyed only by the act-utilitarian principle itself. As far as I can see, though, nothing much hinges on whether or not the reader shares my inclination to describe them as rules or norms; what is significant is rather the substantive character which I attribute to them.

My strategy will be to begin by considering one particular kind of social norm: legal rules. After indicating how an act-utilitarian can consistently urge their enactment and enforcement while retaining the right to deviate from them on direct utilitarian grounds, I shall then move to a consideration of moral norms. My argument shall be that they are sufficiently analogous to legal rules in the relevant respects to be construed as having a similar status—one surely misdescribed as being that of mere rules of thumb. Having answered the question, "How are such rules possible on act-utilitarian grounds?" and having considered why such rules are both necessary and desirable, I shall then turn to a discussion of the manner in which they can serve as reasons for action.

2. *Legal Norms*

There are a great variety of (overlapping!) distinctions to be made amongst different kinds of legal rules.[4] There are those rules that confer powers, and those that impose duties; those that are directed to public officials, and those that concern the private citizen; those that regulate pre-existing forms of conduct, and those that are constitutive of new forms of decision and action—not the least important of which are those constitutional rules which contain formal criteria of validity for legislation and judicial decisions. Whatever may be the case with moral rules, it

---

[4]See my discussion of Hart's distinction between "primary" and "secondary" legal rules in Sartorius, "Concept of Law," Section 3.

cannot be seriously maintained that the act-utilitarian could have no other conception of a legal rule than that of a rule of thumb or summary rule. It would not be claimed that Bentham, from the very outset, was involved in an inconsistency in attempting to develop an act-utilitarian theory of both morals and *legislation*.[5] The reasons for this are not far to seek. Some kinds of legal rules, including the power conferring and the constitutive, are not prescriptive, and are thus not even candidates for being rules of thumb, and yet there is clearly nothing strange about the notion of an act-utilitarian supporting their adoption. Even a typical prohibition of the criminal law does not report what is or has been but rather what should be the case;[6] it may be part of a legal system because it conforms to certain criteria of formal validity even if no bad consequences would follow from performing the acts which it proscribes; and although it typically will, it need not be backed up by coercive sanctions.[7]

Ignoring for the time being the variety of forms which legal norms may take, and confining our attention to the prescriptive provisions of the criminal law, it is equally clear that neither is there any moral or conceptual difficulty involved in an act-utilitarian undertaking the office of legislator, voting for the enactment of a criminal statute and appropriations which sustain a judiciary and law enforcement agencies, and paying his taxes. Nor is there any absurdity in the same individual legislator viewing himself as being morally justified, in his role as a private citizen, in violating a law which he has helped to enact.

Legal prohibitions will not permit a blanket appeal to considerations of consequences as excusing or justifying their violation. For any given law, *some* kinds of utilitarian considerations will typically be allowed to function as excusing, mitigating, or justifying conditions, but never will *all* of the moral grounds for law violation which might be recognized by the act-utilitarian be so treated. The traffic laws, for instance, may recognize a number of different kinds of emergency situations as justifying the exceeding of a posted speed limit, but their purpose would be largely defeated if they permitted individuals to view themselves as exempted from the general standard if they were exceptionally

---

[5]That such an account does not collapse into a rule-utilitarian one has been explicitly noted by Lyons, "On Sanctioning Excuses," 647.

[6]The so-called legal realists would naturally disagree, but a predictive analysis of legal rules has been so thoroughly discredited that I do not believe it is worthy of consideration here. See Hart, *Concept of Law*, Chapter 7, for what comes close to a definitive treatment of the realists' position.

[7]This latter claim is, of course, controversial. But see Hart, *Concept of Law*, Chapter 3, Section 1.

good high-speed drivers, with genuinely high-performance auto-
mobiles, having good reason to be in a hurry to get somewhere.
Too many bad drivers think that they are capable of handling a
car at high speeds when they are not; too many cars that are "un-
safe at any speed" are sold under the guise of having true sportscar
characteristics; some people are always in a hurry. But, of course,
some individuals sometimes will have very good reason to believe
that they ought to exceed the speed limit, knowing that they are
good high-speed drivers, have real sportscars, and that they
should be in a hurry. Even taking into account the likelihood of
being apprehended and punished, they will be justified in breaking the law on act-utilitarian grounds.

The penalties attached to traffic violations could, of course,
be made so severe as to eliminate virtually all such cases; speeding,
for instance, could be made punishable by life imprisonment.
But, for obvious reasons, the price would be too terrible a one for
the utilitarian to pay; rather, he will opt for that least severe
schedule of sanctions which is sufficient to bring the incidence of
speeding down to what is viewed as a socially tolerable level. Even
in a society of act-utilitarians, the very best law that could be
enacted might be one which was sometimes justifiably disobeyed.

There are other options open to the utilitarian legislator who
wishes to discourage a certain kind of conduct. Rather than a
blanket prohibition of acts of kind K, the optimality of an act on
act-utilitarian grounds could be treated as an acceptable legal
defense. Which option ought to be chosen in a given instance
will, for the utilitarian, depend upon empirical considerations
concerning the consequences of choice. As far as my argument
here is concerned, it need only be admitted that there are some
laws the violation of which ought not to be legally defensible on
simple act-utilitarian grounds.[8]

But need justified disobedience be punished? The law does
not apply itself, and most legal systems control the incidence of
legal norms by granting a considerable degree of discretion to
those responsible for their application; police, prosecutors, juries,
sentencing judges. Could not any putative case of justified disobedience to a law always be rectified, in theory at least, by some
sort of adjustment, either in the law, the structure of the institutional roles involved, or the judgments of individual agents?

Although a morally justified law violation followed by the
application of a legal sanction typically does indicate that
something went wrong within the legal system (in the prosecutor's

[8]On what is really the general issue being raised here, see Wasserstrom,
"Strict Liability."

office, perhaps, if not in the legislative assembly), I see no reason to believe that this *must always* be the case. The view that it must be seems to me to represent a failure to appreciate the price that may have to be paid in moral terms if a complex institutional mechanism for controlling human behavior and channeling it into lines that it would not otherwise take is to be workable. To create institutional roles of the sort found within a mature legal system is to put different individuals, including the private citizen, in the position of having to consider quite different kinds of consequences as attaching to the decisions which it is within their power to reach. It is thus no wonder that the decision which ought to be reached (on act-utilitarian grounds) by the occupant of a given office need not mirror or reflect the decision reached (on act-utilitarian grounds) by one who is playing a very different institutional role. Perhaps the cop on the beat had no choice but to make the arrest, but this does not imply that the prosecutor ought to prosecute; this, if not a commonplace, ought to be. No more difficult, in theory, is the case of an individual who ought to break the law, but who also ought to be arrested, prosecuted, found guilty by a jury, sentenced to a jail term by a judge, refused pardon, and then who ought to attempt to jump bail and escape punishment, even though he has no grounds for believing that the legal system ought to be changed in any way.[9] Such situations, where the law is as it should be and a morally justified violation of it ought yet to be legally punished, are, one would hope, rare, and perhaps genuinely tragic. But they are anything but impossible.

There is a fallacious general principle which lends credence to the naive view that the legal prohibition and punishment of morally justified behavior must represent either imperfect human judgment, bad laws, or faulty institutional design. I would like to bring it out into the open here and urge that we have just seen reasons for rejecting it, for we shall encounter it again shortly in the more problematic case of the relation of individual behavior to moral norms. It is what I shall call "the reflection principle," and it embodies the following claim: Where an individual has correctly decided that he ought to do X, any higher-order

---

[9]There is also no difficulty, in my view, in the notion of a civil disobedient, after violating a law which he does seek to have changed, (a) admitting that officials acted rightly in arresting, prosecuting, trying, and convicting him; and (b) attempting to escape punishment. To adopt a definition of 'civil disobedience' which defines such cases out of existence, as most writers on the subject do, is to conceal important issues and create the need for a new term to cover such cases.

judgment about his decision to do X or his actual act of doing it ought to license or approve of, rather than disapprove of or penalize, the decision and/or the act itself.

It is partly because the reflection principle can break down, due to the fact that individuals playing different institutional roles will have different consequences to consider in deciding what to do on act-utilitarian grounds, that a system of legal norms can redirect human behavior into channels that it would otherwise not take. For in addition to indicating the community's belief that acts of a certain kind typically have bad consequences, a prohibition of the criminal law is something which I expect to be applied to me in case of violation, regardless of whether my violation of it is justified on act utilitarian grounds, or would have been so had not the likelihood of the legal sanction entered in as a further relevant consideration. This is because I am aware of the kinds of considerations which must weigh heavily in the minds of those officials engaged in various stages of the process of applying the law. Indeed, insofar as I view myself as an active participant in the support of a legal system, it is a complex system of inter-related roles, structured in terms of differential role-related responsibilities attached to various public offices, that I view myself as supporting. It is not that I expect officials to act other than as act-utilitarians; rather it is that I can anticipate how they will act (as act-utilitarians) in ways which will lead me to act otherwise than I would have had they, and the laws which they are charged with applying, not existed in the first place.

In most general terms, the picture here is that of men deliberately creating a legal system (norms plus officials charged with their application) with the intent of putting others in the position of having to make second-order decisions about their behavior which will channel that behavior into desirable directions that it would not otherwise take. Although he was speaking in terms of self-interest and irrational bias in favor of the near at hand, it is this same general function, understood in much the same way, that Hume had in mind in explaining the origins of government in the *Treatise* (Book III, Part II, Section VII). Insofar as legal norms perform such a function, they are performing what might be viewed as the central function of social norms of any sort. As such, they are surely ill described as being merely rules of thumb.

The natural necessity for backing up the provisions of the criminal law with sanctions can thus be seen to reside in more than the fact that some men must be deterred from intentionally acting in a wrongful manner toward others. As our trite example of the traffic laws illustrates, there are instances in which benevolent men will more often than not be mistaken about what will have the best consequences if they are left to judge matters by their own lights. In such cases, recognizing their own fallibility (or at least that of others), they may appreciate the need for legal sanctions as a mechanism for introducing the further considerations of utility which will steer their behavior onto its proper course. In other instances, the traffic laws again being a good example, individuals acting so as to produce the best consequences will lead to a situation in which all are worse off than they might otherwise be even if no mistaken predictions are made. Here again, a more desirable coordination of individual behavior can be achieved by restructuring individual incentives through the introduction of legal sanctions.

Although the provisions of the civil law are not in the first instance prescriptive, similar remarks nonetheless apply. The laws of contracts, wills, and marriages are conventional means of facilitating voluntarily undertaken private arrangements, and make it possible for individuals acting under the appropriate power conferring rules to bring into existence new structures of legal rights and duties.[10] But to the extent that there is a need for men to be able to place considerable reliance upon others fulfilling such voluntarily created obligations, both good and bad intentions again operating as possible motives for noncompliance, there is a natural necessity for institutional means of *enforcing* the rights in question. And such there are, specific legal enforcers such as the attachment of property being backed up by the most general sanction of the civil law—citation for civil contempt. As with the criminal law, the efficacy of sanctions in the civil law is not to be found so much in the results of applying them to those who fail to fulfill their legal obligations, but rather in the manner in which they lead men to fulfill those obligations which they would otherwise, for whatever reasons, fail to fulfill.

According to this model, law and the coercive sanctions with which it is typically backed need be viewed neither as directly creating a moral obligation of obedience nor as representing the imposition of an alien coercive force upon the individual from above. Between these two extremes, between which much of traditional political theory has wavered, is an account which pictures the rational and moral man as voluntarily participating in the support of a system of norms which will typically redirect his own behavior as well as that of others, and which may, we

---

[10]This way of putting matters is due to Hart, *Concept of Law*, 40.

have seen, punish him for doing that which he ought to do. Although Hobbes and others[11] have argued that rationally self-interested men may agree to establish a system of coercively backed norms which will sanction otherwise self-interested behavior, I do not believe that the analogue for benevolent rather than selfish men has been generally recognized.[12] But if both arguments go through, as I believe they do, then we have the interesting result that there is a need for a system of social norms backed by sanctions regardless of what assumptions one makes (with respect to selfishness versus benevolence, at least) about the psychological nature of man.[13] For benevolent (unlike Hobbesian) men, anarchy or absolutism are not the only alternatives which remain once the notion of political authority or legitimacy has been rejected as a myth. For while retaining the autonomy of moral judgment which accompanies acceptance of the act-utilitarian principle, they may yet support a legal system which will achieve social order by controlling to a considerable extent the consequences of which they, as utilitarians, will have to take account.[14]

3. *Moral Norms*

I shall now argue that the act-utilitarian can give an account of moral norms quite analogous to that outlined above for legal norms. The resulting conclusion will thus be that an individualistic and a social conception of morality are not incompatible, and that one need not abandon act-utilitarianism in favor of some form of rule-utilitarianism or deontological theory in order to provide a way for moral norms to function as more than rules of thumb.

As has already been indicated, my aim is to do more than show that some philosophers, including act-utilitarians such as Smart, have had a mistaken conception of moral rules or of what kind of an account the act-utilitarian can give of them. For critics of act-utilitarianism, we have seen, have argued as follows: Some moral rules (such as those concerning the keeping of

[11]For an interesting and perceptive recent account, see Feeley, "Coercion and Compliance."

[12]But Wasserstrom comes quite close to the sort of position defended here in his "Obligation to Obey."

[13]Compare Buchanan and Tullock, *Calculus of Consent*, 96: "At the constitutional level . . . the purely selfish individual and the purely altruistic individual may be indistinguishable in their behavior."

[14]These remarks are directed to the position taken by Wolff in his *Defense of Anarchism*. More on all of this in Chapter 6 below.

promises) do not permit an individual to justify performing a particular act on the grounds that the performance of that act would produce some slight net advantage over conceivable alternatives in terms of its direct consequences. Such rules are a well-established part of conventional morality and ought to remain as such, perhaps for utilitarian reasons. If any changes in them would be desirable, it is not with respect to their barring of direct appeals to considerations of utility. Therefore act-utilitarianism, which would permit just such appeals, must be rejected.

John Rawls, for instance, claims of promising that

> the point of the practice is to abdicate one's title to act in accordance with utilitarian and prudential considerations in order that the future may be tied down and plans coordinated in advance. There are obvious utilitarian advantages in having a practice which denies to the promisor, as a defense, any general appeal to the utilitarian principle in accordance with which the practice itself may be justified.[15]

Those who argue in this manner are tacitly employing what I have called in Section 2 the reflection principle. For it is assumed that what social morality rightly demands must be reflected directly in the demands made by any acceptable individualistic moral principle. If the social norms definitive of the practice of promising do not permit direct appeals to utility as a justification for the breaking of a promise, and these rules themselves are desirable because of the consequences of their acceptance, then any form of utilitarianism must supposedly reflect this by applying the utilitarian test to general rules rather than particular acts.

By seeing how it breaks down in the case of legal norms, we have already found grounds for rejecting the reflection principle in its full generality. By showing that moral rules may be understood on essentially the same model as legal rules, it will be shown that the reflection principle is not even acceptable when its range of application is limited to morality. Once this has been done, grounds will have been provided for rejecting those arguments, such as Rawls's, which rely upon it.

What must be shown, then, granting that conventional morality ought to contain at least some rules which prohibit direct appeals to utility, is that (1) The rightness of various forms of participation in the support of such rules can be based on the act-utilitarian principle, and (2) The right to violate such rules when so doing would have the best consequences can be retained

---

[15]Rawls, "Two Concepts," 16.

by the individual agent. While the moral norms which an act-utilitarian can consistently support will be seen to have among their functions those attributed to rules of thumb, they will be seen to have other functions as well, and it is because they can and do perform them that they will receive the act-utilitarian's support. As with legal rules, it will be argued that the chief function of conventional moral norms is to redirect behavior into channels that it would not otherwise take. The challenge is to show how moral norms could exist and function in this manner within a society of act-utilitarians. How, in other words, could they possibly be anything more than rules of thumb? To answer this question, I shall constantly seek the guidance provided by the less problematic account of legal rules developd in the previous section. The key will lie in the identification of analogies between the legal and the social sanction and analogies between the ways in which one can be viewed as participating in the support of legal and moral norms.

Many moral philosophers have been inclined to construe the process of social sanctioning on the model of a vengeful God standing in moral judgment on sinful mortals. The social sanction on this model is the overt act of moral condemnation; the mode of individual participation in the support of a shared social morality is conformity to social mores and the expression of blame toward those who deviate from them.

No doubt there are some individuals who are to be found constantly finding moral fault with their fellows. But there is little reason to believe that such excessive moralizing is morally justified, let alone necessary for the preservation of a community's conventional morality. If we look more closely at what we would defend as reasonable behavior among mature adults, what we find is quite different from, and much more subtle and complicated than, what this theologically tainted picture of the process of social norm support suggests. Not only is there a great variety of forms which "the social sanction" takes, but the appropriateness of one form may quite often be seen to depend upon the existence of complimentary forms, not the least important of which is the legal sanction itself.

The model rejected above is perhaps most fitting in the context of what David Falk has called "primary morality."[16] This is the learning context in which the child begins to acquire whatever it is that he will be expected to exercise upon reaching moral maturity. In Western societies, at least, it appears correct to

[16]Falk, "Morality, Self, and Others," 60-61.

claim that it is conventional moral norms which are impressed upon the child by family, peers, school, and church. And it is here that the social sanction bears its closest resemblance to the legal sanction; not only parents, but also teachers and sometimes others will have the license to physically punish deviations from the norms which they are attempting to inculcate.

There is little difficulty in seeing how an act-utilitarian might justify such a process of moral education in a system of norms not permitting direct appeals to utility. A direct attempt to teach only the act-utilitarian principle itself to the child would obviously be disastrous. This is not only due to the fallibility of the child's judgment, but also because one can simply not understand what it is to maximize value until one learns what it is that is to be valued. Thus one of the things that a child must learn through the process of acculturation is, so to speak, his society's "theory of value." The inculcation of rigid norms prohibiting certain kinds of conduct serves the function of teaching the child which interests and satisfactions, whether his own or those of others, are to be taken seriously. Without such a prior understanding, the child could make no sense out of the principle that one is to do that which is likely to have the best consequences.

In the course of his moral development, the child will reach a stage where he will sometimes believe that the violation of a conventional norm is justified because of its consequences, and he will on occasion be correct in his judgment. But he is likely to be incorrect more often than not, and it is thus that he still ought to be discouraged from attempting to decide when a norm ought to be violated on direct utilitarian grounds. Some form of parental blame, disapproval if not punishment, may thus with good reason continue to be applied to violations of conventional norms, even those violations which are in fact justified on act-utilitarian grounds. Therefore, in considering what he ought to do in order to produce the best consequences—when he does consider things in this light—the child will have to consider as a possible consequence of his behavior the incidence of some form of the social sanction. At this stage, we clearly have a situation where a close analogy to the legal case may arise. Because of their quite different positions or roles, the parent may be justified in punishing the violation of a norm which the child was justified in disobeying. The reflection principle, in other words, may break down.

It might be claimed here that there is a significant disanalogy to the legal case in that it is the parent, and not the child, who is participating in the support of the norms which bar direct appeals to utility. Surely the child may lack an appreciation of the situation; but so may his parents. And if the child has reached a sufficient stage of maturity, he may understand the situation quite well. But, more importantly, both the child and the parent, in their own manners, may in fact lend support to the system of norms in a variety of ways. For the child's part, he will typically apply the norms in his relationships with his peers (especially siblings) by basing demands on them, criticizing deviations from them, and justifying his own behavior in their terms.[17] In the normal case, he will support the general system of norms by facilitating his parents' enforcement of them in a variety of ways, the least subtle of which is simply failing to indulge in any drastic form of moral rebellion.

However inadequate the above sketch may be as an exercise in descriptive sociology, I think it reminds us of enough to justify my claim that we have an analogue to the case of legal norm enforcement of the sort which we wished to construct. Both social norms and social sanctions are identifiable, as are quite strong forms of participation in their enforcement. And it is at least coherent to claim that these norms, which typically bar direct appeals to utility, could be sustained by the members of a society on act-utilitarian grounds.

But the child whose moral education I have been discussing becomes an adult, and it will be suggested that it is in a society of adult act-utilitarians that the analogy which I am trying to build breaks down. It will be claimed that, in a society of adult moral agents, men are not cast into the different roles (such as judge and citizen, parent and child) which bring into play the differing considerations of utility upon which my account in large part relies. In such a case, it will be argued, act-utilitarians would view moral rules as nothing more than rules of thumb.

The child does indeed become an adult, and he may fail to become a parent. But a generation of children, in becoming adult, does become a generation of parents. Insofar as the above account of moral education is correct, it thus *is* an account of the place of moral norms in a society of adult act-utilitarians. In characterizing them as parents, I have merely chosen to emphasize that feature of their situation which renders most obvious the need for social norms which bar direct appeals to utility. That this is a contingent feature makes it no less relevant,

---

[17]Thus manifesting what Hart calls the "internal aspect" of rules of obligation; see his *Concept of Law*, Chapter 6, Section 2.

and if act-utilitarianism implies that conventional morality would be dramatically different if we were a last generation of childless human beings, this strikes me as a point in its favor rather than a shortcoming.

My critic will quite rightly not permit the discussion to end here. For even if a society of adults is also a society of parents, adults will often be found employing conventional norms of the kind in question in situations where it is only adult behavior that is a matter of concern. Thus the demand for an account of moral rules within a society of adult act-utilitarians will continue to be pressed.

It is important to note that an implicit assumption behind this demand is that, once being taught conventional norms as a child, one may be able to resist appealing to them as an adult. But this assumption is highly dubious; on the hypothesis that the conventional rules are (among other things) reliable rules of thumb, it may be virtually impossible for an adult to make the sort of psychological adjustments which would be required for him to be able to view them as *only* rules of thumb. It is not simply that once having learned them as a child, I may be unable to resist appealing to them as an adult as a basis for assessing the behavior of others; I may also be unable to resist applying them to my own conduct. Although—looking only to the likely "objective" consequences—I may believe myself justified in breaking a promise on direct utilitarian grounds, for instance, I may realize that I will experience feelings of guilt if I do, and that undesirable consequence may tip the scales back in favor of the promise being kept.

The internal sanctions of guilt, remorse, and anxiety have been stressed recently by Richard Brandt as being among the most significant consequences of an individual's having been brought up in a society within which moral rules which bar direct appeals to utility enjoy a wide currency.

> It is true that the moral system does operate in part by threats: the threat of disapproval by other persons. . . . But the moral system does not work primarily in this way. It works through the fact that a person with a well-developed conscience has a built-in aversion to doing things of a certain sort. The mere thought of doing these things stirs up faint rumblings of anxiety or guilt. And the actual doing of them leaves one most uncomfortable.[18]

Although Brandt believes that the rules which form a moral

---

[18]Brandt, "Utilitarian Theory," 352-353.

system of the sort of which he is speaking are to be understood as those which would be current within a community of ideal rule-utilitarians, it is my contention that they can be accounted for within the framework of act-utilitarianism. For the existence of a moral conscience of the kind which Brandt describes is a predictable consequence of the process of moral education of which I have spoken above. Likely consequences of action are likely consequences of action; the act-utilitarian who finds himself saddled with such a conscience can only view feelings of guilt and anxiety as consequences of action to be given due consideration in deciding what to do. And as was suggested above, a consideration of such consequences will often tip the scales in favor of performing acts which otherwise would not have been optimific on act-utilitarian grounds. If my previous argument concerning the direct utilitarian grounds for teaching conventional norms to children is sound, the only question which remains is whether the adult act-utilitarian, insofar as he is able, should seek to rid himself of his rule-directed conscience.

The answer, I believe, is pretty obviously in the negative. For the agent, likely feelings of guilt, etc., are to be viewed as undesirable consequences of action. But this does not imply that it is undesirable that such consequences exist, even from the standpoint of the agent, let alone society at large. The analogy to the legal case here is clear; that the legal sanction is an undesirable consequence of action does not imply that it is undesirable that legal sanctions exist; quite the contrary, it is only because they have the character of consequences to be avoided that legal sanctions can serve to channel behavior into directions that it would otherwise not take. In the moral case, the built-in aversions which are the consequences of the inculcation of conventional norms are themselves of positive value in that they, too, redirect human behavior in desirable ways. For the norms in question are, by hypothesis, reliable rules of thumb, in that they correctly indicate that the consequences of performing certain kinds of acts are in the overwhelming majority of cases undesirable on balance, regardless of the presence of sanctions. If this leaves room for exceptions to the rules, those which are more than rules of thumb will be so because attempts to identify exceptions to them will more often than not be mistaken. Familiar human failings with respect to lack of reliable information, fallibility of judgment, bias in one's own case, etc., would be present even in a society of ideally moral act-utilitarians. Thus, at the social level, it is reasonable for adult act-utilitarians to continue to enforce some of those norms which they have been taught as children, not only against

others, but against themselves. The results of the adult's conscience being to a certain degree rule-bound are not undesirable,
and thus the rational act-utilitarian will neither seek to modify
his own built-in aversions nor those of others. Although each
individual will (in theory) base each of his decisions directly
upon the act-utilitarian principle, each will be content with the
situation being one in which, among the consequences to be considered, are the predictable reactions of both himself and others
which are based upon conventional norms which do not permit
direct appeals to utility. Each will view the existence of these
norms with their accompanying sanctions as the predictable and
desirable consequences of the independently justifiable acts of
himself and others.

A system of shared social morality is thus a close analogue to
a legal system constructed on an act-utilitarian basis. Considerations of utility lead to the participation of each in the creation
and support of a system of norms which bar direct appeals to
utility and which are backed by sanctions which each has a role
in applying. Although each individual is always to act on the
basis of an act-utilitarian calculation, among the consequences
of his acts which each will have to consider are the likelihoods of
the incidence of these sanctions. Far from being absurd or
paradoxical, we have here merely a particularly important
instance of a peculiarly rational ability which can be described
in highly general terms: A rational decision-maker, on the basis
of a choice criterion C, makes choices at a given time which will
render more or less eligible certain other choices which, at that
time, he can predict he will have to make on the basis of C at a
later time.[19]

A crucial consideration in my argument has been the notion
that, in order for it to be desirable to support a prescriptive norm
which fails to countenance certain exceptions which might be
made out on an act-utilitarian basis, it must be the case that
fallibility, etc., would more often than not lead to mistaken
judgments in attempts to identify those exceptions. It is of some
interest to note that this consideration operates at different
levels, and may in some instances become stronger as we proceed
from the question of violating a given norm to the question of the
desirability of holding someone accountable for a specific norm

[19]A major theme of Schelling's *Strategy of Conflict* is that it will often be
rational, in order to render a deterrent threat credible, for an individual to
divest himself of certain attributes typically associated with rational behavior,
in particular the ability to gather information and have choice options available: as for example, the highway patrolman who writes out the ticket, as a
matter of policy, before leaving his patrol car.

violation, to the further question of holding someone accountable for a failure to hold someone else accountable for the violation of a norm, and so on. Little Johnny might be justified in breaking his promise to his sister Sue but for the fact that his mother would be justified in punishing him for doing this, and his mother might not be justified in punishing him were it not for the fact that her failure to do so would be met with justified disapproval from grandmother. As we move to higher levels, the likelihood of a correct identification of an exception to the relevant rule might diminish, which would render it more likely than it would otherwise be that the initial identification would be mistaken in the first place. This is not to say, of course, that no acts will ever be correctly identified as exceptions, nor that none ought to be. It is merely to indicate the quite complex way in which a system of social sanctions based on shared social norms may act as a sort of feedback mechanism which can radically restructure the sets of considerations of consequences of which the act-utilitarian must take account.

I have spoken above as if overt acts of blame are the typical result of the application of moral norms, but I do not believe that they are. Although blaming others sometimes has its place, there are other ways in which norms are enforced that are equally if not more important. I have already mentioned three: (1) various forms of legal accountability; (2) punishment and other forms of sanctioning in the child-rearing context; (3) self-application.

Correlative to these forms of negative response are forms of positive reinforcement, the social significance of which should not be underestimated. The emphasis here upon blame rather than praise, punishment rather than reward, and guilt rather than heightened self-esteem, is due to the fact that I have taken the prohibitions of the criminal law as the model in terms of which to present the general analysis. But, although I trust that the present account can be extended to such things as ideals, approximation to which is to be rewarded and in terms of which substandard behavior may not be penalized, I also believe that prescriptive norms, backed by various forms of social sanction, play the most central role—legally and morally—in our social lives, at least as we now must live them. Within a society of act-utilitarians, things could perhaps be quite different.

Many forms of nonlegal norm enforcement occur in institutional or quasi-institutional contexts within which specific individuals have the responsibility of applying particular rules. Educational institutions, private and public employers, political parties, churches, private clubs, and so on, are all in large part structured in terms of reciprocal relations of rule-following and rule-applying, and it is this which assures the security of expectations about how those participating in them will behave upon which their existence depends. It is clear that the analysis given above of legal rules and legal sanctioning in terms of well-defined institutional roles can be extended to them. What I suggest is noteworthy is how heavily our society depends upon sanctions other than the moral in order to assure compliance to norms which are felt to be important. Indeed, our reliance upon, and ready resort to, legal and quasi-legal mechanisms of norm enforcement might be claimed to constitute implicit social recognition of the cogency of my argument. For, following Hume's account of the origins of government, I have emphasized the importance and rationality of creating rule-oriented roles and responsibilities which, in a strong way, structure the sets of considerations of consequences of which men must take account.

Within any one of the wide variety of contexts in which some form of sanction may be applied to the violation of a norm, there is the possibility of an antecedent event of an individual being called upon to justify his action. To justify an act, even when it is justifiable, may not be an easy job, and the prospect of having to meet the challenge of justification is thus typically an unpleasant one. There is a sense in which one has been penalized just by having one's behavior called into question, even where blame is ultimately avoided. Such challenging of others, I suggest, is much more frequent than the blaming of them—this, in part, because it is more often justified—but it has, at least in part, the same function as blame itself. That is, the likelihood of its occurrence is a disutility attaching to the performance of certain acts and thus may tip the scales in favor of nonperformance from an act-utilitarian point of view. What must be achieved by the social support of a rule-laden morality is the security of expectations which comes from having good reasons for believing that most people will conform their behavior to certain predictable patterns. Such reasons are in part provided by a shared understanding of the general desirability of at least demanding a justification of acts which are in violation of conventional norms.

I have, then, reviewed some of the chief forms which the nonlegal social sanction may take. I believe it fair to conclude that this review supports my contention that the act-utilitarian can give a coherent and plausible account of moral, as well as legal, rules which bar direct appeals to utility. In performing the central function of channeling human behavior into more desirable directions than it would otherwise take, such rules are clearly functioning as much more than mere rules of thumb.

4. *Conventional Rules as Reasons for Action*

What the consequences of *my* acts will be, and thus whether or not they are right or wrong, will often depend upon the manner in which *others* are behaving, and so, too, for *their* acts, the consequences of which may depend upon how *I* am acting. So, in seeking to do that which will have the best consequences, I must act upon the basis of expectations about how others will behave, which in turn will be based upon my beliefs about how they expect me to behave, for they, too, will be seeking to coordinate their behavior with mine just as I attempt to coordinate my own behavior with theirs. If our phone conversation is interrupted by a broken connection, for instance, I will call you back just in case I believe that you expect that I will call back and that you will thus not attempt to call me back. And your expectation might be based upon a *convention* between us; that is, that the original caller shall attempt to restore broken connections. The convention could, of course, be otherwise—that the one originally called call back, for instance—but there must be some convention between us unless we are to rely upon chance to avoid busy signals in our efforts to restore broken connections.[20] In general, we may wish to describe solutions to such problems of coordinating behavior as *conventions*, and this even in cases where they are not arbitrary, that is, where only one solution to the problem of maximizing utility through coordination exists.[21]

Conventions may take the form of *rules*, which in turn may be understood as systems of *warranted expectations*. As David Shwayder has put it,

> Confining ourselves to community rule, the idea is this: One follows a rule if he conforms to what he sees are the legitimate expectations of others; and the existence of a rule is, moreover, what entitles the others to their expectations, thus rendering them 'legitimate'. A community rule exists if the members of a community regulate their affairs according to what other members of the community would legitimately expect them to do. The rule is at once the expectations one conforms to and what legitimizes or warrants those expectations. The rule is, as it were, a system of community, mutual expectation. When one conforms to a rule he acts in the knowledge or belief that others would expect him so to behave. That the others are entitled to those expectations is his reason.[22]

[20]The example is from Lewis's *Convention*. I have learned much from his account, although I depart from it in certain key respects.

[21]I here follow Hume and depart from Lewis.

[22]Shwayder, *Stratification*, 253.

If my reason for behaving according to your expectations is simply that I do not wish to disappoint you, then my motives are strictly benevolent. If, on the other hand, I will not do my part of a convention unless I also believe that you will do yours, even though if I did my part your interests but not mine would be furthered, then self-interest is clearly playing a crucial role.[23] But of course it may be in the mutual self-interest—the common interest—of the members of a community to conform to a convention if others are so doing, in which case the motives of self-interest and benevolence need not conflict. Given that even the utilitarian must recognize that there is much truth to psychological egoism, he may be led in his disinterested moments to attempt to structure a system of conventional rules—by attaching some form of sanctions to their violation—so as to assure that conformity to them will be in the interest of all or most of those to whom the rules apply.[24]

The social norms which bar direct appeals to utility in the institution and maintenance of which I have claimed the act-utilitarian can consistently participate have the status of conventions in that, even though they may not be arbitrary, good consequences would typically not be produced by any given individual conforming to them unless others were doing so as well. They thus fit Shwayder's characterization of rules as systems of mutually warranted expectations, and it is for this reason that they function as *reasons for action*. For although it is only the act-utilitarian principle itself which has the status of a prescriptive moral principle, in virtue of it more *specific norms may serve as reasons for action in that their existence as systems of expectations implies that failure to conform to them will produce the disutilities associated with the disappointment of those expectations.*

The act-utilitarian is therefore in fact able to give an account of social norms which bar direct appeals to utility as more than mere rules of thumb in a twofold sense. Firstly, they perform the central function of directing human behavior into channels that it would otherwise not take by restructuring the sets of considerations of consequences of which utilitarian moral agents must take account. Secondly, they provide reasons for action in that their conventional acceptance is tantamount to the existence of

---

[23]As it does in Lewis's account but not in Schwayder's.

[24]Just as Hume's rational egoists, recognizing their irrational bias in favor of the near at hand, institute government as a means of seeing to it that the short term interest of some shall be to look after the long range interest of all.

systems of warranted expectations the disappointment of which is a disutility attaching to standard or normal cases of their violation.

5. Hodgson's Argument

I have acknowledged that there is a need which the act-utilitarian can recognize for social norms that bar direct appeals to utility, and I have maintained that the existence of such norms will provide the act-utilitarian with reasons to comply with them. In arguing that such norms may reflect the fact that there are some rules of thumb the exceptions to which cannot be reliably identified, I have sought to meet the objection that misapplications of the act-utilitarian principle would be so widespread as to lead to social chaos. And, by implication, I have contended that once it is understood that conventional social norms to a considerable extent structure the sets of considerations of consequences of which the act-utilitarian must take account, the objection that sometimes it is not right to do that which has the best consequences is at least in part undercut.[25] But what of the claim, implicit in Rawls's "Two Concepts of Rules," and developed at length in Hodgson's *Consequences of Utilitarianism,* that conventional moral rules of the sort in question could not possibly exist within a society of act-utilitarians?

It is clear that it will not do as a reply to Hodgson to argue that there are good utilitarian reasons for the existence of such norms. This is one of *his* points, and it is for this reason that he views his argument against utilitarianism as proceeding on utilitarian grounds. His claim is that a community of rational act-utilitarians would find themselves in a predicament analogous to that of rational egotists in a Hobbesian state of nature: They would recognize the need for conventional rules, and the desirability of the redirection which their existence would give to human behavior, but they could not consistently create or sustain them.[26]

Hodgson would admit that if one could show how the appropriate initial expectations could arise within a society of

---

[25]But, of course, only partially.

[26]In Chapter 14 of *Leviathan,* Hobbes admits that there can be no valid contracts, "social" or otherwise, in the state of nature. The so-called "prisoner's dilemma" finds rational egoists in a similar bind. On this, see Runciman and Sen, "Games."

act-utilitarians in the first place, then an act-utilitarian account of conventional norms could be provided. What he claims is insuperable is the problem of explaining how such expectations could be initially generated. Explicit agreement to abide by conventional rules will not do, of course, for the binding nature of explicit agreements is what is called into question by his claim that the conventional rules concerning promising would be absent. Expression of a firm intention to act in a certain sort of way might be claimed to serve virtually the same function as promising with regard to creating the relevant expectations, but this would be question-begging as well, for the conventions concerning truth-telling are jeopardized by the very same sort of argument that putatively applies to promising.[27]

Let us concentrate on the more fundamental case of truthfulness, rather than promising, for it is clear that if the conventional norms concerning the former could get off the ground, then they could serve (if nothing else could, which I am not willing to admit) as a basis for instituting conventions concerning promising, which in turn could serve as a basis (again, if necessary) for instituting other conventional rules.

The basic point which Hodgson fails to consider, it seems to me, is simply this: "Tell the truth" is not only a conventional norm: it has the independent status of a reliable rule of thumb. But this is itself a sufficient basis for the members of a community of rational act-utilitarians having the expectation that the truth will normally be told. And once those expectations are present, they provide the required sorts of reasons for action, those associated with the disutilities consequent upon the failure to satisfy warranted expectations. And as David Lewis's careful analysis of the sort of practical reasoning associated with conformity to conventional rules demonstrates, even a minimal grain of the relevant initial expectations may be amplified into strong reasons for action. (Recall the pop tune of the 1950's: "I was looking back to see if she was looking back to see if I was looking back to see if she was looking back at me.")

Also, on my account, the appropriate initial expectations would be present in a society of adult act-utilitarians due to the nature of their earlier moral education, which is much concerned, as we have seen, with the inculcation of conventional

---

[27]I am not sure that Narveson does not overlook this point in his interesting attempt to rebut Hodgson's argument in his "Promising," 222-228. It is not overlooked by Lewis in "Utilitarianism," his effective reply to Hodgson.

norms that bar direct appeals to utility. My argument, it will be recalled, was that the resultant psychological propensities would not be viewed as irrational hangovers from childhood to be eliminated through psychoanalysis or moral reeducation by mature adults. But they, too, would provide sufficient foundation for the conventional norms in question.

6. *Collective Action and the Provision of Public Goods*

Throughout this chapter the emphasis has been upon those fallibilistic considerations that provide reasons for backing up what are antecedently reliable rules of thumb with the social sanctions that convert them into genuine social norms capable of directing the behavior of those to whom they apply into channels it would otherwise not take. This focus is surely not misplaced, for the vast majority of those standards of conduct which moral philosophers and laymen would describe as moral rules do have the status of reliable summary rules; in most instances their breach does have worse consequences than would their observance. And while exceptions to them clearly exist, individuals as we know them are notoriously unreliable in identifying them. Truth-telling and promise-keeping, as discussed in the previous section, are paradigmatic examples, and it is for this reason that my reply to Hodgson followed the lines of the general analysis which I have presented so far.

There is, though, a need for social rules which has little or nothing to do with the fallibilistic considerations emphasized so far, a need which I believe has been implicitly although obscurely perceived by Hodgson, Rawls, and others who have found fault with the standard act-utilitarian account of social rules. For their basic point has been that there are instances in which rational act-utilitarians acting on the basis of a correct understanding of what is likely to have the best consequences will fail to provide themselves with common benefits which they could only obtain by acting in accord with binding social rules which bar direct appeals to utility. Thus the general notion that there are basically utilitarian arguments against act-utilitarianism which require the move to alternatives such as rule-utilitarianism and utilitarian generalization.

Illumination is to be found here not so much in the

philosophical literature[28] as in the writings of economists and political scientists concerned with the theory of public goods.[29] A public good (which by this definition may also be a public evil) is something such that if it is available to some members of a (properly defined) group, it is available to the other members of that group free of cost. Examples are clean air, public parks, a stable economy, police protection, and national defense. The problem that much of the current literature in economics and political science has focused upon is simply this: Although appropriately coordinated collective action would be sufficient to provide the members of a group with a public good the benefits of which to each would outweigh the share of the costs to each of providing it, it will not be rational for individual maximizers of expected utility to cooperate toward providing it. Each individual can reason that his own contribution will (typically) be insignificant; either enough others are acting in that manner which will produce the public good, or they are not. In the first case, if the benefit is available to anyone, it is available to him—and free of charge; thus no further benefit, to himself or anyone else, could come from his sharing in the cost of providing it. In the second case, the costs of his acting so as to provide it—that is, in that manner which, if enough others acted in a similar way (which they are not), would lead to its provision—would simply be wasted. So either way, regardless of how others are acting, non-cooperation is that which will maximize expected utility. Each individual reasoning this way, the public good is not provided, and all are worse off than they might have been had they acted differently. The individual members of a group which fails to provide itself with a collective benefit in this way are in what has come to be called an n-person prisoner's dilemma. Much as Hobbesian individuals who are unable to rationally contract themselves out of the state of nature, the choice situation for each individual can be represented as follows, with the individual's preferences over the possible outcomes expressed in descending rank order.[30]

---

[28]But see James Buchanan's apparently unnoticed paper in *Ethics* (1965): "Ethical Rules, Expected Values, and Large Numbers," and in the same journal almost a decade later (1974): Malcolm Feeley, "A Solution to the Voting Dilemma." Mill was of course well aware of the problem, as the Appendix will reveal.

[29]See especially: William Baumol, *Welfare Economics and the Theory of the State;* James Buchanan, *The Demand and Supply of Public Goods;* Mancur Olson, *The Logic of Collective Action;* William Riker and Peter Ordeshook, *An Introduction to Positive Political Theory.*

[30]This (and its mirror image) is the only two-by-two matrix with a strongly stable equilibrium point which is not Pareto optimal.

OTHERS

	Cooperate	Don't Cooperate
Cooperate	2	4
Don't Cooperate	1	3

INDIVIDUAL

It is important to note here that this dilemma of collective action with respect to the provision of public goods does not depend upon individuals acting selfishly; the costs of cooperation outweigh the possible benefits even when the benefits are calculated (as they would be by benevolent individuals) in terms of the entire group to which the public good in question would be available. It is for this reason that such cases are so dramatically different from those having to do with moral rules that are, amongst other things, reliable rules of thumb. Here, the relevant rules—all of the form "Assume a fair share of the cost of providing public good X"—are not such that the consequences of individuals violating them are typically undesirable. The consequences for each individual of all or most others violating the relevant rules are surely undesirable, but for each individual the consequences of his violation are more desirable than those of compliance regardless of how others are acting. Fallibilistic considerations of the sort present with respect to typical moral rules simply do not enter here, for there are no reliable rules of thumb concerning the identification of exceptions to which individuals might be more or less predictably mistaken. Indeed, the reliable rules of thumb with respect to individual action all take the form "Don't cooperate." For this reason it would seem that individuals successfully providing themselves with public goods on the basis of a direct cost benefit analysis with respect to the provision of those goods alone indicates that they are acting irrationally!

A strange case, to be sure; individuals acting irrationally making themselves better off than they would be by acting rationally. So much the worse, some would say, for the concept of rationality—that of utility maximization—upon which the dilemma of collective action is built. So much the better, the act-utilitarian may respond, for an account of morality and rational behavior which can illuminate what would appear to be one of the central reasons why individuals acting in groups often fail to provide themselves with common benefits. For many of the pressing social problems which face us today—pollution, the energy crisis, overpopulation, to name a few—would seem to be susceptible to at least partial analysis in terms of this sort of dilemma of collective action. Understanding such problems may provide a basis for their solution.

"Solutions" may be too pretentious a word, but amongst the possible ways out of such dilemmas that are open for the act-utilitarian to consider would seem to me to be the following:

(1) Although some have claimed that a different analysis applies to small groups,[31] it would seem that at best this is a contingent matter depending upon the probable consequences of individual action.[32] Firstly, with respect to some public goods and some groups—large or small—a particular individual might be in a position to play the role of a public benefactor by assuming the entire cost of providing a given public good when others are unable or unwilling to do so. Although perhaps relatively rare, such benevolence surely is sometimes called for by the act-utilitarian principle. Secondly, and more importantly, particular individuals will sometimes find themselves in a position to influence others in a positive manner by themselves contributing toward the cost of providing a public good. Especially in small groups, some may be in a privileged position to set an example, and if they can predict that it will be followed, and the costs of setting it are not too great, it may be called for by the act-utilitarian principle when the production of a genuine public benefit is in question.

(2) Understanding the dilemma in which they find themselves, individuals may avail themselves of organizations that will provide them with new incentives which will make it in their interest (that is, answer to their preference as either selfish or benevolent men) to act in those ways which collectively will lead to the provision of public goods. Government at all levels, unions (especially the closed shop), and professional organizations which often function as lobby groups can in many ways be viewed as organizations designed to further the interests of individuals who are incapable, acting solely as individuals, of helping themselves. Although some form of compulsion is typically involved—"compulsory" dues and "compulsory" taxation —it may be viewed as rationally self-imposed upon those to whom it is applied. While we may find here a nonrepulsive

---

[31]As does Mancur Olson, *The Logic of Collective Action*, Chapters I and II.
[32]As pointed out by Norman Frolich and Joe Oppenheimer, "I Get By With a Little Help From My Friends."

interpretation of Rousseau's notion of men forcing themselves to be free, the limitations of such solutions must be noted. Firstly, organizations are themselves public goods for those whose interests they are capable of furthering; for individuals to create an organization is thus for them to create a public good; to create an organization may be quite costly ("organization costs"); thus individuals acting freely and rationally as utility maximizers may be unable to organize themselves. The dilemma of collective action may, in other words, arise at the level of creating and sustaining organizations capable of furthering the common interests of their members. One way in which this problem may be avoided is for individuals to avail themselves of already existing organizations created at least in part for purposes other than that of providing public goods for their members. A good example here is the professional organization which provides private goods which its members desire—for example, a professional journal available only to members—and uses the dues collected mainly to provide its members with public goods—for example, through lobbying efforts.

(3) Especially where government regulation is involved, the costs involved in restructuring individual incentives so as to lead to the provision of public goods may exceed or largely cancel out the benefits. Hopefully, alternatives which are less costly are at least sometimes available. According to the analysis contained in this chapter, they often are, this in the form of specific social norms backed by social sanctions which are neither legal nor quasi-legal (that is, enforced by a formal organization against its members). Rational act-utilitarians, on my account, would be willing to support social norms which would provide them with individual incentives to share in the cost of providing public goods; norms backed by social sanctions of sufficient strength so that most individuals would not view acting as a "free rider" as likely to maximize expected utility. The same general account of *how* individuals would support systems of social norms which bar direct appeals to utility as developed earlier holds here as well; but the *why* of the matter, to repeat, is quite different. Fallibilistic considerations with respect to the identification of exceptions to reliable rules of thumb simply do not enter.

(4) Especially in small groups confronting the problem of providing an important public good over an extended period of time, specific social norms requiring social cooperation with respect to the provision of specific goods may develop. Much more significant, though, is the presence of general norms requiring cooperation in general kinds of cases regardless of the nature of

the particular public goods that are in question. There are three candidates to consider here: one bogus, one bonafide, and the other appealing but problematic.

Proponents of utilitarian generalization would of course suggest that each individual ought to cooperate in the provision of a public good when the consequences of everyone's so cooperating would be desirable. But as argued earlier (Chapter 2, Section 2), such a principle either takes into account the way in which others are in fact behaving, or it does not. In the former case, it collapses to the act-utilitarian principle itself and thus can provide no independent basis for cooperation in the provision of public goods. In the latter case, it would lead individuals to assume the sometimes very burdensome costs of cooperation even when not enough others were acting so as to lead to the provision of a common benefit which *would* be provided if—but only if!—enough others *were* cooperating. Where public goods are in question, the typical case is one in which quite a large number of individuals acting in concert is necessary for the production of the desired benefits; the "threshold effects" here are typically so strong that isolated individual action in the face of general noncooperation is especially misguided. Indeed, it may not only be absurdly wasteful, but actually harmful. For although everyone might be better off *if* everyone did X, everyone might be worse off if only some but not all or most did X.

A bonafide principle which the act-utilitarian might support in the same way in which he would support other social norms avoids the absurdities of the generalization principle but requires cooperation when others are in fact cooperating. It is the principle of fair play, one which prohibits "free riding" and requires that the individual assume a fair share of the cost of providing the benefits of social cooperation when he has voluntarily accepted the benefits of others doing their share. As Rawls has emphasized, it bars (is "absolute" with respect to) considerations of utility,[33] and its presence within a society of act-utilitarians would play a significant role in the structuring of the considerations of social consequences of which they, as act-utilitarians, would take account in deciding how to act in those choice situations involving interdependent action of the sort that is involved with the production of public goods. (More on this principle later, Chapter 6, Section 4.) What such a principle would require represents a considerable modification of the original matrix that was used to represent the dilemma of collective action.

[33]Rawls, "Justice As Fairness."

OTHERS

		Cooperate	Don't Cooperate
	Cooperate	1	4
INDIVIDUAL			
	Don't Cooperate	2(3)	3(2)

Here, fairness requires cooperation when others are cooperating in sufficient number to produce the public good, but it permits—in fact, requires, as I construe it—noncooperation when cooperation would be fruitless because of others' non-cooperation.

The principle of fair play may require cooperation within an ongoing practice of mutual cooperation and the past acceptance of common benefits, but it provides no basis for generating such cooperation in the first place. Yet this is precisely what is needed with respect to many serious social problems, ones it is hoped act-utilitarianism provides a suitable moral framework for dealing with. Here it might be thought that what is required is some moral principle that the act-utilitarian could support as a social norm which would yield the same matrix in cases regarding public goods as would the unacceptable generalization principle, namely:

OTHERS

		Cooperate	Don't Cooperate
	Cooperate	1	2
INDIVIDUAL			
	Don't Cooperate	4	3

The line of reasoning, of course, is simply that if each individual would himself prefer to cooperate regardless of how others were acting, then all would in fact cooperate, and the public good would be provided and no one's efforts would be wasted. But any principle which would yield the above matrix must be liable to the same objection as is the principle of utilitarian generalization; it would require wasted efforts of "cooperation"— perhaps not only wasted but even quite harmful efforts—when others were *in fact* not cooperating.[34]

[34]The duty discussed by Rawls to support just institutions would seem to be liable to this objection. See his *A Theory of Justice*, Section 51.

A weaker principle, problematic to be sure and one which I shall not endeavor to develop here, has been suggested by Colin Strang.[35] What it would require with respect to the kind of co-operation necessary to lead to the production of public goods is that individuals present themselves as prepared to cooperate if others are willing to do so as well. Just what this would come to in particular cases is not so easy to say, but sometimes, it is clear, gestures toward cooperation may be made which do not represent a commitment from which one cannot withdraw. In such cases, cooperation can be offered with an eye to how others are in fact behaving; sometimes one's share of the costs can be doled out in small bits contingently upon others cooperating too.[36] Acknowledgment of such a principle as a social norm amongst a society of act-utilitarians would, it would seem, be sufficient to generate forms of social cooperation in the first instance which would not otherwise exist, forms of cooperation sufficient to lead to the provision of common benefits in the form of public goods, and necessary in the absence of private incentives to cooperation of the sort provided by legal sanctions.

My general conclusion, therefore, is that the act-utilitarian is capable of providing an acceptable account of the conventional social norms, both legal and moral, which are admittedly necessary as a basis for the bonds of social union.[37] Later chapters will in large part be concerned with exploring the implications of this account with respect to specific instances of the norms that are constitutive of a just and moral social order governed by the rule of law.

---

[35]Strang, "What If Everyone Did That?," 5-10.

[36]As suggested by Thomas Shelling, *The Strategy of Conflict*, 45.

[37]In his "Forms and Limits," Feinberg has to some degree anticipated the major theme of the present chapter. He there recognizes the distinction between public rules and private principles and argues that an acceptable private principle may have very low utility as a public rule. See especially 377, 379, and 380.

5   *Obligation*

The present chapter is concerned with obligation, especially promissory obligation. My interest in the general notion of obligation stems in part from my belief that the bonds of social union associated with the mutuality of expectations as to how other members of a community will behave are to a considerable degree to be understood in terms of systems of reciprocal obligations. Furthermore, it has been claimed that the act-utilitarian cannot give a coherent account of obligation, nor of the obligation to keep promises in particular. Such an account shall be provided here, and the way will then be cleared for a discussion of political obligation and social contract theory (with its accompanying notion of a tacit promise to obey the law) in Chapter 6, and of legal obligations, both of citizens and members of the judiciary, in Chapters 9 and 10.

1. Promissory Obligation

Critics of act-utilitarianism have often contended that this theory is incapable of accounting for the stringency of certain kinds of obligations, promissory obligations being the most notable example. Sir David Ross, for instance, writes in a familiar passage:

> Suppose . . . that the fulfillment of a promise to A would produce 1,000 units of good for him, but that by doing some other act I could produce 1,001 units of good for B, to whom I have made no promise, the other consequences of the two acts being of equal value; should we really think it . . . our duty to do the second act and not the first? I think not. We should, I fancy, hold that only a much greater disparity of value between the total consequences would justify us in failing to discharge our *prima facie* duty to A. After all, a promise is a

promise, and is not to be treated so lightly as the theory we are examining would imply.[1]

While some have seen such putative counter examples as necessitating either total abandonment or considerable modification of act-utilitarianism, others have remained unconvinced. Jan Narveson, for instance, in his spirited defense of act-utilitarianism, replies:

> If we ask . . . "Why do we have a *prima facie* obligation to keep promises?" the answer is evident. When I promise you to do something, I do so because you are interested in the performance of it, and by promising you that I'll do it, I have led you to expect that I will do it in a way that you would not have expected me to do it if I hadn't promised. Consequently, if I default, it is more serious than if I hadn't promised, because this expectation is then disappointed. . . .
> Thus the excuse "because it was best on the whole for me to break it" is a perfectly proper one, though one which cannot be offered if I do not take into account the disappointment which you will feel if I default, and the extent of your interests which will be unsatisfied by this failure. And this is all there is to it.[2]

When filled out with a discussion of the other sorts of morally relevant considerations to which the act-utilitarian can legitimately appeal, I find Narveson's defense most appealing, but I cannot agree with him that "this is all there is to it." Indeed, I believe that the impasse that apparently exists between the critics and the proponents of act-utilitarianism cannot be understood or resolved until the act-utilitarian comes to grips directly with an important general claim which I take it Ross and many others are making. This is the claim that no *essentially forward looking* consequentialist view of moral obligation can account for the existence of those obligations, such as promissory ones, the reasons for the existence of which are to be found in *chiefly retrospective* considerations. Ross puts the point this way:

> It is plain, I think, that in our normal thought we consider that the fact that we have made a promise is in itself sufficient to create a duty of keeping it, the sense of duty resting on remembrance of the past promise and not on thoughts of the future consequences of its fulfillment.[3]

It seems to me that Ross has a point here that is virtually incontrovertible: If I have promised to do X, then I am under an obligation to do X, and this regardless of the consequences,

[1]W. D. Ross, *The Right and the Good*, 35.
[2]Narveson, *Morality and Utility*, 192-193.
[3]W. D. Ross, *The Right and the Good*, 37.

utilitarian or otherwise. Even if it is admitted that this is a prima facie obligation which might be overridden by utilitarian considerations, the point remains: There exists a sufficient condition for being under an obligation which does not have anything at all to do with the consequences of fulfilling that obligation.

A natural move here is to contend that, although "A promised B to do X" reports a past fact and does provide sufficient grounds for saying that A has incurred an obligation to do X, this is true only because it is *necessarily* true that promises create new expectations, the possible disappointment of which the act-utilitarian can and must take account.[4]

While it is of course typically the case that a promise creates new expectations in the promisee (and perhaps others), it is surely not necessarily true. Suppose that A has promised B to do X, where X is something B believes A would be strongly inclined to do anyway. A has incurred, because of his promise, an obligation to do X, but in such a situation there is no difficulty in assuming that B's expectations have not changed. Being as there are no new expectations, there are no new utilities to consider with regard to disappointed expectations, and we are thus left with what I am taking to be the original problem of how an essentially forward-looking normative theory is to account for the existence of obligations the reasons for which seem to lie primarily in prior circumstances.

The act-utilitarian can provide such an account, I believe, but only upon the basis of an analysis of the concept of obligation that implies that there is no necessary connection between *obligation* and *moral obligation*. If such can be maintained, the act-utilitarian will then be free to contend that only the non-moral features of moral obligation are based upon the kinds of retrospective considerations emphasized by Ross and others, and that the utilitarian consequences of fulfilling or failing to fulfill an obligation are the only considerations that are morally relevant. I shall now turn to an analysis of the concept of obligation which I believe supports just such a view.

2. *Obligations*

Utilitarian and non-utilitarian moral philosophers alike, with the English utilitarians themselves being perhaps the greatest offenders, have typically described normative ethics as

---

[4]Narveson can be read this way in *Morality and Utility*, but his position is clearly different in his later "Promising."

being concerned with the provision of a theory or an account of our moral obligations, implying that there are no philosophically relevant distinctions to be made between what a man *ought* to do and what he may have a *duty* or an *obligation* to do. In recent years, a number of writers have suggested that this failure to distinguish statements of and about obligation from other sorts of "ought" statements represents an important oversight in moral philosophy.[5] It is this oversight which seems to me to be largely responsible for the impasse with respect to the question of whether or not it is possible to provide an acceptable act-utilitarian account of moral obligation. For the clearer one becomes about the concept of obligation, it seems to me, the clearer it becomes that those features of obligation which cannot be accounted for in terms of utilitarian consequences are not morally relevant. (By a "morally relevant" feature of an obligation I mean one that provides a good reason for acting so as to fulfill that obligation.)

It is worthwhile to begin by noting that in our nonphilosophical moments we speak about our moral obligations and duties in a manner quite different from the way in which we describe the other things we believe we ought (or ought not) to do. Although it is natural to speak of my obligations as a husband, father, son, debtor, or teacher, I would agree with H.L.A. Hart that in most contexts it would be "absurd to speak of having a moral duty not to kill another human being, or an obligation not to torture a child."[6] More importantly, the whole language of obligation seems to differ in many significant respects from the terminology we employ when we give moral instruction or advice to others, or pass some form of moral judgment upon their acts. We are often *required*, or it is our *responsibility*, to do that which we are obligated to do, and we often find ourselves in a quite literal sense *held accountable* or *liable* in some specifiable way for a failure to *fulfill* our obligations. Of many (consider legal) obligations, we can say when, and how, and by whom they have been *created* or *imposed*, *incurred* or *assumed*, *changed* or *extinguished* or *transferred*.[7] Although the nature of the language of obligation in and of itself does not settle any philosophical issues, it does serve to focus our attention upon the characteristic features of those situations in

[5]See: Brandt, "Concepts"; Feinberg, "Supererogation"; Hart, "Obligation"; Lemmon, "Moral Dilemmas"; Rawls, *Theory of Justice*, Chapter 6; Whiteley, "On Duties."
[6]Hart, "Obligation," 82.
[7]Compare Hart, "Obligation," 84.

which it is most commonly employed; type situations about which fruitful generalizations might possibly be made. Among the features associated with paradigmatic cases of obligation, I believe that the following are the most important in the present context:

(1) Joel Feinberg has pointed out that the limited contexts in which the language of obligation is most at home are subject to a fairly simple classification.

> We speak of duties and obligations in three different connections. First, there are the actions required by laws and by authoritative command. . . . Second, there are the assigned tasks which "attach" to stations, offices, jobs, and roles. . . . Third, there are those actions to which we voluntarily commit ourselves by making promises, borrowing money, making appointments, and so on. . . . we do this by utilizing certain social contrivances or techniques designed for just this purpose.[8]

(2) An obligation that a person has to perform a particular act arises, not from the intrinsic nature of the act itself, nor from the character of the expected consequences of performing it, but rather from the person finding or deliberately placing himself in the sort of institutional or quasi-institutional context mentioned above. Hart at one time aptly labeled this feature of obligations their "independence of content,"[9] and C.H. Whiteley called attention to what is essentially the same thing when he noted that "[a]n action can be a duty irrespective of its consequences, and one can know it to be a duty without knowing what its consequences will be."[10]

(3) As both Feinberg[11] and Whiteley[12] have noted, we can usually discover what our obligations and duties are in a way that is quite different from any method we might reasonably employ to decide what, all things considered, we *ought* to do. In the normal run of cases, we need do no more than *ask* our bosses or military superiors (if they don't *tell* us), *consult* our appointment books, *read* our contracts, *remember* our promises, vows, and oaths, or *consider* the familial *relationships* which we bear to others. Questions of what we ought, in the final analysis, to do, which of course include questions of whether or not we

---

[8]Feinberg, "Supererogation," 277.
[9]Hart, "Obligation," 100, 102.
[10]Whiteley, "On Duties," 95.
[11]Feinberg, "Supererogation," 284.
[12]Whiteley, "On Duties," 100.

ought to fulfill particular obligations, are, for better or for worse, often not of this sort.[13]

Our obligations can, of course, conflict. Sartre's young Frenchman who is torn between his obligation to remain with an elderly mother who is completely dependent upon him, and his duty to help defend his country during wartime, is a dramatic, but not unilluminating, example. Indeed, although it is at best misleading to speak of the killer or sadist as having failed to fulfill his obligations, I believe that many if not most of the serious moral problems which the normal adult in modern society finds himself faced with can be correctly described as involving a conflict of duties or obligations. Each of the jobs we hold, roles we play, and commitments we make typically carries along with it a host of obligations, and these obligations often come into conflict not only with one another but with our more extensive legal obligations and considered moral judgments as well. It is this fact, I suspect, which led Ross to distinguish *prima facie* from *absolute* obligations.

> I suggest '*prima facie* duty' or 'conditional duty' as a brief way of referring to the characteristic (quite distinct from that of being a duty proper) which an act has, in virtue of being of a certain kind (e.g., the keeping of a promise), of being an act which would be a duty proper if it were not at the same time of another kind which is morally significant. Whether an act is a duty proper or actual duty depends upon *all* the morally significant kinds it is an instance of. The phrase '*prima facie* duty' must be apologized for, since . . . it suggests that we are speaking of a certain kind of duty, whereas it is in fact not a duty, but something related in a special way to duty.[14]

This strange notion of a prima facie duty, which is not yet actually a duty but only tends to be such, has been the cause of some considerable amount of philosophical dissatisfaction. H.J. McCloskey has suggested that Ross should have explicated the notion of an absolute duty in terms of that of a prima facie duty, rather than vice versa, and he argues that an absolute duty is merely a duty to fulfill some one or more of the prima facie duties that characterize a complex moral situation. "The expression 'absolute duty'," he writes, "is simply a shorthand way of referring to the largest sum of fulfillable prima facie duties in a given moral situation . . ."[15]

---

[13]This is of course to deny neither that there are some obligations which are hard to discover nor that people may be mistaken about their obligations.

[14]W. D. Ross, *The Right and the Good*, 20.

[15]McCloskey, "Ross and Prima Facie Duty," 344.

This emendation of Ross, I submit, is even less satisfactory than the original. For there are many instances in which we speak of weighing interests and dividing burdens and risks, and in some of these cases what we in the final analysis ought to do is of such a nature that *none* of our prima facie obligations can be completely satisfied. If I have borrowed $10 from Jones and $10 from Smith, and if I have promised to repay each of them on Friday, then if I only have $10 on Friday, it may be the case (given a suitable further description of the situation) that what I ought to do is to give each of them $5. In such a case, though, there is no plausible description of my prima facie duties such that it can be correctly said that what I have done is to fulfill the largest possible number of them. I have, quite obviously, fulfilled *none* of them, for I still *owe* both Jones and Smith $5 each.

But why talk in terms of prima facie duties at all? The apparent need to do so arises only if one is intent upon construing everything a man ought to do as something he has a duty, or is under an obligation, to do; and this approach, I have argued, only blurs important distinctions. If I have *borrowed* $10 from Jones, I have incurred an obligation (a debt) to repay him. If I have *promised* to repay him on Friday, I have an obligation to repay him on Friday. And these are genuine, bona fide, obligations, and this in spite of the fact that, since my sick child is in need of the medicine that only the money I owe Jones can buy, I *ought* to break my promise to repay him on Friday and, if things are bad enough, perhaps not repay him at all. There is a moral obligation to my child, in other words, which simply overrides whatever moral obligation I have to Jones; what it does not do is to destroy it or render it any the less a genuine obligation.

It is interesting to note how such examples illustrate the quite different ways in which we use the terms 'obligation' and 'ought'. As Brandt puts it,

> . . . if there are two conflicting obligations, recognized as such, and a decision must be made what should be done, we do not normally say, "What then really is my obligation?" To ask this is somewhat odd, since it is already clear that there are two obligations, which conflict. We can ask, of course, which obligation is stronger or more pressing. But the preferred phrasing in the situation is "What *ought* I to do?"[16]

Those moral philosophers who have been content to construe all of the things that a man ought (morally) to do as things that

---

[16]Brandt, "Concepts," 378.

he has an obligation to do, while they may have had some difficulty in explaining the notion of a prima facie obligation, are able to offer a very simple account of the connection that exists between what we ought, and what we are obligated, to do. That I ought to fulfill my obligations reduces, on their view, to the trifling tautology that I am obligated to do that which I am obligated to do. Such a view has been taken by John Searle, who, it is clear, would agree with me both that we are obligated to do only some of the things that we ought to do and that we ought not, in the final analysis, to do some of those things that we are obligated to do. What Searle claims, in other words, is that the principle "If S has an obligation to do X, then S ought, all other things being equal, to do X," is a tautology. And as Searle has correctly noted, *if* the connection between what one is obligated to do and what one ought to do, other things being equal, is analytic, then, since promises do, for instance, create obligations, it will follow that one can derive the statement that I *ought* to meet Jones tomorrow from a report of *the fact* that I promised to do so. [17] And here quite clearly lies the source of the difficulty that the act-utilitarian finds in meeting the objections of a deontologist such as Ross. For if he admits (as he must) that the existence of an obligation can follow from the existence of certain prior facts, and if he also accepts the principle that, *ceteris paribus,* one ought morally to do that which one has an obligation to do, then he cannot avoid the conclusion that retrospective, rather than prospective, considerations can provide sufficient grounds for a judgment about what a person ought morally to do.

Unless he is to deny what is obviously correct in the deontologist's account of obligation, then it is this bridge between the "is" and the "ought" which the act-utilitarian must refuse to cross with one such as Searle. Insofar as one is willing to talk about necessary truths in a natural language at all, I suppose it must be admitted that the principle "If S has a *moral obligation* to do X, then S ought, other things being equal, to do X" is a tautology. But "If S has (any sort of) an obligation to do X, then S ought, other things being equal, to do X" is, I submit, not a tautology, but, at best, a not very reliable rule of thumb. As such, it may provide some basis for an epistemic presumption

---

[17]Searle, "'Ought' from 'Is'", 43-58. This view is retained in all essential respects in Searle's book, *Speech Acts.* Searle hedges as to whether or not the *ought* in question is a *moral ought,* but he clearly intends it to be one which provides a reason for action (175-176). In conversation, Searle has indicated that he prefers to reserve the *moral ought* for "very important questions."

that any given obligation is a moral obligation, but a presumption that may be rebutted is a far cry from a morally relevant reason that must be overriden. What I shall argue in defense of act-utilitarianism is, in brief, that there are obligations that give rise to no corresponding moral obligations, and that the existence of an obligation thus cannot support the assertion that one ought (even *ceteris paribus*) to fulfill that obligation. In order for the existence of an obligation to provide a morally acceptable reason for acting so as to fulfill that obligation, it must be shown either that doing so will have some good consequences or that failing to do so will have some bad consequences.

Consider, for instance, the connection between legal and moral obligation. Suppose a legal system so thoroughly wicked that even a state of political anarchy would be preferable to it: There seems to me to be nothing paradoxical in claiming that the existence of a legal obligation which arose within that system could not in itself provide the slightest grounds for claiming that a corresponding moral obligation existed as well. (This is of course not to deny that there might be other good reasons, such as fear of punishment, for fulfilling such an obligation.) Indeed, what does seem paradoxical is the assertion that even in the wickedest of legal systems there is a moral obligation, even a so-called "prima facie" one, to obey any valid legal rule. It is the utter inability of one who holds such a view to provide any sort of a reason why someone ought to obey a rotten rule created in a rotten system, I believe, that has driven some of the proponents of such a view to the extreme position of claiming that a thoroughly iniquitous legal system is not really a legal system at all.[18] But this latter claim, made in a desperate attempt to save the equally dubious claim that the existence of a legal obligation entails a moral obligation of obedience, has little to recommend it.

I have chosen to speak of legal obligation above because it so obviously fits the pattern of analysis presented earlier. For whether or not one has a legal obligation depends merely upon whether or not one is a citizen subject to a valid rule of law, the validity of a legal rule depending neither upon its content nor upon the consequences of obedience to it, but simply (typically, at least) upon its formal origin. Since there are those, though, who would argue that genuine legal obligations cannot exist in a system that fails to meet certain minimal moral requirements, and who would also argue that there is a moral obligation to

---

[18]See for instance Fuller's *Morality of Law*.

obey any law created in a system that does conform to such minimal standards, I shall turn at this point to a different sort of example.

Although there are some who would argue that a legal system so thoroughly bad that it does not merit any support is not a legal system at all, I believe it will be agreed on all hands that there are some jobs, institutions, and social roles which (at least under normal circumstances) simply should not exist. If it is further agreed that genuine obligations can arise in such contexts, but that their existence does not provide good reasons for action, my point that the bare fact that an act is obligatory does not imply that it is *morally* obligatory will have been made. Thus consider the role of a secret policeman.[19] I believe that the following can be said: (1) If there are secret policemen in a particular state, then the act-utilitarian Jones might have good reasons for becoming one and performing his duties just well enough to be kept on the job, for Jones might know that if he doesn't accept the job, then Smith, the ruthless totalitarian sympathizer around the corner, will accept it and in the course of the zealous performance of his duties do much to weaken the local anti-totalitarian underground movement; (2) In accepting the role of a secret policeman, Jones would be making the best of a bad situation—secret policemen should not exist; under normal circumstances, the practice of maintaining such a group of paid informers is so wicked that it merits no support whatsoever; (3) In spite of the fact that it is a wicked practice worthy of no moral support, acceptance of the role of secret policeman does carry along with it certain duties and obligations: if Jones's superiors order him to spy on the local butcher, it will be his duty to do so.

Given the unfortunate situation suggested in (1), Jones ought to have spied on the local butcher. He had a good, act-utilitarian, reason for doing so; that is, a likely consequence of his failure to do so would be that he would lose his job to Smith. But, given (2), the fact (3) that it was his duty to spy on the butcher does not qualify as an additional reason for saying that he ought to have done so. Indeed, given (2), it is a good reason, which happens to have been outweighed under the circumstances, for his *not* performing the act in question. If it had been Smith who had gotten the job and done the spying, and if he were later required to defend his act, it would be absurd to accept as a relevant defense the fact that he was "only doing his duty." What we would be inclined to say if Smith seriously

---

[19]The example is from Downie, "Social Roles," 29-36.

offered this as his sole defense, I submit, is that he has misunderstood the nature of the challenge with which he has been presented. It is the very performance of his duty which bothers us, in other words, and it is no defense of his act to describe it in the very terms which, given (2), render it morally objectionable. And although Smith's following an order to spy on the local butcher is surely just as much a case of the performance of a duty as Jones doing so, would it not be absurd to say that Smith was fulfilling a *moral* obligation?

The example of the secret policeman is not idiosyncratic. With a little ingenuity, I am confident that the reader will be able to dream up even more disturbing examples of his own. For there are many existing or easily conceivable social practices with associated roles and responsibilities which, although obligations and duties may clearly arise within them, are so bad that they merit no moral support whatsoever. Where such is the case, *obligations* are not associated with corresponding moral obligations.

At this juncture, my account is likely to meet with objections from within the utilitarian camp itself. For although many rule-utilitarians would agree that an obligation or duty is not necessarily a moral obligation or duty, they would argue that, if an obligation arises within an institution or practice which—unlike the cases I've relied upon above—*is* on the whole worthy of moral support on utilitarian grounds, then that obligation is a moral obligation. They would contend, for instance, that although the question of whether or not there is any reason to support a given legal system as a whole is to be answered on utilitarian grounds, the question of whether or not there is an obligation to obey any particular law arising in a system which is worthy of support is not one the answer to which is contingent upon the consequences of obedience. If the question of the system's overall utilitarian acceptability is settled in the affirmative, in other words, it would be contended that there is a moral obligation to obey any particular rule which is a valid law within it. There might, of course, be other reasons to obey it, or it might be that, all things considered, an act of disobedience would be justified, but (it would be urged) there is at least one good reason to obey it, and this is sufficient to establish the existence of a prima facie moral obligation.[20]

Not only does such a view suffer from all of the difficulties connected with rule-utilitarianism (see Chapter 2, Section 2); it

---

[20]Among those to whom this position might fairly be attributed are Toulmin, *Examination*, and Baier, *Moral Point of View*.

also suffers in an acute form from the malady associated earlier with virtually all not-act-utilitarian views (Chapter 2, Section 1). The view avoids the absurd consequence that the obligation to obey the law is absolute; that is, that it can never be overridden. But this raises the question of the manner in which the obligation to obey the law that purportedly derives from the utilitarian merit of the system as a whole is to be weighed against the considerations which in the final analysis might justify disobedience, including considerations of consequences. If this system-related obligation is to have any moral weight, it must, it seems to me, be redescribable in terms of considerations of consequences. But if it is, we are back to act-utilitarianism. If, for instance, it is said that disobeying a law that arises in a system on the whole worthy of support will have the undesirable result of weakening respect for a valuable social institution, and that this is the foundation of the moral obligation to obey, it may be replied that this is a purely contingent matter and that in some cases an act of disobedience might actually strengthen respect for the institution. The arrest, conviction, and punishment of a given law violator might, for instance, especially if well publicized, have a considerable deterrent effect on the behavior of others. Indeed, this is a most familiar claim in the context of utilitarian attempts to justify the institution of criminal punishment. Given the fact, though, that *most* cases of law violation are likely to have some harmful effects on the legal system, if only because they are likely to be discovered and thus put into motion the costly machinery involved in apprehension, prosecution, etc., one can grant the epistemic principle that there is a presumption that one ought to obey any law arising in a system worthy of utilitarian support. In addition, one may even grant, following the analysis of social norms in the previous chapter, that such a presumptive rule of thumb may come to have the status of a conventional moral norm backed up by various forms of social sanction. Although all of this shifts the burden of proof to one who claims that he doesn't even have a good reason to fulfill an obligation which arises within a legal system that he admits is worthy of support, it is quite consistent with specific questions of obedience and disobedience being settled solely on direct utilitarian grounds.

I believe that the act-utilitarian may conclude, then, that although the reasons for the existence of an obligation may lie in the past, as may the grounds for a presumption that a given obligation is a moral obligation, an analysis of the concept of obligation does not show that anything other than a consideration of utilitarian consequences is relevant in determining whether or not any given obligation ought to be fulfilled. The grounds for the existence of an obligation, he may contend, are one thing; the reasons for fulfilling an obligation quite another. Although the deontologist may be correct about the retrospective character of the former, the act-utilitarian need be concerned only with establishing the prospective nature of the latter.

I claim, then, to have laid to rest an objection to act-utilitarianism which, if cogent, would render the discussion of putative counter examples such as that presented by Ross superfluous. For if Ross were correct that "the sense of duty"—understanding by this *moral* duty—rests on "remembrance of the past" and not on "thoughts of future consequences," *any* teleological moral theory would be doomed to failure from the very outset.

3. *Promising: Some Final Comments*

With the ground thus cleared, the act-utilitarian is free to offer an account of those utilities which explain and justify the common conviction that most men ought to keep most of their promises.

(1) With Narveson and others, including Sidgwick,[21] he may point out that a crucial factor is the extent to which new expectations have been created in the promisee that his interests will be satisfied, and this regardless of whether or not the promisor has actually said "I promise," or rather indicated his intentions and created the relevant expectations in some other way.

(2) Based upon his heightened expectations, the disappointment of which is itself a disutility, the promisee may have gone to the expense and inconvenience of making plans whose failure to come to fruition because of the promise being broken would represent a further, and perhaps considerable, disutility.

(3) As the colloquialism "Is that a threat or a promise?" suggests, one only promises to do that which one believes will be in the promisee's interest in the first place. The disappointment of the expectations consequent upon the making of the promise aside, there are thus direct considerations of benevolence which favor keeping it.

(4) Given that the practice of promising is a valuable one, indirect effects upon the practice which might flow from the breaking of a promise are also of some importance. In particular, there is the question of the possible effects of a broken promise on

[21]Sidgwick, *Methods*, 354.

the confidence with which the promisee will rely upon promises, both those of the promisor and those of others, in the future.

(5) Similarly, there is the question of the effects of breaking a promise upon the reputation and future credibility of the promisor himself.

(6) Promises are normally made with the intent of furthering the interests of both the promisor and the promisee; as with legal contracts, the mutuality of interests which they commonly represent may be a strong ground for the confidence that is placed in them. A probable ground for the promisor believing that the best consequences will come from him breaking his promise is thus a changed perception of what his own interests dictate. But men—even moral men—are notoriously biased in favor of their own interests, and their judgments about when they are justified in breaking their promises are to that extent unreliable. Thus the principle that one ought to keep one's promises is not only a reliable rule of thumb; it is a rule of thumb to which attempts to identify expectations will more often than not be mistaken. This second order consideration may also weigh against, although it of course does not absolutely prohibit, the breaking of a promise by one who is aware of his own fallibility.

(7) The conjunction of the above six features of promising is sufficient grounds for it to be rational for a community of act-utilitarians to give the principle that one ought to keep one's promises the status of a socially enforced conventional norm that bars a direct appeal to considerations of utility as the grounds for breaking a promise except when the consequences of keeping it would quite clearly be very undesirable. The existence of the social sanction is thus a further central consideration, and the likelihood of its incidence is sufficient to tip the scales in favor of the keeping of many promises the breaking of which would otherwise appear to be justified on act-utilitarian grounds.

When this last consideration is added to the previous ones, but only then, is it possible to understand how promises can create the security of expectations about how others will behave which permits the future to be tied down in advance in the manner in which Rawls, Hodgson, and others have emphasized. But the account remains, of course, an act-utilitarian one, for once all of the relevant considerations of utility have been taken into account, whether or not any given promise ought to be kept is to be decided solely upon the basis of a consideration of consequences. If the connotations of the deontologist's use of the expression may be put aside, the account may be aptly described as one of the "prima facie" moral obligation to keep promises.

6   *Political Association*

The previous two chapters have already indicated the central elements in my view of political association and the nature of the obligation to obey the law. I have argued that while the act-utilitarian can recognize the need for laws backed by sanctions, he cannot admit the existence of any such thing as an obligation to obey the law as such. In particular cases, the morality of obedience or disobedience is to be determined solely upon the basis of a direct consideration of consequences.

What the present chapter seeks to demonstrate is that the act-utilitarian can go well beyond this and provide an interesting and plausible account of the conditions of political community which represents a genuine alternative to the picture presented by traditional political theory, one which would have government rest either upon force, or expertise, or the general recognition of a moral obligation to obey the law as such. While I shall argue that the claims of power, expertise, and moral obligation are neither mutually exclusive nor jointly exhaustive as alternative bases of the bonds of political association, my own position shall incorporate some of the features of each of these familiar views. For the necessity of the law being backed by sanctions will be acknowledged; the role of nondemocratic elites will be admitted; and, as with the analysis of promising in the previous chapter, the principle that one ought to obey the law will be construed as having the status of a conventional moral norm.

1. Political Association

Political power may be understood as the ability to make or influence decisions which have significant effects upon the well-being of the members of a social group. As such, most men have some political power, and all social groups may be analyzed in terms of the political power relationships which obtain within them. It must be some quite different notion of political power, it would thus seem, that leads anthropologists and others to view some social groups as pre-political.

The apparent contradiction between these two views of political community may be resolved as follows: A political society exists when it is common knowledge amongst the members of that society that political power is concentrated in some determinate person or persons, and the majority of the members of that community to a significant degree form their expectations and make their plans on the basis of the decisions which those in power reach.[1]

If understood in this way, the natural necessity for men forming political associations under all but the most primitive conditions is transparent. Any group of individuals the members of which anticipate remaining in relationships of mutual dependency for any period of time will perceive that it is in their common interest to adopt a procedure for reaching and enforcing decisions which will effect their mutual well-being. They cannot rely solely upon conventional moral rules, not only because the social sanction will typically be too weak to counteract the pulls of psychological egoism, but because even in a society of morally like-minded and unselfish individuals differences in particular cases would arise due to different opinions as to how shared principles applied to socially significant situations of fact. Within a society of act-utilitarians, for instance, much room for disagreement would exist due simply to the considerable uncertainty which surrounds the prediction of what the future consequences of our acts will be. And it is to be assumed that act-utilitarians, like other men, are willing to press their moral claims upon others, especially where these involve questions of social policy.[2] The need for something other than private and uncentralized means of settling such conflicting claims, and of organized procedures for enforcing such settlements without relying upon a resort to self-help, could not long pass unnoticed.

So within all but the most transient social groups there is a need for a political power, a public "umpirage," if not of a

---

[1]Although somewhat similar to John Austin's concept of political society, my notion, unlike Austin's, does not imply the existence of a central sovereign power.

[2]Compare Buchanan and Tullock, *Calculus of Consent*, 4, on the need for a social decision procedure even within a society of altruists.

Lockean law of nature, then at least of the act-utilitarian principle itself. Assuming moral homogeneity, it is the need for what Locke identified as the judicial and executive functions of government—what Hart has recently called rules of adjudication—which is paramount.[3] Given that the subjects of the anthropologist's concern—primitive societies—typically manifest such homogeneity, it is no wonder that the definitions of law which they adopt reflect this (as we have seen in Chapter 3, Section 4). On the other hand, a society which tolerates a considerable degree of moral diversity is more likely to perceive the need for a shared social decision procedure for determining what the rules of the game are going to be as the most pressing; a need for what Locke described as the legislative function of government—brilliantly redescribed by Hart in terms of what he calls rules of recognition and change.[4]

There is no great problem, then, in explaining—at least in general outline—the need for government and the rule of law. Although the ideology of legalism may represent an overestimation of the extent of that need in both the law and morals of the Western world, classical political philosophy surely provides the basis for a plausible and comprehensive account of the necessity for and desirability of law and government.[5] The problem which traditional political theory has *not* solved is rather this: How is political association possible? In particular, how is it that men may be bound together by bonds of political union which stabilize the rule of law without in some way abdicating their autonomy of moral judgment?[6] A stable and effective political community depends upon the individual being able to assume that most of his fellow citizens will obey most duly enacted laws and voluntarily conform to the majority of judicial decisions which settle conflicting claims made on the basis of such laws. Does not the existence of such conformity imply the sacrifice of that individual autonomy of judgment which would permit each individual to act in each case in the manner which he believed was dictated by his considered moral judgments? Is not political anarchy the only form of association which the autonomous moral agent can consistently support?[7]

---

[3]Thus Hart's claim in his *Concept of Law* that it is the rule of recognition which lies at the foundation of a legal system may be misplaced. See Fuller, *Morality of Law*, 144-145, who also cites the anthropological literature.

[4]Hart, *Concept of Law*, Chapter 5, Section 3.

[5]I allude here to Shklar's fascinating and provocative book, *Legalism*.

[6]Compare Rousseau, *Social Contract*, Book I, Chapter 6.

[7]As is maintained by Wolff, *Defense of Anarchism*.

Let us turn to a brief examination of the alternatives with which traditional political theory presents us as possible answers to this question.

2. *Law as Coercion*

According to Hobbes, rationally self-interested men, in order to avoid the sorry condition of a state of nature in which life would be "short, nasty, and brutish for all," would support a system of law which would assure a condition of peace and relative personal security for each by the effective wielding of an overawing regime of coercive force. The penalty attached to the violation of each law would be so great, and the likelihood of its incidence in the case of violation so high, that in the overwhelming majority of cases compliance, rather than disobedience, would be the best bet for the rationally self-interested man.[8] Any given man would have the rational expectation that others would respect his person and property, and honor their contractual agreements with him, for the same reason that he would act in a similar manner toward them: the expected cost of not doing so would be so high as to render it a bad bargain. In those rare instances in which disobedience to law would be likely to promote self-interest, it is what would be demanded by the maxims of rational prudence—which Hobbes calls "the laws of nature."

Hobbes's theory would permit the retention of individual autonomy of judgment; his emphasis on the importance of psychological egoism and the necessity for legal sanctions has considerable appeal; and the general model of rational men deliberately acting so as to restructure the sets of considerations of consequences which will determine their future choices is one with which I am in obvious sympathy.

There are political relations which Hobbes's model does approach capturing: those amongst nation states; that of the partly autonomous political unit forced to pay tribute to an alien external power; that of the member of a politically, economically, and socially disenfranchised minority group within a larger society in which normal political and social relations prevail. But Hobbes's picture is nonetheless not faithful to the realities of political association, either as they normally are or as they could and should be. The element of psychological egoism is blown out of all reasonable proportion, and no consideration at

[8]Hobbes, *Leviathan*, Chapter XV.

all is given to the fact the men often act on the basis of moral considerations which are capable of overriding narrow self-interest. Hobbes is correct that *if* it is *only* the threat of force which underlies the general expectation amongst the members of a political community that the law will typically be obeyed, then that threat must be overawing. But under normal circumstances within a healthy polity, this is not the perception that men have of the foundation of their mutual expectations concerning obedience to law. With good reason, men believe that the basis for obedience to law represents more than the widespread fear of the effective wielding of coercive force by those in power, and they realize that where this is not the case, the situation is undesirable on a number of scores. Not only is it oppressive, but it is typically highly unstable—he who lives by the sword alone is likely to perish by it. Hobbes is right that the glue which holds men together in a stable political union may be viewed as their own deliberate concoction; and it may be a compound one component of which is the fear of the legal sanction. But except in those atypical instances which are both unstable and normally unworthy of moral support, the bonds of social union which are political in character are of more substance than the ties amongst the mutually oppressed.

3. Political Infallibilism

What better form of government could there possibly be than that which guaranteed that those in political power would be incapable of making unwise or immoral decisions? What firmer foundation for the ties of political association than the shared conviction that the law would demand that, and only that, which was morally right? The search for an infallible political decision-making process represents a persistent and still current theme in Western political theory and practice. It underlies the support given to the charismatic and demagogic political leader, and supports the pretensions of theocracy; it led Plato to the ideal of a utopia in which the wisdom of the philosopher king would prevail, while it led Rousseau to the quite different conclusion that, if forced to operate under the appropriate restraints, an infallible legislative majority would express "the general will" and could thus legitimately control a misguided minority by "forcing them to be free."

The assumptions underlying Plato's version of this political ideal, as presented in the *Republic*, are perhaps the most instructive to examine. They include the following: (1) Political decision-making demands knowledge, expertise, and moral insight; (2) Under the right conditions of education and practical experience, those with the requisite initial aptitudes can develop the required qualities of intellect and moral character; (3) Those in possession of the desired political wisdom can be reliably identified, and the nature of their qualifications understood, by those whom they are to govern; (4) Once in power, those who know what is right will not fail to do it.

As the follies of immoral and stupid political leaders continually testify, the first assumption is not to be denied. It is the ambiguous status of the other three assumptions which explains the perennial appeal, as well as the ultimate unacceptability, of the model of an ideal political association resting upon the general recognition of the infallibility of those in power. Our attitudes toward education can only be described as mixed: with Plato, we may acknowledge its great formative influence; but we must admit that we have such a primitive understanding of educational theory and are so inept at educational practice that we could not reasonably share his confidence that we could reliably produce the kind of expertise in question, and this even if there was general agreement (which there is not) as to what in principle it was to consist of. And how is one to distinguish the experts from the charlatans, assuming that they exist to be identified? The democratic electoral process must be viewed as an irrational farce unless one assumes that the electorate at least does better than chance in selecting political leaders, and that much it perhaps does. But how much better than chance? Finally, Plato's conviction that those who know what is right will without fail do what is right is not one which we are likely to share. Although the slogan that "power corrupts, and absolute power corrupts absolutely" is perhaps a cynical oversimplification, blind reliance upon the good will of those in power is equally naive, and considerably more dangerous.

The best that can be said, perhaps, is that the model of the wise and benevolent political leader (or legislature, or electorate) is an *ideal* of which no political society can afford to lose sight, but that extreme caution must be exercised in the light of the fact that the most sincere attempts to attain it in practice are likely to fall far short. Within a broader constitutional framework which does not in general rest upon assumptions implying the infallibility of the political decision-making process, there is perhaps indeed room for the notion that power can safely be placed in the hands of the experts. Chapters 9 and 10 will in fact present a view of the role of the judiciary in a democratic society which may be understood in much this way; similar claims might be made about the practice of basing promotion within all but the highest ranks of the U.S. Foreign Service upon the results of competitive civil service examinations.

Although the ideal of assuring the intrinsic moral merits of what the law demands by guaranteeing the infallibility of those who have the power to make, interpret, and enforce it may be quixotic, it implies something about the grounds of obedience to law which I by no means wish to deny. For what this model of political association forces us to admit is simply this: The law, when it ought to be obeyed, ought to be obeyed primarily because what it prescribes is morally right, and a consideration of its moral merits is thus always appropriate. On this view, the bonds of political community are cemented by a general recognition of the law's substantive moral credentials, and a shared conviction that most men, most of the time, are rational and moral enough to act accordingly.

4. *Political Obligation*

The bonds of social union should not be cemented by force alone, even in those rare instances where this is possible. The ideal of an infallible political decision-making process is in practice unattainable. The only alternative to political anarchy which traditional theory recognizes would identify the ties of political association with the general recognition of a moral obligation to obey the law as such, regardless of the intrinsic merits of what it prescribes or of the likelihood of legal sanctions being applied in the case of disobedience. A political association is on this view at bottom a moral union resting upon common recognition of mutual moral obligations. The members of a political community on this view can have secure expectations that most laws will be obeyed by most men to the extent that they believe that their fellow citizens are inclined to recognize and honor their moral obligations.

Arguments for the existence of an obligation to obey the law as such fall into three chief categories: (1) Those which invoke some sort of a generalization principle; (2) Those which would reduce the obligation to obey the law to a promissory obligation by way of the notion of tacit consent; (3) Those that rely upon a principle of fair play. I shall comment but briefly upon each of these three arguments in turn.

The generalization argument implies that since the consequences of everyone's disobeying the law would obviously be disastrous, any given individual has a prima facie obligation to obey any given law. As was seen earlier (Chapter 2, Section 2), the appropriate reply to the rhetorical question "What would happen if everyone did that?" is simply "Did *what?*" Any conscientious law violator who believed himself justified in violating a particular law would surely not view himself as thereby endorsing indiscriminate disobedience to laws in general, nor would he be oblivious to the importance of considering how his act of disobedience would *in fact* be likely to influence the behavior of others. If, as a matter of fact, a particular act of law violation would be likely to lead to widespread disobedience to laws in general, the act-utilitarian must surely take this into account. But if the generalization principle permits him to do so, and also permits him to treat as relevant the (much more probable) fact that his act of disobedience is *not* likely to influence the behavior of others, then it is indistinguishable from the act-utilitarian principle itself. On the other hand, if the generalization principle does not permit a consideration of how others are actually behaving or are in fact likely to behave, then it has, as we saw in Chapter 2, absurd consequences.[9]

The notion that the citizens of a state may under certain conditions be taken to have given their consent to obey any valid law, whatever its content and regardless of the consequences of obeying it, has had the most widespread philosophical appeal. Indeed, it would seem that social contract theory has even become part of the folk wisdom in the United States, complete with the traditional claim that continued voluntary residence constitutes tacit consent—thus contemporary dissenters confronted with bumper stickers reading "America—Love It Or Leave It." At the time of the present writing, official political rhetoric has become equally sophisticated.

The standard objection to social contract theory seems to me to be conclusive: In order for there to be a (promissory) obligation to obey the law, there must be some act or acts which can be understood as representing full and free consent to do so. Express consent is rare, and even where it is present—as perhaps with naturalized citizens required to take an oath of allegience—its voluntary character is suspect. It is thus that the contract theorist must rely upon the notion of tacit consent—some sign of agree-

[9]On the generalization argument as a basis for an obligation to obey the law, see Wasserstrom, "Obligation to Obey."

ment other than the written or the spoken word. Continued residence is the favorite candidate, but it is only by the wildest stretch of the philosophical imagination that it could be taken typically to be fully voluntary. For the average citizen of the modern nation state, to pack up and leave the country of one's birth and native language—to abandon one's friends, family, employment and cultural ties—is simply not a live option.[10] And even if it were, what—according to the argument of the contract theorist—would be the plight of one who did not wish to incur an obligation to obey the laws of *any* state? Must such an individual spend his life on a raft in international waters?

A further objection to contract theory, on my view, is this: Even if one had promised to obey the law, this would not create a prima facie obligation of obedience to law which was absolute with respect to considerations of utility. On the account of the conventional moral norms which constitute the practice of promising which was given in Chapter 5, it would still be open to the individual citizen to decide each case of obedience or disobedience on its (utilitarian) merits. The only difference that an express or tacit promise to obey the law would make is that it would create expectations the disappointment of which would be a disutility, as well as bring into play considerations concerning the likelihood of incurring the social sanctions associated with the conventional norm that one ought to keep one's promises.

The principle of fair play is this: If one has voluntarily accepted the benefits which accrue from others doing their share by way of contributing what is required of them by the rules of a just scheme of mutual cooperation, then one has a duty to do one's share when it comes one's turn. Failing to assume one's share of the burdens while accepting the benefits which come from others doing so is to be a freeloader; it is to take unfair advantage of those whose compliance with the rules of the practice render freeloading possible.

The principle of fair play has often been claimed to lie at the foundation of a prima facie duty to obey the law; one benefits from others obeying laws which one approves of but with which they disagree, one therefore has a duty to obey those laws that others approve of (if they are valid according to the relevant constitutional criteria) even though one neither approves of them nor benefits from their existence. Although the fair play principle is typically understood to leave open the possibility that

[10]As argued by Hume in "Original Contract."

other moral considerations might in the final analysis justify disobedience to law, direct utilitarian considerations are not taken to be among them. The argument applying the general principle of fair play to political obligation is found in Plato's *Crito*, and was developed at some length by John Rawls in his "Justice as Fairness."[11]

There is an interesting connection between the principle of fair play and the generalization argument: where the former is applicable, so must be the latter. For an individual can have a duty of fair play only if he comes under the rules of a social practice *general compliance* with which produces the *benefits* which he has accepted. If *everyone* failed to do his duty as required by the rules, the practice would collapse, with the *undesirable* consequence that the benefits which are produced by it would be lost.[12]

The fair play principle turns out to be subject to some of the same objections as is the generalization argument. In particular: Even though substantial benefits to himself or others might follow from an individual failing to assume the burdens which a given practice requires him to shoulder, and in spite of the fact that his deviation from the rules of the practice would not cause others to act similarly, he is said to have a duty to conform which cannot be overridden by a direct consideration of consequences. This view seems to me rightly described as involving what Smart has called "rule worship,"[13] and it involves the further absurdity that one would be under a duty to comply with the rules of a joint scheme of cooperation due to the acceptance of past benefits even though others generally were no longer complying. As with the generalization principle, much of the plausibility which the principle of fair play may initially seem to have stems in large part from the implicit but totally unwarranted assumption that a given act of rule violation is likely to have the consequence of causing others to act in a similar way.

Some form of a general principle of fair play does, I suspect, have the status of a conventional moral rule along the lines suggested by the analysis contained in Chapters 4 and 5. The paradigm cases of its application are small group activities in which participation is clearly voluntary and the possibility of withdrawing from the activity remains a live option for all or most participants, while its frequent exercise would in fact

[11]It is also found in Hart, "Natural Rights."
[12]Lyons, *Forms and Limits*, Chapter V, has also noticed the connection.
[13]Smart, *Outline*, 5.

eventually bring the activity to an end. Children playing a ball game and taking turns rotating between desirable and undesirable positions is a good example. If after pitching for three innings Johnny declines to take his turn in left field, perhaps lamely offering the excuse that it is time for his dinner, he is with good reason likely to be met with the charge of "not playing fair."

As applied to political duty or obligation, though, the argument in terms of fair play suffers from the same difficulty as does the contract theorist's argument in terms of tacit consent. It relies upon *voluntary* participation and acceptance of benefits, which, as even Rawls is now prepared to admit, "is difficult to find . . . in the case of the political system into which we are born and begin our lives."[14]

As with contract theory, then, two replies are to be made to the argument that one has an obligation to obey the law based upon a principle concerning what fair play requires by way of mutual cooperation under a just constitution. Firstly, a necessary condition for the application of the principle—fully voluntary participation—is lacking. Secondly, even if the principle were applicable, the intended result—an obligation or duty to obey the law that was absolute with respect to considerations of utility—would not follow. For the principle of fair play has at best the status of a conventional moral norm of the sort described in Chapter 4. Although it was seen that such norms do bar direct appeals to utility in one sense—that having to do with the conditions under which the social sanction will be triggered, they do not generate prima facie obligations of the kind which prevent each case from being decided on its merits upon the basis of a direct consideration of utilitarian consequences.

The germ of truth contained in traditional theories of political obligation seems to me to be this: A viable political association must in the normal case rest upon a generally shared expectation on the part of most of its members that most duly enacted laws will be obeyed, and that most judicial decisions, even those that are legally and morally controversial, will be voluntarily complied with. I shall now turn to an account, in act-utilitarian terms, of the possible genesis of such expectations.

---

[14]Rawls, *Theory of Justice*, 337. Rawls now argues that there is a natural duty to support just institutions in general, and a duty of obedience to law as a way of supporting a just constitution in particular, which is absolute with respect to considerations of utility and which does not rest upon any form of tacit or express consent.

5. *The Utility of Obedience to Law*

Under certain all too familiar conditions, morality might demand rebellion and revolution, rather than support of the existing legal regime. Under other circumstances, especially within minority groups the members of which are the victims rather than the beneficiaries of the forms of conduct which the law requires, there might be a strong moral presumption in favor of disobedience, particularly with respect to certain kinds of laws. I mention this—the obvious—here only to serve as a reminder that it is only under certain conditions that there is anything for the act-utilitarian or anyone else to explain, that is, the character of the legitimate assumption that there is some kind of a presumption in favor of obedience to law.

The account which I shall construct here will rely heavily upon the general position adopted in Chapters 4 and 5, and will proceed by examining in turn what can be salvaged from each of the three views of the nature of political association that I have rejected above in Sections 2-4.

There is much to be learned from Hobbes. Indeed, the core of my account of individual conduct and social norms can be viewed as resulting from the substitution of (at least moderately) benevolent men for selfish men in the Hobbesian model. As did Hume, Hobbes understood that it could be fully rational for individuals guided by a consequentialist choice principle to deliberately create institutions which would restructure the sets of considerations of consequences of which they in the future would have to take account. Although each individual retains the original autonomy of judgment which permits him to decide each case on its merits, his behavior will be directed into channels which it would not otherwise take because each, in conjunction with others, has acted in a manner which effects the eligibility of future candidates for action. A system of laws backed by coercive sanctions has served as our paradigm case.

Although I have followed Hobbes in conceding the significance of psychological egoism, I have not given it the central place that he did. Benevolence also operates as a strong motive, and it could well become stronger than the motive of self-interest in an affluent society (where no individual would ever have to choose between satisfying his own most basic needs and those of others) of act-utilitarians. And even within a society of men motivated solely by considerations of benevolence, I have argued that other sources of fallibility of judgment would exist which, unless corrected, would produce a socially intolerable level of mistaken attempts to identify exceptions to generally reliable rules of thumb. In those instances in which the exceptions to a generally reliable rule of thumb cannot be reliably identified, there are good reasons for giving them the status of legal norms backed by sanctions, thus rendering attempts to identify exceptions to them less likely to appear as optimific on act-utilitarian grounds.

The legal sanction thus need not be viewed by the citizen as the imposition of an alien coercive force from above, but rather may be understood by him as representing the operation of institutions which he and others have the very best of reasons to support. There is power, and there is power. The utilitarian must reject the notion that there is a distinction to be made between legitimate and illegitimate forms of its use insofar as this distinction implies that there is a prima facie obligation to obey those having "legitimate" power or authority.[15] But the utilitarian surely can make a distinction between those political institutions which are worthy of support on consequentialist grounds and those which are not. Where the members of a political association view themselves as mutually supporting structures of legal norms backed by sanctions the existence of which is seen as a positive social benefit, strong ties of community are bound to exist, and individuals are likely to be quite secure in their expectation that most men will voluntarily comply with the law. To borrow Kantian terminology my use of which within an act-utilitarian framework hopefully will not be misleading: The members of a political association view one another as autonomous moral agents subject to laws that they have set unto themselves, and upon whose mutual cooperation the continued stability of their legal and political institutions depends.

Act-utilitarians would of course not seek to give social norms the status of anything *more* than rules of thumb unless they were convinced that they were *at least* generally reliable guides to conduct. Although I have argued that what I called "the reflection principle" in Chapter 4 may break down, and thus that the very best law that might be enacted might on occasion be justifiably disobeyed, this is by no means to deny that the paramount concern of the members of a political community must be to assure that only the best laws possible are enacted and enforced. In light of the curious notions of political society which have found such widespread appeal, it is clear that the obvious has

---

[15]I here follow Wolff, "On Violence."

been lost sight of: The firmest foundation for a stable polity is simply a shared belief among its members that most laws are good, that most men will understand this, and are moral enough in most instances therefore to voluntarily obey them. When political rhetoric begins to concentrate on reasons for obedience which are far removed from such considerations, whether they be quite real (the rubber truncheons and gas grenades of the protectors of law and order), or philosophical fictions (an obligation to obey the law as such, whatever its content and regardless of the consequences of obedience), it is a sure sign that the bonds of political union are in the process of disintegrating.

Plato and Rousseau understood all of this quite well, and although we may not share their faith in the possibility of providing institutional guarantees that only good laws will be enacted, the act-utilitarian must recognize that it is a contingent question whether or not it would be rational to defer to the judgments of a class of putative experts on certain matters. Indeed, the crucial question is not whether or not one ought to recognize expertise of the sort which leads one to conclude that one must have been mistaken if one finds oneself in disagreement with the experts. It is rather this: Is it possible to identify experts who are reliable enough to warrant transferring to them considerable institutional power to make and enforce political decisions, and whose institutional role it is rational to support even when considerable doubts exist as to the wisdom of particular decisions which they reach? Where such an institutional transfer of political power is reasonable, as I believe it is in the case of the judiciary, common knowledge that this is so will provide a basis for the shared conviction that it may sometimes be necessary to obey the law simply to avoid the damage which would otherwise result to a valuable social institution. (But the question of likely institutional effects is, of course, an empirical one.) A further element in the bonds of political union, in other words, is the common conviction among the members of a community that their political and legal institutions—imperfect as they may be—are good enough to be worthy of continued support.

When they are present to a sufficient degree, as they often are, the factors considered above provide sufficient grounds for members of a political community to expect that most laws will be obeyed by most men most of the time. Not only will they have such expectations; they will arrange their affairs and make their future plans on the basis of them. The disappointment of these expectations, the interference with those arrangements, the frustration of such plans—all are disutilities associated with disobedience to law of which the act-utilitarian can and must take account. The situation, in short, is *as if* men had promised to obey the law, or recognized some other basis for an obligation to do so, such as considerations of fair play. The purpose of traditional theories of obligation, in other words, is to explain how it is that obedience to law could be generally relied upon, as it admittedly must be, within a stable political community. What we have seen is that this may be explained without positing any principle of obligation independent of the act-utilitarian principle itself.

A final concession may be made to the traditional view that there is a prima facie obligation to obey the law as such, independent of, and absolute with respect to, considerations of utility. It is this: Where things are as they should be with respect to institutional forms and the wise and moral use of political power, the presumption that any given law ought to be obeyed may be so strong as to warrant the members of a society of act-utilitarians giving the principle that one ought to obey the law the status of a conventional moral norm. Whether or not this is so is, of course, a contingent matter, and as the analysis presented in Chapter 4 demonstrated, such a conventional norm may be supported by one who retains the right to deviate from it on direct utilitarian grounds. The role which such a norm may play in a democratic society will be explored in the context of an examination of majority rule in the next section. Its bearing upon the morality of civil disobedience will be discussed in Section 7.

6. *Majority Rule*

In the *Second Treatise*, Locke writes as follows about marjority rule:

> For when any number of men have, by the consent of every individual, made a community, they have thereby made that community one body, with a power to act as one body, which is only by the will and determination of the majority; for . . . it is necessary the body should move that way whither the greater force carries it, which is the consent of the majority: or else it is impossible it should act or continue one body, one community . . . and so everyone is bound by that consent to be concluded by the majority. . . .
> And thus every man, by consenting with others to make one body politic under one government, puts himself under an obligation to everyone of that society to submit to the determination of the majority, and to be concluded by it; or else

> this original compact . . . would signify nothing, and be no
> compact, if he be left free, and under no other ties than he was
> in before. . . .[16]

We have already seen ample reason to reject Locke's claim, echoed by many later writers, that agreement to majority rule would "signify nothing" unless it were understood to imply the recognition of a moral obligation to obey the laws enacted by the majority. If the majority is given the *power* to enforce its decisions, and those decisions are most often reasonable, it can get along quite well without its being acknowledged to have any moral authority to command obedience.

The as yet unanswered question which is raised by this quotation from Locke is rather this: Does majority rule have any special credentials which entitle it to the utilitarian's support in preference to other forms of government? In attempting to answer this question, I shall consider majority rule as a legislative decision procedure, and avoid the considerable complications which are introduced by representation, political parties, electoral processes, etc. The model will be the idealized one of direct majority rule, where all sane adult citizens participate directly in the voting process.[17] Except where otherwise noted, the procedure will be one where a simple majority (51 percent) carries.

Locke seems to have believed that there is something natural about majority rule, but although in a given historical context it may have a certain salience due to its familiarity, the same may be said of many other forms of government.

The contract theorist will naturally tell us that majority rule is that form of self government to which men would voluntarily consent. Not only does this beg the question of *why* they would consent to it, but it is not sufficient to give majority rule any special title; men could equally well promise to obey the legislative decrees of a benevolent despot.[18] So the question remains: Would the members of a community of act-utilitarians have grounds for believing that majority rule had anything special to recommend it?

The answer must surely be that it depends upon the circumstances. The naive view that majoritarian democracy is the best form of government for all civilized men is simply untenable—an unsupportable maxim of modern political

---

[16]Locke, *Second Treatise*, Sections 96 and 97.
[17]See Wolff, *Defense of Anarchism*, 34-37, on the technology of what he calls "instant direct democracy."
[18]Wolff, *Defense of Anarchism*, 41-42.

rhetoric. As Plato realized, any form of government rests upon certain assumptions about the level of knowledge of, and the kind of information available to, those in political power. Majority rule makes sense only if particularly strong assumptions are made about the level of intelligence and understanding of the general populace, these assumptions in turn implying a great deal about prevailing educational practices and systems of public information. Also, I suggest, it must be assumed that most participants, either through motives of benevolence or enlightened self-interest, will attempt to enact legislation that will promote the common good.[19] For although there are some decision problems which demand for their solution little more than an identification of what is in the mutual self-interest of each, there are others where selfish interest will dictate compromises which will put everyone in a worse position than he would have been if benevolence had been an operative motive.[20]

When the appropriate assumptions can reasonably be made, majority rule does have a number of features which would recommend it to a community of benevolent men. As has often been noted, it is perhaps the safest possible hedge against the abuse of political power. Also, political participation may be enjoyed by the members of a community in its own right. Furthermore, men take positive pleasure in their belief that what they think ought to be the case is the case. When the majority has its way, one knows that at least 51 percent of the people will experience the satisfactions associated with their belief that the right legislative decision has been made, and this even though the future consequences of their act may cause all to regret it. (Although such satisfactions of the majority will typically outweigh the analogous dissatisfactions of the minority, things can be otherwise. If a bare majority has little confidence in the correctness of its decision, while a substantial minority is firmly convinced that the majority view is grossly mistaken, the situation is likely to be reversed. On the other hand, though, such considerations can and should be given weight prior to voting by act-utilitarian legislators; just how much weight raises general questions about political tolerance which shall be dealt with in Chapter 8.[21])

---

[19]Compare Barry's discussion of Rousseau and the general will in "Public Interest."

[20]For example, the coordination problems discussed by Lewis in *Convention* and the prisoners' dilemma.

[21]We also have here a clear case of the need for interpersonal utility comparisons.

In a society of act-utilitarians about which the required assumptions concerning knowledge, intelligence, and goodwill can be made, there is an especially potent argument in favor of majority rule which is deserving of much more attention than it usually receives. Within such a community of morally like-minded individuals, differences on issues of social policy would rest on differences concerning the consequences of alternative acts of legislation. The differences, in short, would be cognitive in nature; it would make complete sense to speak of the majority or of any given individual as being right or wrong, correct or incorrect. But where such is the case, a mathematical formula due to the French mathematician Condorcet is applicable.[22] What it implies is that the reliability of the group's decision under majority rule is *considerably greater* than the reliability of any randomly chosen individual member of the group. As the size of the group grows larger, or as the proportion of votes needed to carry is increased beyond a simple majority, the reliability of the majority decision increases dramatically.

Where it is assumed that each (or the average) voter is right in v of the cases, and wrong in e of the cases ($v + e = 1$), and h voters vote Yes, while k voters vote No, the probability that the h members are right is given by the formula:

$$\frac{v^{h-k}}{v^{h-k} + e^{h-k}} .$$

Thus the following:

Number of Voters	% Required to Carry	Individual Reliability	Group Reliability
1,000	51	51%	69.00%
10,000	51	51%	99.97%
1,000	60	51%	99.97%

One must, of course, assume that the average voter is more often right than wrong; otherwise Condorcet's formula is a potent argument *against* majority rule. But given the not unreasonable assumption of a bare minimum of individual reliability, we have here a powerful argument in favor of majority rule as a legislative decision procedure.[23] Ironically, it rests, as

[22]First called to my attention by Barry, "Public Interest," 13.

[23]Wolff, *Defense of Anarchism*, 58-67, contains an excellent introductory discussion of those logical properties of majority rule which might be viewed as the basis for arguments *against* it. For more advanced discussions, see Arrow, *Social Choice*; Black, *Committees and Elections*.

does much else of what I have claimed about act-utilitarian grounds for supporting conventional social norms, on fallibilistic considerations. Support of majority rule as an institutional decision procedure would be viewed by act-utilitarians as the most general possible method for dealing with their manifest unreliability as individuals. Although they would not recognize any moral obligation to obey the laws enacted by the majority, they would have good reasons for giving the majority the institutional means for enforcing its decisions. And given the fact that the majority decision is more reliable than the judgment of the average individual, they would also have good reasons for supporting a conventional moral norm which barred direct appeals to utility as a ground for justifying disobedience to law.

7. *Civil Disobedience*

Civil disobedience as a form of nonviolent political protest has enjoyed an increasing currency and has received considerable attention throughout the world in recent years. Although it has spawned a flood of philosophical comment and analyses, contributions which are likely to be of any lasting interest have been few and far between. Perhaps the reason for this is that there is in fact very little of special philosophical significance to be taken note of. The phenomenon of civil disobedience is surely an apt vehicle for raising general questions in moral, political, and legal philosophy, but it is far from clear that it raises any important issues in its own right.

On the face of it, there is little more for the act-utilitarian to do than to note that acts of disobedience to law, civil or otherwise, are to be justified, like any other kind of act, in terms of their consequences. Although I have already gone beyond this in suggesting that under the appropriate circumstances there may be reasons for giving the principle that one ought to obey the law the status of a conventional moral norm, I believe that there is a bit more that can, and should, be said.

Although the philosophical essentialism underlying attempts to define necessary and sufficient conditions for an act's being an act of civil disobedience must be rejected, it is important to note the features present in typical cases. They include the following: The act is nonviolent; it is public; it is intended to call attention to the existence and nature of a law or government policy which the protestor believes, on moral grounds, ought to be changed; the disobedient is prepared to accept the legal consequences of his act, including arrest and the possibility of eventual fine or imprisonment.

With the possible exception of the core feature of moral protest, the features mentioned above are to be understood as merely highly likely means for succeeding in getting a sincere message of protest across to those to whom it is addressed. Under special (and not so special) circumstances, one or more of them might be absent without the act in question ceasing to be a genuine act of civil disobedience. If it is the general public or a substantial segment thereof to whom the message of protest is directed, the public nature of the act is a practical necessity. And the message is most likely to be understood if it is not accompanied by violence; as is well understood by those legal authorities who seek to veil it by themselves provoking the violence which is bound to receive the bulk of the publicity. The willingness of the disobedient to accept arrest and punishment may be necessary as a means of convincing a skeptical public of the sincerity of his convictions, although this will often be amply clear on other grounds. A better reason for the disobedient accepting the legal consequences of his act may simply be that this is the only way in which he can raise the issues he is concerned with in court, which may be an appropriate place to raise them if the grounds of moral protest are also grounds for questioning the legal validity of the law or policy in question. This also explains why it is typically the law to which he objects that the protestor will violate, even though some other nonviolent illegal act might be a more effective means of getting the message across.

Two features not mentioned above strike me as the most significant in the context of the present inquiry concerning the relationship between individual conduct and social norms. Firstly, an act of civil disobedience may be distinguished from other nonviolent forms of political protest, such as conscientious objection, in that it represents an appeal by the protestor to moral principles which he believes the members of the community share with him. Understood in this way, the disobedient is simply choosing an especially dramatic and probably costly way of forcing the community to reconsider the law or policy being objected to in the light of its own best judgment.[24] Secondly, the protestor is seldom acting alone, but usually is a member of a group. More importantly, and suggestive of the same point, the disobedient typically is moved to act in part

---

[24]See Rawls, *Theory of Justice*, Sections 55 and 56.

because he has considerable support for his moral convictions from a substantial segment of the more enlightened members of the community of which he is a part. The question of historical fact which emerges from the conjunction of these two features is this: Within a given community, has the civil disobedient more often than not been eventually acknowledged to be justified in his protest, and has civil disobedience proven to be an effective means of bringing about desirable changes in law and government policy? Where the answer is in the affirmative, as it clearly is in the United States today, this is sufficient to countervail the presumption against disobedience to law created by a conventional moral norm that one ought to obey the law. Indeed, one might even claim that under certain circumstances not only should a conventional moral norm that one ought to obey the law recognize civil disobedience as an exception, but that within certain communities it in fact does so. Consider, for instance, the university subculture in the United States today. Similar remarks could be made about the reaction within certain communities to illegal work stoppages. There are, in short, certain kinds of acts of disobedience to law which, in virtue of the motives, status, and numbers of those who participate in them, may have a presumption of moral justifiability *in their favor.* Where the burden of moral proof lies is, we have seen, an empirical question for the act-utilitarian. It cannot be assumed that it must always be upon he who would disobey the law; in spite of the general character of rules of thumb and the lack of reliability with which exceptions to them may be identified, a conventional moral norm to the effect that one ought to obey the law can recognize at least some exceptions.

Although it is important that those legal authorities—especially prosecutors—who have considerable discretion in deciding how to react to acts of civil disobedience take such considerations into account, it would be naive to assume that any legal system could be structured so as to provide ultimate legal vindication of each and every act of morally justified disobedience. The reflection principle, in other words, may break down at the interface between individual moral judgment and justified institutional response with regard to civil disobedience, just as it may with respect to other kinds of acts.[25]

[25]Ronald Dworkin, in his "Civil Disobedience," seems to come dangerously close to denying this.

7   *The Just Society*

A stable social order in large part depends upon a common conviction that basic social institutions—economic, political, educational, etc.—are just. But one of the most persistent complaints against act-utilitarianism is that it is unable to account for our considered moral judgments concerning social justice. The fundamental principles of a just moral and political order, it is contended, demand that utilitarian considerations sometimes be subordinated to individual claims of entitlement based upon principles of just desert. Whether it be political liberty, economic benefits, or personal freedom that is involved, it is contended that act-utilitarianism would override the morally legitimate claims of the individual as a means of furthering the common good. If men are to be treated as moral ends rather than as mere means to the satisfaction of the interests of others, and are to be secure in their expectations that they will receive from their social institutions that which they are due, principles of distributive and retributive justice which are independent of, and absolute with respect to, the principle of utility must, it is claimed, prevail.

I shall reserve discussion of those features of distributive justice that have to do with political liberty, equal opportunity, and personal freedom until the next chapter. In this chapter, I shall attempt to defend act-utilitarianism against the charge that it would permit the unwarranted sacrifice of the some to the' many (or the few, for that matter) with respect to the distribution of economic burdens and benefits (distributive justice) and the application of legal sanctions (retributive justice).

1. Utilitarian Principles of Justice

The approach which I shall adopt is in large part dictated by the general account of individual conduct and social norms developed in Chapters 4 and 5. Let me sketch it here, and reply to the charge that it is inconsistent with act-utilitarianism.

Principles of distributive and retributive justice serve primarily as criteria for evaluating the design and operations of those social institutions which determine the pattern of expectations within a community as to how the primary objects of human desire will be distributed and what kinds of claims upon them will be recognized as legitimate. An economic system with its associated wage, price, and tax mechanisms; a political constitution; legal rules concerning private property; a penal code—all are institutional vehicles for determining how the primary goods of self-esteem, the means of material well-being, political power, personal liberty, and social opportunity will be distributed amongst the members of society.[1] Although individual acts and agents may be spoken of as just and unjust, thus suggesting that there are quite general principles of justice with a very wide range of application, the institutional application is nonetheless primary. Indeed, the just act is often simply that which is required by the constitutive rules of a just institution.

Previous chapters have argued that act-utilitarians might often recognize the need for, and thus rationally participate in the creation and support of, conventional moral norms which bar direct appeals to utility. Such are rational means for directing behavior into desirable channels that it would otherwise not take, and their existence is the basis for many of the secure expectations that an individual may have as to how members of his community will behave. On the basis of such expectations, plans may be made and coordinated in advance, and the individual can predict the consequences of his voluntary acts with a reliability which otherwise would fail to obtain.

The principles of social justice, in my view, are the most fundamental guidelines for the design and operation of those social institutions which generate individuals' expectations about what claims they will be recognized as having on the distribution of those primary goods which virtually all men desire. With regard to both distributive and retributive justice, I shall argue that there are certain salient features of man and his world which provide the best of reasons for act-utilitarians to establish and support institutions which conform to familiar liberal notions of social justice. Furthermore, I shall contend that there are conditions under which it is reasonable for some principles of

[1]The notion of primary goods is from Rawls, *Theory of Justice*, 62 and following pages.

justice to be given the status of conventional moral norms which bar direct appeals to utility and not merely that of rules of thumb for institutional design.

John Rawls has recently contended that the choice and public acceptance of principles of justice by the members of a hypothetical community of rational utilitarians would be tantamount to their abandonment of utilitarianism as a moral theory. If it is believed that the direct employment of the act-utilitarian principle itself in the distribution of primary goods would have undesirable consequences, and if principles of justice which are absolute with respect to considerations of utility are instead chosen as the basis for designing and criticizing institutions created for that purpose, utilitarianism, it is claimed, has been rejected.[2]

A major purpose of this essay has been to demonstrate how and why just this kind of claim is radically mistaken.

Do Hobbesian individuals, creating and supporting institutions and social (primarily legal) norms which penalize otherwise self-interested behavior, abandon either psychological or ethical egoism? By establishing rules of justice do they thereby become just in some sense which is inconsistent with them continuing to act solely on the basis of the maxims of rational prudence? The answer, quite clearly, is that they do not. As we have seen, they have merely restructured (out of self-interest) the set of considerations of future consequences of which they—continuing to act always and only on the basis of self-interest—will have to take account.

Likewise, act-utilitarians remain act-utilitarians as long as it is only the act-utilitarian principle which they recognize as the ultimate prescriptive criterion for individual moral choice. If they choose to support a conventional moral norm concerning the making and keeping of promises which bars direct appeals to utility, they have not thereby abdicated the right to decide each case on its direct utilitarian merits, but merely restructured (in a radical way, to be sure) the set of consequentialist considerations which will determine where the merits lie. If they support a constitutional democracy and adopt majority rule as a social decision procedure, what is in question are the atomic although coordinated individual acts of individual agents each of which may be justified on direct act-utilitarian grounds. They are not to be understood as having adopted the view that what the majority decides, rather than what the act-utilitarian principle

---

[2]Rawls, *Theory of Justice*, 181-182, 502.

determines, is the ultimate arbiter of what is morally right, nor have they incurred even a prima facie obligation to obey the laws enacted by the majority.

Similarly, support of principles of justice which bar direct appeals to utility, and active participation in the creation and maintenance of institutions which satisfy those principles, in no manner imply that the act-utilitarian principle has been abandoned. Each individual remains free to decide each case on its direct utilitarian merits, but where the merits lie will depend in large part upon the institutional framework within which individual choices are made. Although the design of that framework may be guided by principles of justice which bar direct appeals to utility, the theory remains an act-utilitarian one if the choice of those principles is itself based on direct utilitarian considerations.

I conclude, then, that the act-utilitarian can seriously and consistently consider concrete proposals for principles of social justice, viewing them either as possible constitutional limits on legislation, more specific legal norms, conventional moral rules, or merely rules of thumb as guides to institutional design. Whatever the principles of justice which he adopts, and whatever the manner in which he adopts them, his grounds for doing so will be direct utilitarian ones which he by no means need subsequently abandon as his sole prescriptive guide to individual moral choice.

2. Justice as Fairness

John Rawls's *A Theory of Justice,* an extensive development of his 1968 paper, "Justice as Fairness," is surely the most comprehensive, careful, and persuasive non-utilitarian account of social justice to be found in the philosophical literature. Although an attempt to do justice to Rawls's entire theory is well beyond the scope of this essay, a few comments on some of its noteworthy features are in order. Before turning to a discussion of the specific principles of distributive justice which he defends, I shall first comment briefly on Rawls's conception of the particular form of social contract theory within the framework of which his account is developed.

Justice as fairness is a mere fragment of a comprehensive moral theory of *rightness as fairness.* The principles of right in this view are those which would be unanimously chosen by individuals in a hypothetical original position in which none would be aware of those inequalities, arbitrary from a moral point of view, which permit natural men to take unfair advantage of one another. Mutually self-interested men with roughly similar needs and abilities, acting behind a veil of ignorance as to what their particular life plans and social position will be in the real world, must reach agreement in advance on those principles which will serve as the basis for the design and criticism of their fundamental social institutions insofar as they are concerned with the distribution of primary social goods. Although self-interested, they are free from envy, and are subject to the constraints of having a morality in the sense that each will conform to the principles originally agreed upon even if so doing works to his disadvantage in specific cases once the veil of ignorance is removed. As Rawls himself emphasizes, this conception of morality makes the theory of right in general, and thus the theory of justice in particular, part of the more general theory of rational choice. What is right is what is in accord with those principles which would be chosen by rational men in a hypothetical position of fair equality as the best means of promoting their individual ends. Moral principles are the result of a fair bargain amongst equals.

Regardless of what view he takes of the principles of justice (or any others) that would be adopted under such circumstances, this conception of moral theory is one which the utilitarian must reject. Even though Rawls admits that with slight changes in the motivation assumptions which characterize his description of the original position, it is the utilitarian principle, and not his principles of justice, which would be adopted as the fundamental charter of society,[3] all of this must be deemed irrelevant by the utilitarian. Most men as they are exhibit an inclination to act upon both benevolent and selfish motives. The act-utilitarian's conception of moral theory is that it appeals directly to the former, psychological egoism being just one of a number of empirical facts which must be taken into account in the application of the utilitarian principle. Rawls, on the other hand, treats the inclination to further narrow self-interest not only as a psychological fact but as the fundamental basis for the concept of morality itself. Although he hedges on his description of what self-interest comes to,[4] his view is essentially Hobbesian, even

[3]Rawls, *Theory of Justice*, Sections 27 and 28.
[4]Rawls writes of his hypothetical men in the original position that "although the interests advanced . . . are not assumed to be interests in the self, they are the interests of a self that regards its conception of the good as worthy of recognition and that advances claims in its behalf as deserving satisfaction." *Theory of Justice*, 127.

though he must assume that men are benevolent enough to be willing to save for the benefit of future generations and are subject to what he calls "the constraints of having a morality." [5] Indeed, both the strictly Hobbesian man and the benevolent man may reply to Rawls that they fail to see the relevance, to them, of the principles which Rawls's hypothetical men (essentially Hobbesian, but of limited benevolence in certain crucial respects) *would* adopt under hypothetical conditions which fail to obtain in their real lives. The consistent Hobbesian, who finds himself in a real world where some *can* take advantage of others, will see no reason to conform to the principles of justice when so doing would be contrary to the dictates of narrow self-interest, and he will not be moved by a consideration of what is in the interest of future generations. The utilitarian will not be surprised if it turns out that the principles of justice which would be adopted by essentially Hobbesian men are not the same as those which merit support on the basis of a principle of benevolence.

I conclude, therefore, that Rawls's argument for his principles of justice in terms of the notion of which principles would be adopted in the initial position of fair equality as he characterizes it carries little weight, wherever it may lead. What remains is the notion that acceptable principles of justice are those which best accord with particular considered moral judgments about matters of social justice, and are consistent with the other principles contained in a comprehensive moral theory. Of course, if it turns out that such substantive principles are the ones which would be adopted under the hypothetical situation as Rawls describes it, this would give a privileged position to arguments from his hypothetical situation to other moral principles. My own view is that the principles which Rawls defends neither are in accord with our considered moral judgments nor are they the ones which would be adopted in the initial situation, even as Rawls describes it.

3. Distributive Justice: Rawls's Account

The act-utilitarian is concerned only with the sum total of satisfaction consequent upon the distribution of any fixed quantity of goods and services; where they lead to the same net utility level, he is indifferent to the pattern in which either the

---

[5] See Rawls, *Theory of Justice*, 128 and following pages, on the just savings principle and the motivational assumptions needed to derive it. On the constraints of the concept of right, see Section 23.

satisfactions or that which produces them is distributed. Potshots may be taken at act-utilitarianism by pointing out that unequal distributions may thus be viewed as either indifferent to or even preferable to equal ones on the grounds that a failure to satisfy the desires of some is compensated for by the satisfactions of others. To such complaints the utilitarian may reply that the plausibility of such putative counter examples typically rests upon confusing the pattern of goods and services with the pattern of distribution of the associated satisfactions. There are sound empirical grounds—considerations of envy, diminishing marginal utility, etc.—for the act-utilitarian not being indifferent to the former. But, the utilitarian may ask, what *reasons* can be given for preferring one distribution to another when the levels of satisfaction associated with both—*all* things considered —are equal? To answer such a question, one must have a comprehensive non-utilitarian *theory* of justice.

And this is what Rawls has. The two principles of justice which he argues would be adopted in the original position of fair equality are:

First Principle
Each person is to have an equal right to the most extensive total system of equal basic liberties compatible with a similar system of liberty for all.

Second Principle
Social and economic inequalities are to be arranged so that they are both:
(a) to the greatest benefit of the least advantaged, consistent with the just savings principle, and
(b) attached to offices and positions open to all under conditions of fair equality of opportunity.[6]

The priority rules which hold among these principles—a crucial feature of Rawls's theory—prevent liberty from being traded off for either economic advantage or greater opportunity. Likewise, fair opportunity cannot be traded off for greater social or economic advantage. All take priority over maximizing the net sum of satisfactions.

It is clear that political liberty and socio-economic opportunity—which Rawls takes to constitute the basis of the all-important primary good of self-respect—have been given a central place in the theory. I shall defer a specific discussion of them until the next chapter. Here, I shall concentrate on the general conception of justice which Rawls presents, and the second part of the second principle—the difference principle—in

[6]Rawls, *Theory of Justice*, 302-303.

particular. Some quite general considerations will demonstrate, I believe, that Rawls has failed to provide a plausible alternative to a utilitarian account of distributive justice.

The difference principle represents the unwillingness of Rawls's hypothetically situated individuals to gamble on landing in a less advantaged position than they can assure themselves of as the price to be paid for the higher payoffs attached to other positions which they might have the good fortune to find themselves occupying once the veil of ignorance is removed. Unequal social and economic benefits are acceptable only if their existence works out to the benefit of the least, as well as the more, advantaged. Each individual, in acting as if he assumed that he would turn out to be one of the least rather than the more advantaged, is, as Rawls once put it, acting as if his own worst enemy would put him in his social and economic place. [7]

Rawls's hypothetical individual acting behind a veil of ignorance is employing what decision theorists call the *maximin rule* for choice under conditions of uncertainty. [8] The decision-maker is viewed as having to make a choice amongst a finite number of alternative acts with each of which is associated a finite number of possible outcomes, [9] which one will eventuate if the act is performed depending upon which of a number of possible states of affairs obtain in the world. Since probabilities cannot be assigned to these different states of nature, they cannot be assigned to the outcomes associated with each act-state pair. The decision-maker therefore cannot employ that decision rule, appropriate for choice under conditions of risk, which requires choosing that act which has associated with it the highest expected utility. The maximin rule requires one to play things safe and to perform that act which has associated with it the highest minimum payoff. For example, if the rows in the matrix below are associated with acts and the columns with states of nature, the maximin rule requires performing the (second) act associated with the second row.

$$\begin{bmatrix} 2 & 64 & 200 \\ 3 & 75 & 50 \end{bmatrix}$$

[7] Rawls, *Theory of Justice*, 152-153.

[8] For a general discussion of a variety of criteria which have been proposed for rational choice under uncertainty, see Luce and Raiffa, *Games and Decisions*, Chapter 13.

[9] For there to be a genuine choice problem, at least one act must have more than one possible outcome associated with it, and there must be at least two acts with different possible outcomes.

Although such a conservative maxim is sometimes warranted, it is surely no more an appropriate *general* solution to the problem of choice under uncertainty than is the highly optimistic *maximax* criterion, which opts for the choice of that act with which is associated the highest maximum payoff (which is found in the first row in the above matrix). Uncertain mother nature (or one's fellow man) is neither an evil demon nor a Santa Claus, and thus neither extreme pessimism nor extreme optimism is warranted as a general policy to adopt in situations of choice under uncertainty. As Rawls himself admits, if one considers the series of gain-and-loss tables:

$$\begin{bmatrix} 0 & n \\ 1/n & 1 \end{bmatrix}$$

for increasing n, some point must come at which it is rational to choose the first row rather than the second.[10]

While Rawls realizes that the maximin rule is not an appropriate general principle for rational choice under uncertainty, he contends that there are certain conditions under which its employment is reasonable, and that these conditions in fact are present in the situation in which his hypothetical men perceive the need to reach agreement on principles of justice. These special conditions are the following: (1) There is a certain ground-floor satisfaction level which can be attained as a sure thing. (2) What can be attained—possibly, but with unknown probability—above the ground level is of diminishing marginal value. (3) Falling below the ground-floor level of satisfaction is of great (and perhaps increasing marginal) disvalue.[11] Under such conditions, it is clear that the decision-maker is well advised not to risk falling below that ground-floor satisfaction level of which he can assure himself by performing one of the acts contained in the set of options available to him.

Since Rawls is assuming that all of his hypothetical men will employ the maximin rule in the original position in their choice of principles of justice, he must be assuming that their utility functions are similar in the above noted respects with regard to primary goods, whatever may be the difference in their utility functions over the nonprimary goods which they will also find themselves desiring as natural men once the veil of ignorance is removed.

---

[10]Rawls, *Theory of Justice*, 157.
[11]Rawls, *Theory of Justice*, 154-155.

But now consider the following: The existence of similar utility functions and diminishing marginal utility are the precise grounds upon which the act-utilitarian principle implies that utility will be maximized by an equal distribution of social and economic benefits. And Rawls's assumptions are even stronger than these, although they of course imply them. Add to them the quite plausible assumption that it would not be worth the social cost to attempt to identify individual differences in utility functions over primary goods even when it might be assumed that they in some small measure existed, and it is clear that the act-utilitarian would have the best of reasons for creating and supporting economic and social institutions which would assure that the ground-floor satisfaction level was attained by all. Under these assumptions, the specter of the few (or the many) being deprived by the utilitarian of the primary satisfactions of human life in order to promote the greater happiness of others simply vanishes. If Rawls is entitled to use these assumptions at the very foundation of his theory, as underlying the rationality of the choice of the maximin rule for choice under uncertainty, the utilitarian is surely entitled to employ them in *applying* his fundamental moral principle.

So the act-utilitarian will have little difficulty in justifying distributions of primary social and economic good which are intuitively just, at least with respect to the provision of a certain social minimum. But what about the distribution of surpluses above that minimum?

It is here that Rawls's principles and the utilitarian principle diverge in their implications; but it is just at this point that Rawls's argument concerning the use of the maximin rule and the choice of his principles of justice breaks down as well. For if assured of attaining the ground level of satisfaction in question, why would not Rawlsian men welcome the existence of inequalities which did not work out to the benefit of the least advantaged so long as they were given a fair chance of occupying the positions to which the greater advantages were attached? Indeed, although the value of further primary goods beyond the ground floor level may be of decreasing marginal utility, the utility function need not be continuous, but may move in steps, as indicated by the dotted, rather than the solid, line in the map which follows. [12]

[12]As suggested by Simon, *Models of Man.*

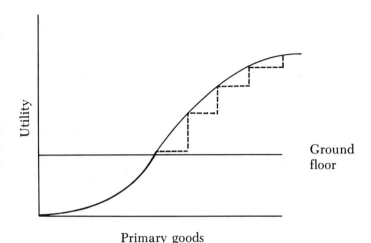

Primary goods

Where the primary good in question is money, for instance, each step may represent the value of an indivisible consumer item, where the value of each penny one has saved jumps considerably as soon as one has saved enough money to purchase the desired item. Where individual utility curves above the ground floor can be represented in this way, it is surely just to distribute primary goods in a manner which permits some to reach higher steps even though others may not benefit from their doing so. Following Rawls's principles might put everyone above the ground floor, but no one as high as the first step above it. Rawls's self-interested individuals, I suggest, would surely view it as a reasonable gamble to violate his principles—especially the difference principle—under such circumstances. The utilitarian would do so, of course, simply on the grounds that the substantial gains to some outweighed the small losses to others.

In placing so much emphasis upon the primary good of self-respect, Rawls is perhaps suggesting that to abandon the maximin rule would be to risk being deprived of those social and economic advantages which are the chief bases of self-esteem. But in spite of its great significance, this would be to blow out of all proportion the extent to which individual self-esteem is or need be predicated upon the individual's success in the competition for scarce primary goods. It would be to assume that the *minimum* satisfaction level for the primary good of self-respect is the absolute attainable *maximum*. But if this were the case, no economic or social inequalities whatsoever would be acceptable, for whatever their *social* or *economic* advantage to the least advantaged, this would be outweighed by their resulting loss in self-esteem. Absolute social and economic equality, with its implications of a fairly primitive state of economic development, would be required.

Indeed, above the ground-floor level after which point diminishing marginal utility sets in, the difference principle, which demands that all inequalities work out to the benefit of the least advantaged,[13] has some curious consequences.

Rawls calls attention to two empirical conditions which may, but need not, characterize the relationship between the benefits and burdens of some and those of others.[14] When *chain connection* holds, *if* the advantages to some representative man raise the expectations of the least advantaged representative man, then they raise the expectations of all representative men in between. For example, if the advantages of the entrepreneurial class raise the advantages of the unskilled laborer, then—where chain connection holds—they raise the expectations of the semi-skilled. When expectations are *close-knit*, it is impossible to raise or lower those of any representative man without raising or lowering those of *all* other representative men.

As stated, neither of these conditions logically implies the other.

Let us now explore the implications of the difference principle under the four possible combinations of these conditions:

(1) Where both chain connection and close-knittedness hold, Rawls admits that the difference principle has the same implications as the principle of average utility.[15]

(2) Consider the case where neither chain connection nor close-knittedness hold. It is then possible that a *great* improvement in the advantages of the most advantaged is called for by the difference principle because they produce some *slight* advantage for the least advantaged, while they worsen the situation of those in positions in between. Might not those in the middle positions claim that they have *unjustly* had their interests sacrificed, especially if the level of well-being of those in all of the middle positions could have been substantially increased by leaving the satisfaction levels of the two extreme positions as they were?

(3) Now suppose that chain connection obtains, but that

---

[13]Rawls, *Theory of Justice*, 83, introduces further qualifications which permit inequalities that don't work to the benefit of the least advantaged when they are at no cost to them.
[14]Rawls, *Theory of Justice*, 80-83.
[15]Rawls, *Theory of Justice*, 82.

close-knittedness does not. If the antecedent in the conditional definition of chain connection is satisfied, all is well. But suppose it is not. Then the difference principle may demand that *all* representative men but the least advantaged forego *substantial* benefits so that the least advantaged may enjoy some *slight* increment in their schedule of benefits.

(4) Finally, consider the case where close-knittedness obtains, and the advantages of some representative man are in fact raised. Even if the condition of chain connection fails to obtain, the implications of the difference principle would again seem to be acceptable.

There are, it thus appears, only two cases in which the difference principle has acceptable results: (a) Where chain connection holds, and the advantages to any given representative man do raise the expectations of the least advantaged; (b) Where close-knittedness obtains, and the advantages of some representative man are in fact raised. But (a) and (b) are very likely *not* to hold in typical cases in which the difference principle may be applied; they are *very* strong conditions. I thus conclude that where the difference principle diverges in its implications from the principle of utility, it is more likely than not to have unacceptable consequences.

These difficulties would be great enough even if the number of individuals in each class of representative men was the same; where the number of those in the most and the least advantaged classes is few, and that of those in the middle positions is many, the implications of the difference principle may border on the absurd. Those in the middle positions, numbering in the tens of thousands, might be required to forego substantial benefits so that a few hundred in the lowest class might benefit—however slightly—from the enormous benefits conferred upon the handful who occupied the most advantaged positions.

The general complaint, of course, is that the difference principle totally disregards the magnitude of relative gains and losses. Except where the payoffs to the least advantaged are the same under all alternative distributions (which is highly unlikely), it is indeed only to the payoff schedule of the least advantaged that it pays heed. As A.K. Sen has put it, with maximin justice "there is *no* trade off" between the satisfactions of some and those of others.[16]

[16]Sen, *Collective Choice*, 139. Two reviews of *Theory of Justice* which are especially clear on these sorts of difficulties with the difference principle are Arrow, "Ordinalist-Utilitarian Notes"; and Nagel, "Rawls on Justice." Many of the above criticisms of Rawls are also found in Barry, *Liberal Theory*.

4. *Distributive Justice: A Utilitarian Account*

The utilitarian, I have argued above, may criticize Rawls on the very same score on which Rawls and others have objected to utilitarianism: The principles which he adopts would lead to the unjust sacrifice of the interests of some to those of others. But assuming that interpersonal utility comparisons may be put upon a firm foundation, the act-utilitarian must admit—indeed, urge—that unequal distributions may sometimes be justified because the satisfactions of those who receive more outweigh the dissatisfactions of those who receive less. This is an undeniable consequence of act-utilitarianism which will be welcomed by benevolent men.

To the charge that the act-utilitarian is thus committed to treating (at least some) men as means rather than as moral ends, thus depriving them of the basis of self-respect, a number of replies are in order. Firstly, insofar as an individual act or social policy will result in damage to the self-esteem of some of those who are likely to be affected by it, this is an important disutility of which the act-utilitarian can and must take account. Indeed, he may even agree with Rawls's suggestion that self-respect is the most important primary good, although he will of course refuse to give it *absolute* weight. Secondly, it may be argued that in the only clear sense that can be given to this notion, the act-utilitarian does treat all men as moral ends: It is only their satisfactions and dissatisfactions which are held to be of value, and the preferences of each are given the same absolute weight on an intersubjective scale of value. All men, and their happiness and unhappiness, are treated as being of equal moral worth. Thirdly, insofar as unequal distributions of the things that men desire are justified on the grounds that the happiness of some outweighs the unhappiness of others, it is reasonable to assume that many of these inequalities will be randomly distributed over time. The one who benefits from the sacrifices of others today is likely to be called upon to subordinate different interests of his own to those of others tomorrow. In the proverbial long run, inequalities may balance out in a manner which permits each to view himself as having received roughly equal treatment with others. It is a defect of many contemporary social institutions that some receive more, and others less, of virtually everything over time. But who would seriously suggest that such institutions could be justified in terms of the utilitarian principle? Finally, benevolent men will not only take positive pleasure in knowing that the burdens which they assume enhance the well-being of others; they will view themselves as most fully realizing their potential to act as moral agents in those instances in which they voluntarily accept those disadvantages which work to the advantage of others.

As has already been suggested, though, there is, in spite of the above, good reason for limiting the scope of the direct operation of the utilitarian principle when it comes to the distribution of primary social goods.

In many instances, equal distribution (up to a certain ground-floor level, at least) is called for by obvious but all too often ignored features of a world in which the majority of people are ill-fed, ill-housed, ill-clothed, and uneducated. Roughly equal needs for (similar utility functions over) primary social goods, diminishing marginal utility of those goods past a minimum attainable by all, and the inefficiency of constructing mechanisms which would be sensitive to differences where they do exist—all are the best of reasons for designing institutions which conform to traditional liberal ideas of social justice.

Where basic needs and desires are no longer in question, though, there is nothing inherently immoral about designing institutions which will foster inequalities the justification of which lies simply in the fact that some need pay only a modest price to considerably heighten the satisfactions of others. This is not to deny, of course, that one may have more confidence that institutionally fostered inequalities are justified when, as is demanded by Rawls's principles, the inequalities appear to work out to the advantage of others than those whom they most directly and substantially benefit. A system of higher education to which there is limited competitive access, but which is supported by a tax burden shared by all, perhaps may not be justified by either of these principles taken in isolation, although it may be by their conjunction. On the one hand, it must be admitted that all are being required to make a small contribution to the support of an institution the primary and substantial beneficiaries of which are those who receive the education, and associated earning power, in question. On the other hand, failing widespread benevolence, the system would probably be politically unacceptable if it were not also believed that the better educated would in the long run make valuable contributions to the general social good which would otherwise be lost.

Rawls's admission that the principles with which his theory is concerned are to a considerable extent ones of what he calls *pure procedural justice,* consistent with any de facto distribution of primary goods which yields the required payoff schedules for his representative, average men,[17] serves to highlight the point that what just institutions do is to create and maintain certain stable sets of expectations amongst the members of a social group. It is like knowing that a game of chance is fair; if fairly played, the outcome is just, whatever it may be. But although I don't know whether I'll win, lose, or come out even, I do know a number of things which permit me to make rational decisions (in terms of betting behavior) that I could not otherwise make. So with just institutions: They support rational expectations which permit those whose lives they affect to make plans and take risks which it would otherwise be irrational for them to undertake. Viewed in this manner, they are but another instance of conventions which serve to redirect human behavior into channels which it would otherwise not take by restructuring the sets of considerations of consequences upon which those employing a consequentialist choice principle will base their decisions.

There is no doubt but that a community of rational act-utilitarians would perceive the desirability of institutional mechanisms for distributing primary goods which subordinate direct considerations of utility to simpler and much more predictable considerations. Without them, the security of expectations required for the formation of rational long range life plans would to a considerable degree be lacking. To what extent such institutions would conform to Rawls's two principles of justice is an empirical question the answer to which must depend upon the contingent features of any actual social situation. But I am confident that there are few, if any, real historical contexts in which it is plausible to claim that it would be reasonable to attempt to meet all of the demands made by Rawls's principles. Even admitting that what Rawls's principles require may be overridden, if not by considerations of utility, at least by other considerations of justice, and leaving aside the difficulties with them already mentioned, the priority rules associated with them— which cannot be abandoned without abandoning the theory— would seem to prohibit just the sort of trade-offs which are demanded by the realities of social existence. Whereas political liberty and equal opportunity are, according to Rawls's principles, to strictly dominate considerations of social and economic advantage, this is just the sort of justice the achievement of which may appear to be a hollow victory indeed for those who live under relatively liberal governments and yet exist from day to day without knowing where their next meal is

---

[17]Rawls, *Theory of Justice*, Section 14.

coming from. Most inhabitants of undeveloped countries, I
suspect, would with good reason take the view that Rawls's
principles had the priorities reversed from their most plausible
natural ordering.

With respect to the distribution of social and economic
benefits, I thus conclude that what justice demands can only be
determined by the application of the act-utilitarian principle to
complex problems of institutional design under concrete social
conditions, there being at best a presumption in favor of equal
distribution of certain primary goods (up to a point) under
conditions of abundance and equal need which are admittedly
quite widespread. As far as principles of distributive justice
which have to do with economic and social advantages are
concerned, the act-utilitarian will thus view them, with caution,
as little more than rules of thumb. Except within the most tech-
nologically and socially static societies, economic and social
conditions are simply too variable and changeable to warrant
such principles being raised to the status of conventional moral
rules, let alone constitutional guarantees. With respect to retributive justice and personal as well as political liberty, we shall
see, the status of principles of justice may be quite different.

5. *Retributive Justice*

The generic notion of retributive justice subsumes both legal
and moral responsibility. Although I shall confine my remarks
primarily to the legal case, they are intended to apply, *mutatis
mutandis*, to morality as well.

Few today would deny that the institutional goals which
justify the enormous expense to which society goes to inflict
suffering on people in the name of the law are utilitarian in
character. Deterrence, reform and rehabilitation, and the prevention of resort to self-help are generally acknowledged as the
primary reasons for maintaining a system of legal punishment.[18] Likewise, there is widespread agreement that a
utilitarian account of the severity of the legal sanctions attached
to various offenses is also plausible.[19] Even those who wish to
retain capital punishment as the maximum or mandatory
sentence for certain offenses (kidnapping, air highjacking,

[18]The question of just how well the criminal law accomplishes these goals is
a difficult and controversial one which fortunately need not be answered here.
[19]Including Rawls in "Two Concepts."

murder of police officers) are inclined to argue in terms of the need for strong deterrents, rather than retributively in terms of what the criminal has coming in virtue of the moral turpitude of his offense.[20]

Where retributive theory continues to thrive is with respect to questions of responsibility. Who is to be punished? Only those, it is answered, who have broken the law and are responsible for so doing. Neither the innocent, nor those who are not responsible for their acts, may ever justly be punished. But, it is contended, the act-utilitarian might justify precisely such injustices in terms of consequentialist considerations. Legal officials acting on act-utilitarian grounds might conspire to frame and severely punish an innocent man in order to "set an example" during a crime wave where none of the real culprits have been apprehended. The criminal law might have a greater deterrent effect if certain traditional excusing or mitigating conditions, such as insanity, which some break the law in the hope of shamming if apprehended, were eliminated altogether. These, genuine possibilities on act-utilitarian grounds, would be absolutely prohibited by the deontologist's principles of justice, whether or not he be a retributivist.[21]

Rule-utilitarianism, it has been claimed, is the only form of utilitarianism which can account for our intuitive conviction that there is something unjust about "punishing" either the innocent or those who are not responsible for their acts.[22] The rules constitutive of the institution of criminal punishment are to be justified on utilitarian grounds, but the specific acts of those charged with enforcing and applying the law are not. Rather, their acts are to be justified in terms of the rules in question, and any discretion which they have to appeal to direct utilitarian considerations must be one which is granted to them by those rules. There are obvious utilitarian reasons, it is contended, for framing the institution of the criminal law in terms of rules which deny officials the discretion ever to consider "punishing" the innocent, and which retain as well the traditional battery of legal excuses—infancy, insanity, duress, etc. Basically, these reasons all revolve around the desirability—indeed, the necessity —of men being able to have secure expectations about what the consequences of their voluntary acts will be. Although legal

---

[20]But see the brilliant defense of retributivism in Morris, "Persons and Punishment."

[21]See the essays in Hart, *Punishment and Responsibility*.

[22]Rawls, "Two Concepts," and Brandt, "Utilitarian Theory," are the most notable examples.

sanctions may be needed to direct human behavior into channels that it would otherwise not take, the purpose of having them would in large part be defeated if men could not reliably predict that they could voluntarily avoid them by acting in certain ways. The apprehension which one would constantly live under in a Kafkaesque world in which one might be "punished" although innocent or not responsible is so great that it can hardly be imagined. As Rawls has put it,

> [P]unishment works like a kind of price system: by altering the prices one has to pay for the performance of actions it supplies a motive for avoiding some actions and doing others. . . . [A]n institution which is set up to "punish" the innocent, is likely to have about as much point as a price system (if one may call it that) where the prices of things change at random from day to day and one learns the price of something only after one has agreed to buy it.[23]

All of the above points can be accommodated within the framework of *act*-utilitarianism. One of the major themes of this essay has been that the act-utilitarian can consistently participate in the creation and support of structures of social rules which function as more than rules of thumb and, in a sense, bar direct appeals to utility. A system of criminal justice is as clear a case of this as one could hope to find. Not only does it establish a system of "prices" attached to acts which it is within the province of the private citizen to perform, it also controls the behavior of those officials who are charged with the enforcement of the criminal law by attaching "prices" to their acts as well. Far from granting officials the discretion to "punish" innocent men, the hazards associated with unpredictable behavior on the part of legal officials are so great that they will be avoided by making those officials liable to severe legal penalties for such things as false arrest, interference with a citizen's civil rights, perjury, etc. Indeed, laws against entrapment are some evidence that even a minimum of official tampering with the association between fully voluntary conduct and the incidence of the legal sanction is viewed as being so fraught with danger that it is worth paying a high cost (in terms of the acquittal of known criminals) in order to discourage it.

Putative criticisms of act-utilitarianism built upon the familiar theme of punishing the innocent, then, are without foundation at the level of institutional design. All of the dangers supposedly associated with act-utilitarianism simply serve to highlight the importance of certain considerations of which the

---

[23]Rawls, "Two Concepts," 12.

act-utilitarian is fully capable of taking account. As soon as the critic goes beyond the bare assertion that the act-utilitarian might sometimes find reason to "punish" the innocent to a discussion of what is so wrong with such a possibility, he is to be found appealing to straightforward utilitarian considerations.[24]

The critic will be quick to point out that in my account of individual conduct and social norms all individuals, including legal officials, remain free to act upon the basis of a direct consideration of utilitarian consequences, whatever the nature of the institutions and social norms which structure such considerations. Although the features of institutional design which I have mentioned may render it quite *unlikely* that legal officials acting on utilitarian (or egotistical) grounds will view the framing of an innocent man as likely to have the best consequences, cases can be imagined where, all things considered, this would appear to be called for by the application of the act-utilitarian principle.

All of this must be admitted. But once a case is convincingly described in which it is clear that the framing of an innocent man *would* have the best consequences, even given due consideration to the likelihood of the subsequent punishment of those who have framed him, the result is one that the act-utilitarian should by no means seek to avoid. Although the importance of such life-boat examples to moral philosophy can be overemphasized, it is an undeniable fact of our moral experience that sometimes it is the lesser of two evils that must be chosen. Avoidable and predictable human suffering is tolerated by almost any familiar social practice which involves the allocation of scarce resources, the only plausible rationale for this being in terms of the maximization of the sum total of human satisfactions. Unless one believes that there is some central moral distinction to be made between the "statistical lives" of the predictable victims of avoidable automobile crashes, industrial accidents, and communicable diseases, on the one hand, and the lives and fortunes of known individuals identifiable by proper name, the suffering of the innocent must be accepted as a virtually unavoidable aspect of human life.[25]

Similar remarks apply to questions of legal responsibility. A systematic and general failure to permit individuals to avoid the incidence of legal sanctions by successfully pleading lack of *mens*

[24]As with Rawls, "Two Concepts," and frequently with Hart, *Punishment and Responsibility.*
[25]The notion of statistical lives is from Fried, *Anatomy,* Chapter XII.

rea would produce a level of insecurity and anxiety so intolerable as to virtually militate against the continuation of many socially desirable forms of human interaction. Although the criminal law might have a greater deterrent effect if traditional legal excuses were eliminated altogether, this because there would then be no possibility of shamming them, the price, in utilitarian terms, would simply be too great a one to pay.

Although the general absence of the possibility of appealing to traditional excusing and mitigating conditions as a means of avoiding legal sanctions would surely be intolerable, this is not to say that exceptions do not exist. Strict and vicarious liability are familiar phenomena in the civil and to some degree in the criminal law, and it is clear that a consistent utilitarian rationale can be provided for them. But, in the main, even they do not function so as to make legal sanctions strictly unavoidable, but rather push back to an atypically early stage the point at which voluntary choice must be exercised if certain kinds of consequences of one's acts are to be predictably avoided.[26] One may be strictly liable in the criminal law for selling adulterated food or drugs or serving alcoholic beverages to a minor, for instance, but then one can always get out of the business in question if one thinks that the risks are too great. More problematic is the notion of holding all the members of a group responsible for a wrong committed by one of its members, known or (more typically) unknown. In the normal case, the utilitarian surely will find good reason to reject resort to such practices; but as many elementary school teachers would be quick to suggest, here, too, one can easily conceive of situations in which invoking group responsibility would be the lesser of two evils.

In sum, there are typically the best of reasons for making the incidence of social sanctions, whether legal or moral, contingent upon the performance of prior acts which the individual agent could have voluntarily chosen not to perform. As with the practice of promising, retributive justice is structured in large part in terms of retrospective rather than prospective considerations, although the rationale for both is nonetheless a direct utilitarian one. In both cases, too, the practice may be viewed as aimed at giving individuals as firm a basis as possible for forming rational expectations about what the consequences of their voluntary acts and those of others are likely to be. To this end, social norms constitutive of the practice of promising bar direct appeals to

---

[26]The point is well made by Wasserstrom in "Strict Liability."

utility as grounds for the breaking of a promise, and these norms make a difference in the nature of rational expectations because they are backed up by social sanctions. Similarly, legal sanctions, in order to be able to function as a sort of price system effectively channeling voluntary choice behavior into lines that it would otherwise not take, must in the main be withheld from the innocent and those who are in some manner not responsible for what they do. In the interstices of such practices, though, there is room for each individual to decide each case on its merits on direct utilitarian grounds. All things considered, including the demands of social norms and institutional practices worthy of the act-utilitarian's support, promises must sometimes be broken, and the innocent sometimes made to suffer.

8   *Liberty*

Various conceptions of distributive justice constitute moral responses to the fact that men's needs and desires exceed what is available by way of social and economic resources. For the act-utilitarian in particular, a just distribution is one which achieves an optimal allocation of advantages and disadvantages under conditions of scarcity. Non-utilitarian conceptions, such as Rawls's, may require different patterns of distribution, but both utilitarian and non-utilitarian views typically are in accord at least to the extent that they recognize that under conditions of scarcity inequalities may be justified. Things are quite different with respect to political liberty and fair opportunity to compete for favored social and economic positions. These are not scarce resources, but the creatures of institutional design; they can, and sometimes should, be made available equally to all. Indeed, although I have rejected the strict lexical ordering which Rawls imposes upon his principles of justice, I agree with him that where a certain minimum of social and economic advantage can be attained by all consistently with the maintenance of a system of equal political liberty and fair equality of opportunity, the latter is what social justice normally requires. On my view, of course, the requirements of social justice are simply those of the act-utilitarian principle as applied to questions of institutional design under particular social conditions. The possibility of formulating general and nearly universal principles of political liberty and fair opportunity merely reflects the fact that there are nearly universal features of men's social situation which call for similar institutional responses in spite of the existence of great diversity on other scores.

I shall construe the notion of political liberty narrowly here, understanding by it the pattern of legally protected rights with respect to participation in the political process. Personal liberty,

on the other hand, I shall understand as the freedom which an
individual is accorded by legal and social institutions to engage
in those activities which he desires to engage in without interference. The notions of political liberty and personal freedom as
thus construed are not mutually exclusive; freedom of political
association, for example, is an instance of both. But the distinction is nonetheless important, for a concern with personal
freedom, we shall see, demands that a prominent place be given
to considerations which play only a minor role when it is
questions of political liberty in the narrow sense that are at issue.

I shall turn first to a consideration of the act-utilitarian basis
for principles of equal opportunity, and then to those of political
liberty. A discussion of personal liberty, in particular of the
libertarian principle defended by Mill in *On Liberty*, will
conclude the chapter, representing what I believe is one of the
more important and interesting applications of the general
position developed in Chapter 4.

1. Fair Equality of Opportunity

Insofar as inequalities in the distribution of social and
economic advantages and political power can be justified, there
is a question of who it is that is to be given access to the
privileged positions. Traditional liberal ideals of fairness demand
that equal opportunity be accorded to all, and contemporary
social action movements reflect the fact that such ideals are still
very much alive, and yet fall far short of social reality. What
basis might the utilitarian find for such demands for equal
opportunity?

To answer this question, one must return to the question of
what justifies the inequalities in the distribution of advantages
which gives rise to it in the first place. In the most general terms,
the argument of the last chapter was that what justifies differential treatment of a given person or class of persons in the distribution of advantages must in the final analysis have to do with
the maximization of the satisfactions either of those directly
benefited or of others. But this implies that either the given
person or class of persons directly benefited has a greater capacity to achieve satisfaction by being accorded greater advantages
than others, or else that they rather than others being accorded
certain advantages will work to the advantage of others who are
not directly advantaged. We saw, for instance, that unequal
distribution of educational resources may bring into play both

sorts of considerations. On the one hand, some, because of greater aptitude or motivation, might be claimed to be in a better position to themselves benefit from the advantages of, let us say, a college education. On the other hand, regardless of whether *they* enjoy or profit by it, allocating educational resources to some rather than others may be justified on the grounds that there is a differential in talent which will permit some to get more out of their education than others and thus make a greater contribution to society at large when they bring their educated talents to bear upon the solution of social problems.

The important thing to note about both of these arguments is that they justify an unequal distribution of a scarce social resource on the grounds that there is an identifiable differential either in individual capacity to experience certain sorts of satisfactions, or else in the capacity to contribute to the satisfactions of others.

The primary argument for fair equality of opportunity must therefore be this: Where differentials of the sort which justify unequal distribution of social and economic advantages or political power are in question, a fair competition is the most reliable way of identifying those who possess the relevant capacities. With respect to most social practices in which justifiable inequalities are to be found, there is simply no biological or hereditary key as to who—in terms of the rationale of the practice in question—ought to occupy the privileged positions. In most instances, the choice of a selective device is clearly more rational than the use of a random one. So the question is simply what sort of a selective device is the most efficient and reliable from the standpoint of the differential capacities which are to be identified. Some form of a fair competition is typically called for. And as the experience of some American universities with the admission of the so-called educationally underprivileged, and the experience of professional sports teams with the supposedly undersized, illustrate, the most efficient and reliable way to identify those with the required capacities may simply be to permit individuals to compete directly with one another (as in "open" training camps in professional football) or against some objective standard (as in some universities) by giving them the opportunity, at least for a time, to occupy the advantaged roles and positions to which they aspire.

Rawls has claimed that to deprive individuals of fair equality of opportunity is to deprive them of one of the most important bases of self-esteem.[1] The psychological effects of such abominations as institutionally enforced racial segregation bear Rawls out to a considerable degree. Individuals are inclined to adopt self-images which reflect the images which others have or seem to have of them, and even "separate but equal" treatment is bound to suggest that some men are viewed as being more equal than others. But this argument for fair equality of opportunity is surely one to which the act-utilitarian can appeal at the level of institutional design, self-respect being one of the primary objects of human desire, and the failure to achieve it thus being a disutility of considerable weight.

What Rawls fails to consider, though, is that the argument may cut two ways. Those who fail to win access to the privileged positions which are attached to practices within which there is fair equality of opportunity may consider that they have only themselves to blame, and suffer a substantial blow to their self-esteem. Although they may view themselves as having been treated as equals in terms of equally deserving a chance, they may view their failure to succeed in a fair competition as a sign of their proven unequal worth. The utilitarian will, of course, be sensitive to such considerations, and will thus refuse to endorse fair competition as the universal solution to the problem of identifying those with the talents and capacities called for by the unequal advantages attached to particular social practices.

I conclude, then, that under social conditions which are surely widespread, but far from universal, the act-utilitarian will support social practices and institutions which generate social and economic inequalities, or inequalities in political power, only when there are associated institutional mechanisms which provide a fair opportunity for those who are interested to compete for the most advantaged positions.

We have here an almost pure case of a problem in institutional design, and once the act-utilitarian has acted so as to create such institutions, the only further acts to consider are those which contribute to their maintenance and support. Although individual acts which take place within existing institutional frameworks are of course to be justified on direct utilitarian grounds, the institutions definitive of patterns of opportunity to achieve the most privileged social positions naturally structure the sets of relevant utilitarian considerations to a considerable degree. For the private individual, the positions which he has a fair opportunity to compete for largely determine the set of options available to him by way of education, employment,

---

[1]Rawls, *Theory of Justice*, Section 14.

occupancy of political office, etc. For those responsible for the administration of systems designed to assure equal opportunity, their position is analogous to that of those responsible for the administration of a system of criminal justice. Although they might in particular cases view it as desirable on direct utilitarian grounds to deny institutionally-guaranteed opportunities which it is within their *power* to withhold, they will not find themselves vested with the *authority* to exercise their personal discretion in such matters, and they may indeed be liable to legal sanctions if they are apprehended in an attempt to deviate from the specific rules in terms of which their offices and responsibilities as administrators are defined. The model here, I hope, is by now familiar and unproblematic.

2. *Political Liberty*

Insofar as political liberty is understood to refer to the right to occupy political office, I understand it to be encompassed by principles of equal opportunity. Equal opportunity to run for political office, in spite of the great opportunities it provides for demagogy and deceit, is still perhaps the most reliable way to identify the talent which is obviously required for the making of intelligent political decisions. Also, the more open the opportunities to compete for political office, the less likely is political power to fall into the hands of a self-perpetuating elite over time, thus providing some degree of protection against its abuse in a world of less than ideally benevolent men.

So by political liberty, then, I understand the right of the citizen to play an active and meaningful role in the selection of political leaders, whether through the mechanisms of majority rule or some other means (and there are other means). As so construed, my remarks about majority rule in Chapter 6 apply, *mutatis mutandis*, to the question of the desirability of institutions which foster political liberty. It may be added that political freedom may be an important basis of the primary good of self-respect, and that the broader the base of political power amongst the citizens of a state, the greater the degree of control which they are likely to have over their political leaders. But as was urged in Chapter 6, the desirability of extending political liberty to a significant degree depends upon the level of intellectual abilities which are required for its informed exercise among those to whom it is extended. Under the appropriate conditions there are the strongest of direct utilitarian considerations in favor of full and equal political liberty, and those conditions do in fact prevail in many modern nation states. Where the requisite conditions are lacking, though, the call for political liberty may be no more and no less than a dangerous bit of political rhetoric.

3. Personal Freedom

Originally published in 1859, Mill's essay *On Liberty* is devoted to the defense of

> one very simple principle, as entitled to govern absolutely the dealings of society with the individual in the way of compulsion and control. . . . That principle is that the sole end for which mankind are warranted, individually or collectively, in interfering with the liberty of action of any one of their number is self-protection. That the only purpose for which power can be rightfully exercised over any member of a civilized community, against his will, is to prevent harm to others. His own good, either physical or moral, is not a sufficient warrant.[2]

Over a hundred years of controversy have surrounded this declaration of principle, for there are difficulties in interpreting it, in reconciling it with Mill's act-utilitarianism, and in defending it under any particular interpretation. These problems are given an increased urgency by the recent surge of interest in, and heated controversy over, specific instances of the legal enforcement of morality. And their solution represents an important challenge to one, such as myself, who believes that act-utilitarianism can be elaborated in a manner which provides a significant role for libertarian principles which bar direct appeals to utility.

I shall seek to clarify and defend Mill's principle through a discussion of the position which Lord Patrick Devlin has taken on the enforcement of morality, with particular attention to the critical reaction which Devlin has provoked from H.L.A. Hart and Ronald Dworkin. An examination of the exchange amongst them will reveal that what is by far the most significant source of controversy over the enforcement of morality has come to be progressively concealed from view.

Although I shall focus on the enforcement of sexual morality by the criminal law, the issues are much broader than this. First, it is clear that the law is concerned with much more than *sexual* morality, and that it is not only the criminal law which manifests

2Mill, *On Liberty*, 13.

such a concern. Second, it is obvious that many, although not all, of the issues which emerge arise in contexts other than the legal, such as the question of what role a system of public education ought to play with respect to the inculcation of moral and political principles. Indeed, what is at issue in most general terms is the right of the individual to be free from interference of any sort on the part of society.

One further caveat is in order before turning to Lord Devlin. We are concerned here with the question of what critical principles, if any, ought to limit a society's right to enforce its positive morality through the vehicle of the criminal law, regardless of the costs or constitutional consequences of doing so. All of the parties to the dispute, in other words, recognize that there might be constitutional barriers to the legal enforcement of a particular moral prohibition, or that the costs of enforcement in any given case might outweigh the putative benefits.[3]

In recommending that private homosexual acts between consenting adults no longer be made criminal, and in endorsing the existing law under which acts of prostitution as such were not punishable, the 1957 Report of the Wolfenden Committee in England asserted that unless crime is to be equated with sin, the law should not attempt to regulate all private morality.[4] Two years later, Lord (then Justice) Devlin delivered his now famous Maccabean lecture in jurisprudence, "The Enforcement of Morals."[5] In this lecture, and in a variety of other publications,[6] he has attacked the Millian stand taken in the Wolfenden report, and countered with his own view that society has a prima facie right—perhaps even a duty—to enforce its positive morality through the vehicle of the criminal law.

As both Hart and Dworkin have noted, there are two independent arguments which may be attributed to Devlin.[7] Briefly, they are: (1) A shared morality is as necessary to a given society's continued existence as is a stable government; society thus has just as much of a right to penalize deviations from its shared morality as it does to prohibit treason—in either case it is simply asserting its right to prevent its own social disintegration. (2) The bare fact that a great majority of the members of any

[3]For an excellent treatment of this aspect of the issue, see S. Kadish, "Overcriminalization."
[4]Wolfenden Committee, *Report*, Section 62.
[5]Reprinted as "Morals and the Criminal Law."
[6]A number of Devlin's essays are reprinted in Devlin, *Enforcement*.
[7]Ronald Dworkin, "Lord Devlin"; Hart, *Law, Liberty, and Morality*, and "Social Solidarity."

given community believe that a certain kind of act is immoral is in itself a reason for a member of that majority to view its legal prohibition as prima facie right (or even obligatory).

The first argument, which Hart aptly labels "the disintegration thesis," rests upon certain empirical assumptions about the effects on a society of a failure to enforce its positive morality through the criminal law. The second argument does not appeal to a consideration of consequences at all, but rather asserts a direct moral right on the part of society to "follow its own lights," as Dworkin puts it. I would like to consider certain features of these arguments, and the replies which have been made to them by Hart and Dworkin respectively, in turn.

The disintegration thesis need not detain us long. Surely Lord Devlin is correct in maintaining that there is at least some sense in which "society may use the law to . . . safeguard anything . . . that is *essential* to its existence."[8] But as Hart has pointed out on a number of separate occasions,[9] the empirical assumption that it must legislate sexual morality in order to avoid disintegration is simply without foundation. Although there may be what Hart has called a "natural necessity" for society to provide some minimal protection of persons, property, and promises in order to continue in existence, there is no evidence whatsoever that there is any similar need to prohibit homosexuality, prostitution, etc.

It is Devlin's second argument, asserting the right of society to follow its own moral lights, which is to my mind of the greatest interest. As Dworkin notes, one has to some degree to read between the lines to find it in Devlin,[10] and it is not clear that Devlin himself would view it as separable from the disintegration thesis. Indeed, Dworkin's own description of the argument does not square very well with the understanding which he seems to have of it when he turns to its criticism. As *described* by Dworkin, the thesis is that society has a right to prohibit those acts the performance of which would bring about significant changes in those social institutions upon which the society places an especially high value. Understood in this way, the argument "does not claim that (mere) immorality is sufficient to make conduct criminal."[11] But as *analyzed* by Dworkin, the argument seems to be that the principled belief that a certain kind of conduct is immoral *is* a sufficient ground, other things being

---

[8]Devlin, "Criminal Law," 11; emphasis added.

[9]In addition to the works cited in note 7 above, see Hart's "Immorality and Treason."

[10]Ronald Dworkin, "Lord Devlin," 992.

[11]Ronald Dworkin, "Lord Devlin," 993.

equal, for seeking to have it made illegal. If I can convince you
that my belief that homosexuality is immoral is based upon
moral principle, rather than mere prejudice, emotional reaction,
or mistaken conception of fact, writes Dworkin, "you will admit
that so long as I hold my moral position, I have a moral right to
vote against the homosexual, because I have a right (indeed a
duty) to vote my own convictions."[12]

Now although my representation of the views of either
Dworkin or Lord Devlin as to what Devlin's argument really
comes to may not be completely accurate, it seems to me that
some such principle of entitlement is the chief ground upon
which most proponents of the legal enforcement of morality
would rest their case. If one sincerely believes that the performance of a certain kind of act is wrong, what better reason
could one have for seeking (through the vehicle of the criminal
law, if that is necessary, and the costs aren't too great) to prevent
it? Indeed, even Mill wrote that "We do not call anything wrong
unless we mean to imply that a person ought to be punished in
some way or other for doing it—if not by law, by the opinion of
his fellow creatures; if not by opinion, by the reproaches of his
own conscience."[13]

Many recent discussions of the enforcement of morality,
taking place in a climate where the virtues of tolerance are at
least paid lip service, have generally concealed the real roots of
controversy by typically concentrating upon what are at best
only secondary considerations. Writers such as Lord Devlin and
Norman St. John-Stevas,[14] on the other hand, writing under the
heavy and frankly admitted influence of a religious morality,
sincerely believe that certain kinds of behavior are immoral or
sinful which others, particularly those with a utilitarian perspective, find either unobjectionable or at worst pathetic. No
wonder they differ as to what ought to be prohibited by the
criminal law. Their real differences are on the moral merits; talk
of the disintegration of society, the costs of enforcement, and so
on, represents secondary considerations which, although
sometimes surely quite relevant, are *only* secondary.[15]

Ronald Dworkin's attack on Devlin is quite different from
Hart's attack on Devlin's disintegration thesis because Dworkin is
more sensitive to the real basis of Devlin's position. "What is
shocking and wrong," writes Dworkin, "is not his (Devlin's) idea
that the community's morality counts, but his idea of what

[12]Ronald Dworkin, "Lord Devlin," 995.
[13]Mill, *Utilitarianism*, 60.
[14]St. John-Stevas, *Live, Death.*
[15]Compare Louch, "Sins and Crimes."

counts as the community's morality."[16] As this passage indicates, although Dworkin casts the dispute between Lord Devlin and himself in moral terms, the difference is framed in terms of what counts as the positive morality of a community, not in terms of a difference in personal views as to what qualifies as an acceptable set of principles of critical morality. Although there is little doubt that Dworkin's view of substantive harm and immorality differs substantially from Devlin's, it is not his strategy to appeal to it. Rather, agreeing with Lord Devlin that a man has not only the right but the duty to vote his moral convictions, Dworkin attempts to argue that most opposition to homosexuality, pornography, and so on, cannot be defended as a matter of *principled moral conviction*. It is only those moral convictions which can be defended in terms of consistent reasons and principles which one is entitled to impose upon others, Dworkin argues, and *this* principle of entitlement is itself relevant because it is part of the positive morality of the community of which both he and Lord Devlin are members.

> Even if it is true that most men think homosexuality an abominable vice and cannot tolerate its presence, it remains possible that this common opinion is a compound of prejudice (resting on the assumption that homosexuals are morally inferior creatures because they are effeminate), rationalization (based on assumptions of fact so unsupported that they challenge the community's own standards of rationality), and personal aversion (representing no conviction but merely blind hate arising from unacknowledged self-suspicion). It remains possible that the ordinary man could produce no reason for his view, but would simply parrot his neighbor who in turn parrots him, or that he would produce a reason which presupposes a general moral position he could not sincerely or consistently claim to hold. If so, the principles of democracy we follow do not call for the enforcement of the consensus, for the belief that prejudices, personal aversions, and rationalizations do not justify restricting another's freedom itself occupies a critical and fundamental position in our popular morality. Nor would the bulk of the community then be entitled to follow its own lights, for the community does not extend that privilege to one who acts on the basis of prejudice, rationalization, or personal aversion. Indeed, the distinction between these and moral convictions, in the discriminatory sense, exists largely to mark off the former as the sort of position one is not entitled to pursue.[17]

Dworkin's argument is a significant and novel attempt to defend a libertarian position in terms which the legal moralist is

[16]Ronald Dworkin, "Lord Devlin," 1001.
[17]Ronald Dworkin, "Lord Devlin," 1000-1001.

himself constrained to accept, and this without taking joinder directly on the issue of the substantive moral merits of homosexuality, prostitution, or other practices. I agree with Dworkin that the principle of political morality to which he calls our attention would be widely accepted by reflective citizens and legislators in our community, and I would also argue that it would find support within a society of act-utilitarians. But while I also believe that there are at least some instances in which an appeal to such a principle would be sufficient to defend a libertarian position, the view surely does not represent a fully adequate response to the position of the legal moralist.

In the first place, it is not clear just how Dworkin's principle of entitlement is to be interpreted. Two interpretations suggest themselves, neither of which is satisfactory.

Perhaps all that is required is that *there exist* some reasoned principle in support of a widespread belief that a certain kind of conduct is wrong. It need not matter whether most people would appeal to the principle in support of their beliefs; all that need be demanded is that the principle in question be consistent with whatever other moral principles are attributed to them. Now this interpretation is surely too weak. Unless one wishes to dismiss belief in God and an afterlife as irrational as such, which Dworkin surely does not, it will not be difficult to concoct religious arguments to support the position of the legal moralist. Although many such arguments will fail to impress a number of us, and in spite of the fact that we might be inclined to label them irrational, they are not of the sort to be disqualified by Dworkin's notions of arbitrariness, prejudice, irrationally mistaken conception of fact, rationalization, pure emotive reaction, and so on.

The second possible interpretation would demand not only that there exist a principled basis for the conviction that a certain kind of conduct is wrong, but that the majority of those who believe it to be wrong do so because they in fact consciously hold to the principle in question. But this interpretation is clearly too strong. As Dean Rostow has convincingly argued,[18] the moral convictions of most men are at best only partially based upon explicit principles; for the most part they represent the uncritically accepted results of processes of acculturation of which those who hold them are but dimly aware. Were Dworkin to demand that they be much more than this, he would, I suspect, be denying the community's positive morality any right to be enforced through the law at all.

[18]Rostow, "Enforcement of Morals," 78.

Indeed, when pushed for an interpretation of the notion of a reasoned or principled basis for a moral conviction which would at least be sufficient to exclude such things as pure "gut reaction" and rationalization, it seems that it is difficult to go far beyond the views of Lord Devlin himself. For although Devlin has been taken to task by Hart, Dworkin, and others for treating the widespread existence of *feelings* of "reprobation" and "disgust" toward certain kinds of behavior as sufficient warrant for prohibiting it, his view is in fact more complicated, and more plausible, than this. The presence of such feelings is at most merely necessary, and not sufficient, for Devlin,[19] presumably because they are only evidence of the depth of the conviction that a certain kind of conduct is wrong. And they must be present after calm discussion and deliberation on the issue of immorality, and must yield a judgment of unanimity amongst "reasonable" men.[20]

My conclusion, then, is that the libertarian will receive some—but little—solace from the claim that it is only a community's *principled* moral convictions that it is entitled to enforce through the criminal law. For under any plausible interpretation of "principled" that would entitle it to enforce anything, this would provide no assurances whatsoever of the kind given by Mill's principle, that is, that one will remain free to engage in certain kinds of activities regardless of the rationality of other people's objections to them.

There is a second difficulty having to do with the *status* of Dworkin's principle of entitlement. It is relevant, he claims, because it is a recognized part of *our* shared political morality. But suppose a community failed to accept such a restrictive principle, and rather put a premium upon individuals acting on their own impulses as determined by their spontaneous reactions of the moment? Would such a society in Dworkin's view be entitled—indeed, even have a duty—to enforce its shared morality whenever a consensus existed, regardless of how arbitrary or irrational their convictions might be? Here again, Dworkin's concession to the legal moralist must be simply too great for the libertarian to tolerate.

The question remains, then, of whether or not there are any critical principles to which the libertarian might appeal which would delimit some sphere of human conduct as absolutely outside of the legitimate range of coercive social control.

One looks here, not to Hart's criticisms of Devlin's dubious disintegration thesis, but to his discussion of Mill's principle in

---

[19]Devlin, "Criminal Law," 17.
[20]Devlin, "Criminal Law," 17-22.

Law, Liberty, and Morality. What one finds is, I am afraid, quite disappointing.

Hart writes that Mill's protests against paternalism were excessive, and argues that Mill's principle must be modified so as to permit interference with individual liberty on frankly paternalistic grounds.[21] Legal interference, Hart contends, may be warranted either to protect others from harm, or to prevent the agent from harming himself. However, Hart claims that such modified principles would not be inconsistent with opposition to the use of the criminal law for the enforcement of morality as such.[22]

It is here that Lord Devlin has had a field day with Hart's position.[23] If it is right to prevent an individual from inflicting a physical harm upon himself, or to prevent him from consenting to the infliction of such a harm by another, how can it be wrong to protect him from inflicting moral harm upon himself? Does Hart mean to distinguish physical from moral paternalism? Or is there some novel distinction to be made between moral paternalism and the enforcement of morality? Lord Devlin is at his best in pointing out the obvious reasons why Hart is in no position to give affirmative answers to these questions, and his discussion makes it quite clear that—as suggested earlier—he believes society has a right to prevent harms and immorality, whether physical or not, simply because they are wrongs. Once one amends Mill's principle in the manner suggested by Hart, the only grounds upon which a controversy over a specific prohibition may be fought out are in terms of the nature and magnitude of the putative harm and the cost of preventing it through the use of the criminal law. The libertarian has been deprived by Hart of any principled basis for denying that *all* wrongful acts, other things being equal, ought to be prevented, if necessary through the vehicle of the criminal law.

It has been my argument that both the legal moralist and the libertarian must agree that an individual or a community is entitled to seek to prevent that which is sincerely believed to be immoral. This would strongly suggest that specific disputes between them can only be resolved by taking a stand on the moral merits, although this is of course consistent with a stand on the merits generating general restrictive principle which would limit the application of the principle that error has no rights. But what this demands is that the libertarian put forward some substantive conception of what it is that determines the moral merits,

[21]Hart, *Law, Liberty, and Morality*, 32.
[22]Hart, *Law, Liberty, and Morality*, 33.
[23]Devlin, "Social Reality," 124, 132-139.

and argue in terms of it. But this is just what writers such as Hart
and Dworkin have conspicuously failed to do. It is therefore
no surprise that they fail to support the Libertarian position
of the *utilitarian* J.S. Mill. For although a libertarian principle
such as Mill's may transcend—indeed, is designed to transcend—
particular differences on the merits in specific instances, it must
be based upon some concrete conception of the right and the
good. In what follows, I shall therefore seek to indicate what I
take the implications of act-utilitarianism to be with respect to
the enforcement of morality.[24] Specifically, the paradigms which
I have in mind are homosexuality, prostitution, contraception,
and pornography. With respect to all of these there are certain
considerations which must be given special emphasis by the
act-utilitarian, not the least of which, we shall see, is an
emended version of Mill's absolute prohibition on legal
paternalism.

In the first place, it is clear that the utilitarian holds a theory
of value quite different from that implicitly or explicitly assumed
by those who take a traditional religious perspective on such
matters as sexual morality and birth control—and this is the
perspective of most, if not all, legal moralists. The utilitarian will
view questions of morality and immorality only in terms of
ascertainable harms and benefits as reflected in the desires and
aversions, satisfactions and dissatisfactions, pleasures and pains,
of sentient creatures. Where many find immorality and sin, the
utilitarian will often find little, if anything, to complain about.
In some instances, such as birth control, he will view as
positively desirable what others may find morally objectionable.
To conceal such differences in substantive moral viewpoints is
only to court confusion.

Secondly, it is clear that the utilitarian must place a very
high value upon the personal freedom interfered with by the
legislation of morality. Such freedom has instrumental value in
that it permits people to chose that which they desire, the
satisfaction of such desires being the sole intrinsic value for the
utilitarian. And insofar as most people prefer to be free to
choose, not being interfered with has intrinsic value as well.
Now I do not mean to claim that the non-utilitarian cannot place
a high value upon human freedom; Devlin, for instance, clearly
has considerable regard for it. What I do mean to point out is
that the utilitarian is directly committed to demanding a justification, in terms of harms to be prevented or benefits to be won,
for any interference with human freedom, for on his theory there

---

[24]As with Rawls, "Two Concepts," and frequently with Hart, *Punishment
and Responsibility.*

is the strongest of presumptions that there are significant dis-utilities associated with it.

In *On Liberty*, Mill quite properly emphasized the great instrumental value of individual liberty, not only for the individual, but for society at large as well. Many libertarians obviously share Mill's sentiments, but the question remains as to how the act-utilitarian could without inconsistency propose an *absolute* prohibition upon acts of any generic kind, let alone paternalistic legislation. In attacking Mill's principle in his *Liberty, Equality, and Fraternity* in 1862, James Fitzjames Stephen concluded that this question simply could not be answered. His argument is that no matter how great the value of freedom, the utilitarian is committed by the very nature of his position to deciding each case of putatively justified paternalism on its individual merits. His quite plausible suggestion is that it must at least sometimes be justified on direct utilitarian grounds.

> If . . . the object aimed at is good, if the compulsion employed is such as to attain it, and if the good obtained over-balances the inconvenience of the compulsion itself, I do not understand how, upon utilitarian principles, the compulsion can be bad. I may add that this way of stating the case shows that Mr. Mill's "simple principle" is really a paradox. It can be justified only by showing as a fact that, self-protection apart, no good object can be obtained by any compulsion which is not itself a greater evil than the absence of the object which the compulsion obtains.[25]

Contemporary writers such as Hart,[26] believing that there are numerous instances in which the law is justified in protecting individuals against themselves, have implicitly or explicitly adopted Stephen's position. They have followed him in rejecting Mill's principle, and have accepted his claim that such an absolute prohibition cannot be given a consistent act-utilitarian defense. They have thus deprived themselves of the most important argument which the libertarian might bring against the legal moralist which would transcend substantive disputes concerning the morality or immorality of specific kinds of acts.

Now is Hart so obviously correct in suggesting that we have a more realistic conception of human nature than did Mill, and that it is thus clear to us that paternalistic legislation will sometimes be justified on direct utilitarian grounds, whereas Mill mistakenly believed that it never was?[27] Optimism with respect

---

[25]Stephen, *Liberty, Equality, Fraternity*, reprinted in part in Radcliff, *Limits of Liberty*, 51.

[26]See also Gerald Dworkin, "Paternalism."

[27]Hart, *Law, Liberty, and Morality*, 32-33.

to the progress of human knowledge is surely admirable, but it simply does not ring true to suggest that a mere century could, in this context, make that much difference. If it is obvious to us that paternalistic legislation is sometimes warranted on direct utilitarian ground, it must have been so to Mill as well.

I believe that it was, and that close attention to Mill's argument for his famous principle will reveal that his argument is not only consistent with, but retains great plausibility in spite of, the frank admission that there are specific instances in which paternalistic legislation could be justified on direct utilitarian grounds. The point, in brief, is that with respect to positive law Mill must be taken to be arguing on something like the constitutional level. Just as one might argue in favor of First Amendment freedoms while acknowledging that without such barriers to legislation there are instances in which legal interference with the press, say, would be clearly desirable, so one may advocate a constitutional barrier to legal paternalism while at the same time admitting that in its absence specific bits of paternalistic legislation might be justified.

How might one so argue? The analysis presented in Chapter 4 above contains the answer. Assume: (1) that most acts of kind K are, on utilitarian grounds, wrong, although (2) some acts of kind K are, on utilitarian grounds, right, but that (3) most attempts to identify the exceptions to the rule of thumb "Acts of kind K are wrong" are mistaken because there is no reliable criterion by means of which exceptions to the rule may be identified. Where these conditions are satisfied, the act-utilitarian has good reasons for acting so as to prevent anyone from *ever* performing an act of kind K.

One would be inclined to argue this way with respect to First Amendment freedoms: (1) Most governmental attempts at interference with, say, freedom of the press, have had bad consequences, and are thus wrong on utilitarian grounds; (2) But one can of course think of specific instances in which governmental interference with a given publication would have good consequences; (3) On the other hand, were government to have the legal authority to decide that something was a genuine exception to the hands-off policy indicated by (1), more often than not decisions to interfere would be mistaken, with bad consequences in specific cases, and a "chilling effect" in general on the press stemming from fear that the power would be abused. Therefore, an *absolute prohibition* on governmental interference with the press is that policy choice—erected to the status of a constitutional guarantee—which will have the best consequences in the long run. Although this may not be very elegant as a piece of constitutional analysis, it should suffice to remind us of a familiar and reasonable pattern of argument which is totally consistent with an act-utilitarian position. That the *act* in question is one of choosing a general constitutional *rule* makes it no less of an act.

Although Mill has not to the best of my knowledge been explicitly interpreted in this manner,[28] there is little doubt that he argues for his principle in just this way. For the utilitarian, what is right and wrong is directly linked to the experienced satisfactions and dissatisfactions of those affected by any act, and the individual is of course the best judge of what he finds satisfying and what not. The individual, in short, is a better judge than society of what is in his own interests. Mill's argument against paternalism is that even where it is motivated by good intentions, it is more often than not misguided, with resultant harm rather than benefit to the individuals concerned, and the further harm to society at large which stems from its failure to profit by what might have been in any case an instructive "experiment in living."

> The strongest of all the arguments against the interference of the public with purely personal conduct is that, when it does interfere, the odds are that it interferes wrongly and in the wrong place. On questions of social morality, of duty to others, the opinion of the public, that is, of an overruling majority, though often wrong, is likely to be still oftener right, because on such questions they are only required to judge of their own interests, of the manner in which some mode of conduct, if allowed to be practiced, would affect themselves. But the opinion of a similar majority, imposed as a law on the minority, on questions of self-regarding conduct is quite as likely to be wrong as right, for in these cases public opinion means, at the best, some people's opinion of what is good or bad for other people. . . .[29]

What Mill here identifies as "the strongest of all the arguments" in support of his principle has been systematically ignored by commentators. But it *is* a strong argument, and in fact appears to be the only one to which the act-utilitarian could

[28]But Devlin at least seems to realize that Mill's principle is to be understood at something like the constitutional level. See his "Mill on Liberty," 102-103.

[29]Mill, *On Liberty*, 102. Lest the reader suspect that this quote represents a *too* careful and selective reading, let me note that it in fact represents a considerably tempered version of the position which Mill took on governmental interference with individual liberty a number of years earlier in his *Political Economy* (1848). He there wrote (311) that not only do "people understand their own business and their own interests better . . . than the government does, or can be expected to do," but that they "care for them more" than government as well. See also 151, 304 and following pages, 317, 325.

consistently appeal in an attempt to give Mill's principle the absolute status which Mill quite rightly required for it. In addition, it would seem to be the only *kind* of argument which is not damaged by the claim that there are *specific instances* in which paternalistic legislation (were it not prohibited) would be justified on utilitarian grounds.

I have suggested that Mill may be interpreted as arguing at the constitutional level for the adoption of a legal barrier to paternalistic legislation. So he might. But in the context of current controversy concerning homosexuality, etc., where such a constitutional limitation is lacking, it is clear that the libertarian must appeal to the principle rather as one of conventional political morality, similar in status, but obviously opposed, to Dworkin's principle that a man is entitled to attempt to impose his principled moral convictions upon others.

It is interesting to note that Mill understood quite well the posture of the legal moralist whom in terms of his principle he was attempting to counter. "Nine-tenths of all moralists and speculative writers," he notes,

> teach that things are right because they are right; because we feel them to be so. They tell us to search in our own minds and hearts for the laws of conduct binding on ourselves and on all others. What can the poor public do but apply these instructions and make their own personal feelings of good and evil, if they are tolerably unanimous in them, obligatory on all the world? . . .[30]
> . . . Who can blame people for desiring to suppress what they regard as a scandal in the sight of God and man?[31]

"The only tenable ground of condemnation" of those who would enforce their moral views on others, Mill concludes, "would be that with the personal tastes and self-regarding concerns of individuals the public has no business to interfere."[32]

I believe history bears Mill out in his claim that paternalistic legislation is in any given instance likely to be misguided, but this, as Mill apparently failed to realize, is not sufficient justification for an absolute barrier to paternalism. As explicitly noted above, it is also required that there be no reliable criterion in terms of which exceptions to the general rule—exceptions which are admitted to exist—can be identified. Many, I suspect, would suggest that Mill's principle must be modified in light of the fact that there are certain limited classes of exceptions which *can* be reliably identified, and I am inclined to agree with them.

[30]Mill, *On Liberty*, 103.
[31]Mill, *On Liberty*, 105.
[32]Mill, *On Liberty*, 104-105.

Mill himself admitted that children and the "uncivilized" were to be exempted from the application of his principle, and there is little doubt that he would have been willing to add the senile and the mentally infirm as well. Why should we recognize *these* exceptions? Clearly they are not ad hoc, but are rather all instances of kinds of persons whose capacity to make choices which will lead to the satisfaction of their actual needs and desires is in some manner limited or not fully developed. In such cases, the utilitarian can justify interference in terms of either the individual's existing needs and desires as the individual himself perceives them, or else in terms of needs and desires which it can with great plausibility be argued that the individual will himself eventually come to recognize. Thus the familiar, but cogent, argument for compulsory education. But if such is the principle upon which exceptions may be based, it would appear that it would license other forms of interference as well. For there are instances in which it is empirically demonstrable that people will act against their own interests if not coerced into acting otherwise; thus statutes making compulsory the wearing of protective helmets by motorcycle riders, and others prohibiting swimming after dark at unguarded beaches.[33] Where identifiable classes of individuals can be shown to be likely to manifest choice behavior inconsistent with their preferences as those preferences can be unproblematically attributed to them, the odds may change in favor of interfering with their personal liberty, if necessary, in order to protect them against themselves. Mill's principle can and should be modified accordingly.

Although this suggested emendation is in line with our perhaps more enlightened views about the fallibility of human judgment, it will not compromise the usefulness of Mill's principle to the libertarian. For the striking fact about the views of the legal moralist is that, in urging that homosexual acts, and so on, be prohibited because they are harmful or immoral, he must employ a concept of harm and immorality which bears no significant relationship whatsoever to the needs and desires of those individuals whom he would seek to protect against themselves, as those individuals quite consistently perceive their own needs and desires.[34]

I have identified three closely related features of a utilitarian defense of libertarianism: (1) A conception of value closely tied to the interests of individuals as they themselves perceive them; (2) an especially strong conception of the value of personal freedom

[33]These examples are from Gerald Dworkin, "Paternalism."
[34]Compare Chapter 2, Section 6, this text.

of choice; (3) a principled objection to interference with self-regarding conduct. We have seen that both (2) and (3) rest largely upon (1). And it has been admitted that the real basis of the controversy between the utilitarian and the legal moralist lies in their quite different conceptions of what is of value and moral significance. Is there, then, any reason to believe that the legal moralist could be persuaded to accept an emended version of Mill's principle, the chief argument for which rests upon a conception of human well-being which he clearly rejects?

The utilitarian relies upon his own conception of value in arguing that the individual is the best judge of what is for his own good, and Mill's argument would be cogent even within a society of avowed utilitarians. Those who base their moral views on religious authority of course believe that they know the moral truth, and are thus not likely to be impressed with the claim that they may be mistaken in imposing their views of human goodness and well-being on others. Were *they* members of a community of morally like-minded individuals, they would reject Mill's principle. But as a member of a morally heterogeneous community, the legal moralist might indeed agree that legal interference with self-regarding conduct is more often than not misguided, and thus accept some form of Mill's principle. Especially in a pluralistic democratic society, where one day's majority may be the next day's minority, the legal moralist may urge the adoption of principles of tolerance simply as a matter of self-protection. He may view it as a real evil that he is not able to prevent others from acting in ways that he believes to be immoral, but he may view it as an even greater evil himself being forced by others with different moral views to act in ways which he views as wrong. Within a pluralistic society such as our own, it is thus to be hoped that the libertarian has available to him, in an emended version of Mill's principle, a principle of tolerance which might actually be used to persuade others with substantially different views on issues such as homosexuality to abstain from legal interference. The reaction of many church leaders to U.S. Supreme Court school prayer decisions surely suggests that broad principles of the kind in question can win shared agreement among those who hold widely divergent views about the substantive merits of their application in specific instances.[35]

But the virtues of the non-utilitarian's acceptance of a Millian principle of tolerance reveal its defects. The principle that error knows no rights continues to lurk in the background; as suggested above, it is only the utilitarian who is willing to

[35]See Krislov, *Supreme Court*, 205-206.

accord error some rights in terms of a principle of tolerance even when he finds himself among those who are morally like-minded. Insofar as the non-utilitarian's acceptance of a principle of tolerance is a form of self-protection, he has no reason to accept it in a morally homogeneous community. Neither does he have any reason to extend the protections it affords to those who are too weak to represent a real threat to him within a pluralistic society. Indeed, in spite of the considerable degree to which the virtues of tolerance are extolled in our society, many would claim that as a matter of fact genuine tolerance is extended only to those groups which are strong enough to post a genuine political or economic threat to other groups.[36]

In another vein, it might be argued that a pluralistic society requires observance of principles of tolerance in order to avoid the breakdown of law and order. The enforcement of legal prohibitions which a substantial proportion of the community believe to be lacking in moral foundation may not only be very costly, but is likely to weaken respect for the legal system in general among those who view themselves as being repressed rather than protected against themselves. But this argument is no better than the last, and in fact has similar implications. For we know all too well that just as often as not the majority can succeed quite well in enforcing its view upon even a substantial minority, and where the minority in question is insubstantial, the level of its respect for the legal system in general may not be viewed as counting for much.

Defenses of tolerance in terms of political expediency carry weight in a pluralistic society, and are surely relevant. But the danger in them lies in the fact that if they are taken to be the *only* defenses, tolerance may come to be viewed as increasingly dispensable as society becomes increasingly homogeneous, each increase in legal moralism itself playing a causal role in increasing the level of homogeneity over time, this in turn justifying further repression. As Mill well understood, the result might be a society which, lacking the experience of a variety of instructive experiments in living, would itself be the eventual loser. The utilitarian argument for Mill's principle of tolerance is therefore anything but superfluous, for it would appear to be the only argument which finds a firmer foundation for that principle than some form of political expediency.

The legal moralist will, of course, be quick to point out that he would not view himself as being treated with excessive tolerance should the law be radically changed so as to reflect the

[36]See Wolff, "Beyond Tolerance."

utilitarian's view of what morality, as tempered by Mill's principle, demands. As far as he would be concerned, a world in which homosexuality, prostitution, pornography, and so on were legally permitted would be a world much changed for the worse, and it surely could not be said to be a world which showed much respect for or toleration of *his* moral views. For his views demand that such activities, which he believes to be immoral, be prohibited. All of this must be admitted, As has been emphasized throughout, the root of the controversy between the legal moralist and the utilitarian lies in their quite different conceptions of what constitutes the right and the good. Since they both share the view that wrong ought, other things being equal, to be prevented, they cannot both be satisfied.

There is, though, a form of tolerance which the utilitarian will extend to the legal moralist which the legal moralist has seldom been kind enough to extend to his opponents in return. This form of tolerance has little to do with Mill's principle, but is simply an extension of the general utilitarian concern with the prevention of avoidable human suffering and dissatisfaction. For, again given the principle that wrong ought to be prevented, the legal moralist will be quite understandably dissatisfied at knowing that what he believes to be immoral acts are not being deterred by force of law; if he is a retributivist, he will be further disturbed by the fact that what he believes to be immoral is being permitted to go unpunished. Such dissatisfactions will be given due consideration by the utilitarian, and although it is unlikely that they will ever lead him to change his position on any significant issue with respect to the enforcement of morality, they may surely lead him to temper the manner in which he will present his case, and are likely to influence the nature of the details of the legislation which he will propose. This sort of tolerance is most significant as it operates outside of the law, however, and may strongly influence the nature of the interpersonal relations among those who hold divergent moral views on admittedly sensitive subjects.

Hart has taken such strong exception to the above claim that he is worth quoting at length:

> [A] right to be protected from the distress which is inseparable from the bare knowledge that others are acting in ways you think wrong, cannot be acknowledged by anyone who recognizes individual liberty as a value. For the extension of the utilitarian principle that coercion may be used to protect men from harm, so as to include their protection from this form of distress, cannot stop there. If distress incident to the belief that others are doing wrong is harm, so also is the distress incident

to the belief that others are doing what you do not want them to do. To punish people for causing this form of distress would be tantamount to punishing them simply because others object to what they do; and the only liberty that could coexist with this extension of the utilitarian principle is liberty to do those things to which no one seriously objects. Recognition of individual liberty as a value involves, at a minimum, acceptance of the principle that the individual may do what he wants, even if others are distressed when they learn what it is that he does—unless, of course, there are other good grounds for forbidding it. No social order which accords to individual liberty any value could also accord the right to be protected from distress thus occasioned.[37]

This is surely one of the strongest, and most puzzling, statements to be found in Hart's voluminous and valuable writings. In giving consideration to such distress, the utilitarian is surely not suggesting that anyone has an *absolute right* not to be subjected to it, but merely that it is a relevant consideration which ought to be given due weight. And it is hard to believe that there are any instances in which giving it heed would lead to legal prohibitions that would not have been otherwise justified on utilitarian grounds. For, as Mill made quite clear, it is future generations whose interest often ought to guide legislation, and with a view to mores changing as a result of legislation, the distress of those who would be displeased or even anguished by legislative repeal of specific legal prohibitions is not likely to count for much. Consider, for instance, homosexuality. Some would, of course, be distressed if the law were to become more permissive with respect to it. But it is not likely that future generations will hold such views, and, even if they do, what about the distress caused to homosexuals who find themselves heavily penalized for their peculiar way of expressing what are among the most basic of human desires? Certainly any reasonable balancing of satisfactions and dissatisfactions would at best justify little more than protecting the legal moralist (and others) from homosexuals flaunting their idiosyncrasies upon the public in the same manner and to the same degree to which heterosexuality is promoted through such means as commercial advertising.

Most men do, and all men should, I thus conclude, experience some distress in knowing that what they sincerely believe to be wrong is in fact the case. Non-utilitarians are no exception, and I see no reason to believe that the utilitarian cannot safely and openly acknowledge this.

[37]Hart, *Law, Liberty, and Morality,* 46-47.

9   *The Rule of Law*

I have sometimes argued, and more often simply assumed, that a stable social union in large part depends upon human behavior being effectively subject to the governance of general rules. This enterprise—"law" in the broad sense as defined by Lon Fuller—is one upon whose success rational expectations about how others will behave and what the consequences of one's own acts will be to a significant degree depend. In this generic sense of law, social norms of a variety of sorts, including the legal and the moral, may be understood on essentially the same model—thus the general structural analysis of Chapter 4. As such, law is a virtual necessity as a condition of social community. Less universal, perhaps, is the necessity for law in the narrower and more familiar sense which connotes the existence of legislatures, courts, policemen, and so on; one can at least conceive of a close-knit community of benevolent men relying upon the social sanction alone as the means of directing human behavior into channels that it would otherwise not follow. Under the conditions of the modern nation state, though, the specifically legal is the form of social ordering and control upon which men are bound to continue to most heavily rely. Such a claim need not imply an uncritical acceptance of a dogmatic ideology of legalism.[1] It is quite compatible with the admission that there are important domains of human action and interaction which are simply not suited to the governance of general rules of any form. But the legitimate need for legal ordering in the narrow sense is so omnipresent under the conditions of modern social life that the notion of the rule of law could be neglected in the present account only at the price of the greatest incompleteness. For modern man, the conditions of social union are in large part legal, and any

[1] I allude here again to Shklar, *Legalism.*

analysis—normative or descriptive—of the relationship between individual conduct and social norms must take this into account.

Questions concerning the existence of a prima facie obligation to obey the law as such aside (Chapter 6), there are a number of problems to be resolved concerning the nature of the rule of law. What is it? What are the conditions necessary for its effective maintenance? What are the moral implications of having achieved it? The present chapter seeks to provide answers to these questions, with considerable attention being given to Lon Fuller's account of what he calls "the internal morality of law" and to his analysis of the concept of adjudication as well. The following chapter will be primarily concerned with a question which this chapter leaves unanswered but in large part attempts to define: What is the institutional role and responsibility of courts of law, especially with respect to the employment of moral standards as a basis for decision, within a system of constitutional adjudication such as our own?

1. The Internal Morality of Law

Lon Fuller's *The Morality of Law* has received exceptionally harsh treatment from most analytically inclined philosophers of law.[2] A more sympathetic understanding of his views than they have taken follows, I believe, from splitting apart, and then recombining, some of the different threads in what is a quite complex position, one which I do not think is fully articulated in *The Morality of Law* itself. I shall thus begin here with Fuller's notions of law and legality; in Section 2 I shall turn to his valuable but little discussed views on the nature of adjudication; and in Section 3 I shall consider the claims he makes concerning the nature of the connection between law and morality. My own position on the central issues will emerge as a response to his own.

Law, for Fuller, is a purposive enterprise—that of subjecting human behavior to the governance of general rules—and is thus to be understood in explicitly teleological terms. His question is: What are the conditions, both minimal and optimal, which are necessary for the success of that enterprise? Surely this is *a* valuable way of looking at law, and a much needed complement to the equally valuable static and structural approach of legal positivists such as Kelsen and Hart. And the notions of necessity and purpose employed are by no means objectionable as bits of metaphysical nonsense. Laws, when they have a rational foundation, do have

[2] A list of the reviews of the first edition of *Morality of Law* is to be found in the second edition.

the purpose of directing human behavior into lines it would not otherwise take. And the necessity in question may even be understood best in terms of Hart's notion of *natural necessity*. For one can take Fuller to be claiming that there are certain salient but contingent features of man and his world which provide the best of reasons for proceeding in certain ways rather than others in attempting to subject human behavior to the governance of general rules. A minimal satisfaction of the conditions associated with the enterprise of law-making and law-applying is necessary if one is to be described as having achieved even minimal success; on the other hand, their complete satisfaction is an unattainable ideal which nonetheless ought to control the aspirations of those who would seek to realize the rule of law. Fuller's eight conditions, observance of which represents adherence to the internal morality of law, are the following:

1. There must be rules—that is, general standards of conduct.
2. The rules must be intelligible to those to whom they apply.
3. The rules must be promulgated.
4. The rules must be prospective.
5. The set of rules must be logically consistent.
6. It must be physically possible to comply with the rules.
7. The rules must be stable—that is, not changed from day to day.
8. The rules must be applied to the cases to which they are understood to apply by those charged with their application.[3]

Fuller's discussion of these eight criteria—the need for satisfying them, the particular practical obstacles to doing so, especially the complex ways in which they can come into conflict with one another as well as with substantive aims—is comprehensive, illuminating, and important. Indeed, his discussion might with some justice be claimed to be the most sensitive and instructive account of legality and the associated aspects of the rule of law in the jurisprudential literature. Insofar as conformity with at least the minimal requirements of the internal morality of law can be rendered likely by placing legal restraints upon legislatures and courts, there is much for the utilitarian to learn here about various aspects of institutional design. But while I have some reservations about details, no attempt shall be made to summarize Fuller's discussion of these eight conditions. This would take us too far afield, and the most important general point—that the act-utilitarian can consistently take the kinds of considerations which they suggest into

[3]Fuller, *Morality of Law*, Chapter 2.

account at the level of institutional design—should at this point not be in need of further argument.

What of the second order claims which Fuller makes concerning the consequences of compliance or noncompliance with the internal morality of law? Surely one must agree with him that a total failure to satisfy any one of these criteria, or a great enough failure to satisfy a number of them, would be aptly described as resulting in "no law at all."[4] Likewise, there is nothing mysterious about his related notion that the existence of a legal system is a matter of degree, depending upon the degree to which the conditions of legality are met; this simply follows from his understanding of law as a purposive enterprise which can meet with varying degrees of success. This is not to say that a definition of law which would treat its existence as an all or nothing affair might not be equally valuable in other contexts.[5]

More problematic is Fuller's contention that the observance of the internal morality of law by those in power is the foundation for a bond of reciprocity between the citizen and the state. "Government says to the citizen in effect," writes Fuller, "'These are the rules we expect you to follow. If you follow them, you have our assurance that they are the rules which will be applied to your conduct.'"[6] Doubtless this kind of mutuality of law observance and law application does provide the basis for *a* form of reciprocity between the citizen and his government, and, perhaps more importantly, amongst citizens themselves. Surely it is one basis for the sorts of structures of mutual expectations which provide reasons for action for the act-utilitarian.

What is perplexing is rather Fuller's further claim that "when this bond of reciprocity is finally and completely ruptured by government, nothing is left on which to ground the citizen's duty to observe the rules."[7] Although, strictly speaking, this statement implies (is in fact logically equivalent to) only the claim that the observance of the internal morality of law is a *necessary* condition for the existence of a moral obligation of obedience to law on the part of the citizen, it is clear that Fuller understands it to be a *sufficient* condition as well. And this is because he believes that observance of the requirements of legality places considerable restraints upon the substantive aims which particular laws may be employed to further. There is, he contends, an "affinity between legality and justice."[8]

[4]Fuller, *Morality of Law*, 39.
[5]Perhaps a failure to realize this explains the especially unsympathetic response of Ronald Dworkin, "Philosophy, Morality, and Law," 676-678.
[6]Fuller, *Morality of Law*, 39-40.
[7]Fuller, *Morality of Law*, 40.
[8]Fuller, *Morality of Law*, 159.

Fuller's critics have not only rejected this claim; they have perceived nothing by way of a significant argument in its support.
But although I, too, accept the positivist's dictum that "law as it
is is one thing, as it should be, quite another," I also believe that
there is much more to be said, and that Fuller in fact says a good
deal of it. In particular, I believe that there is an argument to be
reconstructed in support of Fuller's position, and that even if its
conclusion must ultimately be rejected, it is of sufficient interest
to make the effort well worthwhile.

2. *Adjudication*

In two important but seldom discussed papers, Fuller has
concerned himself with the general concept of adjudication.[9]
Like others,[10] he is interested in the question of what features of a
dispute render it an appropriate subject for judicial resolution—
"justiciable," as the international lawyers put it—but the novelty
and chief value of his contribution is that it focuses primarily on
the prior and more basic question of what distinguishes adjudication from other forms of dispute resolution and, more
broadly, decision-making. As Fuller notes, tossing a coin, voting,
and bargaining are all means by which a social decision can be
made, and, like adjudication but unlike decision by executive
fiat, they each may offer those affected by the decision some role
in the process by which it is reached. What distinguishes adjudication from other forms of social decision-making and
dispute resolution, according to Fuller, is the particular mode of
participation in the decisional process which it provides an
institutional guarantee of for interested parties.

> Adjudication we may define as a social process of decision
> which assures to the affected party a particular form of parti-
> cipation, that of presenting proofs and arguments for a de-
> cision in his favor. . . .
> Whatever protects and enhances the effectiveness of that
> participation, advances the integrity of adjudication itself.
> Whatever impairs that participation detracts from its
> integrity. When that participation becomes a matter of grace,
> rather than of right, the process of decision ceases to deserve
> the name of adjudication.[11]

Fuller provides us with an illuminating discussion of what he
might well have called "the internal morality of adjudication,"

[9]Fuller, "Collective Bargaining," especially 19-42; Fuller, "Forms and
Limits."
[10]See for instance Marshall, "Justiciability."
[11]Fuller, "Collective Bargaining," 19.

and his contention that there are greater demands of rationality upon adjudication than upon many other forms of social decision procedure is a theme that I shall pick up on later in my discussion of the judicial role. For the present, though, suffice it to note that Fuller seems to associate adjudication with the judicial function of law application—the last of the eight conditions which constitute the internal morality of law as described above. Now surely the rule of law could be maintained in accordance with other forms of rational jucidial decision procedure— decision by well-informed judicial fiat, for instance. But to make sense out of Fuller's position on the connection between the internal morality of law and its substantive content, I believe that we must assume what is not explicitly noted in *The Morality of law*, that adjudication is *the* form of judicial law application.

If adjudication is distinguished by the fact that it assures the interested parties of an opportunity to participate in the decisional process by presenting "reasoned proofs and arguments" in their own favor, what is to be said about the character of such argumentation? Although I shall have much more to say about this in the next chapter, for the purposes at hand it is sufficient to note that Fuller throughout his long career has stoutly maintained that proof and argument in the judicial context is primarily concerned with the *purposive interpretation* of binding legal standards, whether they be precedents, statutes, or constitutional provisions.[12] The conclusions of legal arguments take the form of assertions of claims of rights and obligations, Fuller observes, and assume a background body of shared principles and rules against which such claims may be rationally tested.[13] Hard cases demand that difficult problems of interpretation of such standards be solved, but it is only because interpretation is purposive in nature, bringing to light the latent aims of extant judicial standards, that it has been possible for the common law to go through a process of "working itself pure from case to case."[14]

The general picture which emerges, then, is that the rule of law establishes an institutional framework which guarantees that those affected by controversial applications of general rules will be afforded an opportunity to argue their claims as to what rights and obligations are implied by such rules in a manner which will force a consideration of the substantive purposes which underlie them. This institutional assurance that a "tracing

[12] See Fuller, *Law in Quest of Itself*, for an early statement of his views.
[13] Fuller, "Forms and Limits," 26-27.
[14] Fuller, "Positivism and Fidelity," 474.

out and articulation of shared purposes"[15] will occur surely establishes *a link* between a procedural morality of law and the substantive content of particular rules.

3. *The Connection Between Law and Morals*

Fuller's argument is as follows: (1) The existence of a legal system implies that the internal morality of law is being observed to at least a certain minimal degree; (2) Observance of the internal morality of law places significant restraints upon the substantive aims which can be furthered by particular legal rules—that is, it assures that they will to a certain degree be just and moral; (3) The resulting substantive morality of law is sufficient to ground a moral obligation (presumably a prima facie one) of obedience to it.

I have not taken issue with (1), although I view it as either a stipulative definition or a statement of natural necessity rather than as a necessary truth. For the most part, Fuller's critics have not challenged (1) either, nor have they objected to the inference from (2) to (3); an inference which I clearly reject in Chapter 6. It is rather (2) which has been the primary concern of Fuller's critics, and it shall be mine as well. For although it may imply nothing directly about the citizen's obligation of obedience to law, the claim that the observance of certain procedural requirements is sufficient to assure at least a certain minimal goodness in the substantive content of particular laws is surely a significant one for the utilitarian. If true, it would provide him with the very best of reasons, other things being equal, to support institutional mechanisms which would guarantee, as far as possible, that those procedural requirements would be met by those having the power to make and apply the law. The question, then, is: What leads Fuller to adopt the position expressed in (2)? To answer this question, I believe that one must consider what Fuller has to say about the internal morality of law in the light of his views concerning adjudication and purposive interpretation.

Fuller's critics have for the most part employed a divide and conquer strategy with respect to his claim that observance of the internal morality of law puts restraints upon the possible content of particular laws strong enough to assure their conformity to even minimal standards of substantive morality. Cannot the most wicked laws be intelligible? Self-consistent? Promulgated?

[15]Fuller, "Forms and Limits," 52.

Possible to comply with? Uniformly applied? Prospective? Stable? Although the answer to each of these questions must obviously be in the affirmative, the critics have, I believe, missed the forest for the trees.

Fuller himself cautions that the eight principles which comprise the internal morality of law do not lend themselves to separate categorical statement,[16] and much of his account is taken up by an analysis of the quite complex relations amongst them. All of this should suggest that one consider what connection might exist in his view between substantive moral aims and the internal morality of law by viewing the latter holistically, rather than in terms of the separate criteria which make it up. What, then, is the net result of observance of the internal morality of law? In a word: *publicity*. The promulgation of intelligible prospective rules which it is believed the courts will apply, rules which are stable, consistent, and possible to comply with, is a public declaration of the strongest sort of the direction which government is seeking to give to the citizen's behavior through the use of coercive power.

The implications of this must, I believe, be understood in the light of Fuller's view that the legal system employs adjudication as its institutional procedure of dispute resolution, and his claim that the resolution of legal disputes typically calls for the purposive interpretation of extant legal standards. For the observance of the internal morality of law within a framework which provides an institutional guarantee that those affected may directly participate in the process of searching out the purposes behind particular laws provides considerable assurance that those purposes cannot be effectively concealed by those in power. The element of publicity associated with observance of the internal morality of law puts the citizen on notice as to the direction in which government seeks to control his behavior. Adjudication in terms of purposive interpretation permits him to force those in power to answer the question of *why* they are doing what they are doing. The substantive aims of those in power will inevitably be revealed. It is Fuller's position, I believe, that the necessity of such revelations of purpose will force substantive aims to successively approximate to standards of moral goodness over time. Quite simply, his view is that "evil cannot stand the light of day." In a revealing passage in his well known exchange with H.L.A. Hart in the *Harvard Law Review*, Fuller states what I am taking to be the core of his position:

[16]Fuller, *Morality of Law*, 104.

. . . Professor Hart seems to assume that evil aims may have as much coherence and inner logic as good ones. I, for one, refuse to accept that assumption. I realize that I am here raising, or perhaps dodging, questions that lead into the most difficult problems of the epistemology of ethics. Even if I were competent to undertake an excursus in that direction, this is not the place for it. I shall have to rest on the assertion of a belief that may seem naive, namely, that coherence and goodness have more affinity than coherence and evil. Accepting this belief, I also believe that when men are compelled to explain and justify their decisions, the effect will generally be to pull those decisions toward goodness, by whatever standards of ultimate goodness there are. Accepting these beliefs, I find a considerable incongruity in any conception that envisages a possible future in which the common law would "work itself pure from case to case" toward a more perfect realization of iniquity.[17]

And in *The Morality of Law*, we find the following:

. . . I have spoken as if the affinity between legality and justice consisted simply in the fact that a rule articulated and made known permits the public to judge of its fairness. The affinity has, however, deeper roots. Even if a man is answerable only to his own conscience, he will answer more responsibly if he is compelled to articulate the principles on which he acts.[18]

These passages have been largely overlooked by Fuller's critics,[19] and they have thus failed to come to grips with what surely is, as Fuller himself describes it, one of "the most difficult problems of the epistemology of ethics." For Fuller is basing his argument on a view—one which goes back at least as far as Plato—with an appeal which is at least as great as the difficulties which exist in understanding and evaluating it. His position on the connection between a procedural morality of law and the substantive content of particular laws is anything but the simple-minded and obviously false assertion that an intelligible rule must be a good rule, a rule that is promulgated must be a good rule, etc.

As I have interpreted it, Fuller's position is not to be understood primarily in terms of "the assertion . . . that coherence and goodness have more affinity than coherence and evil." Rather, as the second passage quoted above and the second part of the first passage suggest, the fundamental assertion has to do with the capacity of human beings to continue to support evil aims once they have been forced to critically reflect upon what

[17]Fuller, "Positivism and Fidelity," 474.
[18]Fuller, *Morality of Law*, 159.
[19]Ronald Dworkin, "Philosophy, Morality, and Law," 672, alludes to the former and dismisses it as "entirely mysterious."

their aims really are. Fuller's view, as I understand it, is that this capacity is minimal. Like Plato and other philosophical rationalists, Fuller is assuming a strong connection between virtue and knowledge; a problematic conception, to be sure, but one with a venerable enough history to merit it more serious attention than Fuller's critics have accorded it.

If I have correctly identified Fuller's overall argument concerning the connection between law and morals, what is to be said about it?

I have already (Chapter 6) indicated my reasons for rejecting the view that there is a prima facie obligation to obey the law as such, whatever may be claimed about its content. If the procedural framework within which the law is created and applied provides some assurance that its substantive content (that is, for the utilitarian, the results of individuals complying with it) will be good, this, although surely desirable, at best creates an epistemic presumption—which may be overridden—that it ought to be obeyed. Such a presumption, we saw in Chapter 5, is a far cry from a prima facie moral obligation which must be outweighed by countervailing moral considerations.

Observance of the internal morality of law within a system of adjudication where purposive interpretation plays a dominant role in judicial argument does serve, as Fuller contends, to bring to light the substantive goals of particular laws and judicial decisions, and thus subjects them to moral scrutiny. It also permits them to be evaluated in terms of whatever overarching constitutional standards may exist which it is within the power of the judiciary to apply. Surely these are the best of reasons for conforming to the principles of legality and guaranteeing the institutional forms associated with the notion of adjudication.

But what about Fuller's central claim that "when men are compelled to explain and justify their decisions, the effect will generally be to pull those decisions toward goodness . . ."? Plato had a comprehensive theory—of knowledge, morality, and human motivation—which would support such a position, but it is not a theory which is likely to find many adherents today. Can Fuller's claim be given some plausibility on any less dubious a foundation? I believe that it can—*some* plausibility. Firstly, whatever the ultimate explanation may be, there seems to be some empirical evidence in support of such a claim. The greatest atrocities are typically perpetrated behind a veil of secrecy; the wickedest policies often seem to lack any consistent basis in terms of principled purposes, even evil ones. U.S. imperialism in Southeast Asia is a current, and prime, example. There is, then, some evidence that evil cannot stand the light of day, and, even in spite of contrary evidence, the inclination to explain immorality in terms of irrationality or ignorance is hard to resist. Hope springs eternal, and even the mildest optimism about man's potential to achieve progress as a moral being within a social community leads one to hope, if not with firm conviction to believe, that open and rational discussion of decisions of social policy will, at least over time, "pull those decisions toward goodness."

Some evidence, *a degree* of justified optimism—these are one thing; a blind faith in institutional forms (which I by no means wish to ascribe to Fuller)—this is something else again. As with majority rule as a legislative decision procedure, institutionalization of the requirements of legality and procedures of adjudication are at best only partial guarantees that the right and the good shall prevail. Even when conforming to the requirements of legality, a majority, even of benevolent men, might do great wrong. Even when confining themselves to the role of adjudicators, courts may reach decisions which are both legally and morally mistaken. Other assurances, other safeguards, against the abuse of the power to make and apply the law, it is surely rational to seek.

4. The Rule of Law

Let us assume that the conditions obtain under which it is reasonable to support majority rule as the form of legislative decision procedure (Chapter 6, Section 6). Compliance with the principles of legality on the part of legislators and courts need not be left wholly to their discretion; it may to a considerable degree be compelled by constitutional provisions or conventional social norms governing legislative and judicial practice. Witness constitutional requirements of promulgation and bans on *ex post facto* laws with respect to the former, and canons of judicial interpretation concerning intelligibility and the possibility of compliance with respect to the latter. As Fuller reminds us, though, although minimal compliance with the principles of legality is, and may by law be made to be, a matter of duty, it must in large part remain an ideal often rightly compromised in the light of the conflicting demands presented by complex social situations.

Assume as well that adjudication is the institutionally guaranteed form of judicial decision procedure; the guarantees again being a mixture of constitutional requirements and well-entrenched judicial practice.[20] Such may be a response to men's natural desire to participate directly in the reaching of those decisions which most deeply affect them; a desire nurtured by general attitudes toward participatory democracy associated with the institutionalization of majority rule. More deeply, a rational justification for the support of adjudicative forms may be found in the kind of considerations suggested by Fuller's argument: Adjudication provides an opportunity for the citizen to assure the continued articulation of the latent purposes behind the laws to which he is subject, thus permitting a public moral appraisal of them much closer than would otherwise be possible, as well as exerting whatever pull toward goodness may be exerted upon a government which is forced to explain and justify its decisions, if only in legal terms.[21]

The fallibility of law-making procedures remains substantial, even if one assumes general benevolence amongst those entitled to participate in the legislative process. Not only is there the classic case of the threat which a majority may pose to a minority, there is the undeniable fact that certain decisions reached by a majority might work to the great disadvantage of all, present and future. Where certain generic kinds of decision can be identified beforehand as of a sort more likely than not to be mistaken, with no reliable criterion being available for identifying the exceptional cases, substantive constitutional restrictions on the legislative power are in order. Thus the character of the argument for some form of Mill's anti-paternalistic principle in the previous chapter, and the suggestion that this form of argument might be extended to other, more familiar, constitutional guarantees as well. The Bill of Rights is far from perfect, and surely subject to judicial abuse, but it is a model for a most important element in the rule of law, one which manifests man's occasional genius for coming to grips with the need to structure the framework within which his own deliberations and decisions take place.

The crucial element in the rule of law which yet cries out for analysis—both descriptive and prescriptive—is that of the judicial role and function as a form of adjudication. I shall here sketch the prescriptive argument which I believe supports the

[20]Far from being mutually exclusive, the former may in fact demand consideration of the latter. Consider, for instance, the "due process" clause of the U.S. Constitution.

[21]Perhaps this provides some explanation of the strong resistance of the U.S. government to the raising of the issue of the constitutionality of the Vietnam War in draft evasion and other sorts of cases.

view that the institutional role and responsibility of the courts in a constitutional democracy should be limited to that of applying the law rather than making it. In the next chapter I shall turn to the much more difficult task of arguing that what *should* be the case *could* be, and indeed *is*, the case within legal systems such as our own.

The position to be supported is this: If possible, the institutional role and responsibility of the courts within a constitutional democracy should be to adjudicate conflicting claims presented as a matter of felt legal right on the basis of established legal standards. A court of law should be bound to base its decision on a determination of pre-existing legal rights and duties; in adjudicating a dispute, it should have no business in creating new legal relations, or in appealing to anything other than legal standards. Although others engaged in the process of law enforcement and application (policemen, prosecutors, juries, sentencing judges) should perhaps be granted, explicitly or implicitly,[22] considerable personal discretion in applying the law, judicial adjudicators should have none.

Two related but independent arguments, both based upon straightforward utilitarian considerations, support this view of the institutional role in which courts of law should be cast.

In the first place, there are those considerations which support majority rule as the favored form of social decision procedure. Given the practical impossibility of placing the judicial decision-making function in the hands of a democratic assembly under modern conditions, the judicial role is of necessity confined to a relative few. By virtue of their highly specialized training and experience, their considerable power and their small number, the members of the judiciary constitute a genuine political elite. And if the judicial role is to be an impartial one of adjudication, judges must be insulated from untoward influences by removing them to a considerable degree from the control of the public which they are to serve. Thus familiar practices with respect to the recruitment and institutional accountability of judges; most importantly, the practices of executive appointment rather than election as well as life tenure accompanied by the virtual practical impossibility of judicial recall.[23] If courts were to have the authority to make law, they would constitute a legislative elite in a very pure form

---

[22]For an especially valuable discussion, see Kadish and Kadish, "Rule Departures"; also their recent *Discretion to Disobey*.

[23]I am indebted here to the very perceptive discussion in Weiler, "Two Models."

indeed. But the very arguments which favor majority rule as the form of legislative decision procedure as against some form of nondemocratic elitism imply that the law-making power should be the exclusive province of the majority. They militate against entrusting a judicial elite with the awesome power to make the law as well as to apply it.

In the second place, there are the requirements imposed by the nature of adjudication itself. If the parties to a dispute are to have a meaningful role in the process by which the decision is reached which resolves it by having the opportunity to present arguments in support of their claims of right, there must be some set of shared pre-existing standards around which the issue can be joined. The rational adjudication of a dispute can not take place in a vacuum, and neither can it occur in a context within which the decision-maker is free to make up the rules as he goes along. There must be a shared conception of which reasons and arguments will be treated as relevant, and which will not.[24] Were all of the moral considerations which might be deemed relevant by the adjudicator or either of the parties, if the issue were to be decided *de novo* in an extralegal setting, to be admitted as relevant in the judicial context, controversies could seldom be narrowed to the point where a convincing case could be made that the decision reached represented the proper resolution of the competing claims of right and obligation at issue.

It might be argued in reply here that all concerned could be brought to understand that adjudicators would employ the act-utilitarian principle itself in the resolution of disputes. Pre-existing legal standards, whether of legislative or judicial origin, would serve the citizen as more or less reliable guides as to how the courts would decide, but they would be subject to modification—including outright abandonment—should the circumstances appear to dictate that this would have the best consequences. Adjudication, it might be claimed, would be preserved as the form of institutional decision procedure insofar as the parties to the dispute were given the opportunity to present reasons and arguments in their own favor based upon the direct application of the act-utilitarian principle itself. Indeed, if it were common knowledge amongst the members of a community that the members of the judiciary were act-utilitarians, how else could one expect them to act? As act-utilitarians, must they not decide each case on its direct moral merits in terms of which decision is likely to have the best consequences with respect to all

[24]Fuller, "Forms and Limits," 60-62.

who will be affected by it? Courts could take account of pre-existing legal standards, surely, and of the consequences of their decisions with respect to discouraging or encouraging reliance upon them, but how could consistent act-utilitarians treat such standards as anything more than the other "givens" of which account must be taken in making a direct utilitarian calculation of probable consequences?

The above argument—roughly that of Richard Wasserstrom's *The Judicial Decision*, at least with respect to judicial reasoning in common law areas,[25] rests on two misconceptions. The first concerns the implications of the adoption of act-utilitarianism. The second is with respect to the relationship between the judicial resolution of live legal controversies and the manner in which extant legal standards control behavior outside the courtroom.

A consistent act-utilitarian, in principle, is of course to decide each case on its direct merits in terms of probable consequences; to fail to do so is to cease to apply the act-utilitarian principle. A judge who is an act-utilitarian is no exception. But, to return to the major theme of this essay, this is quite consistent with there being the best of utilitarian reasons for subjecting the judge to social norms which bar direct appeals to utility. The role and responsibility of the judge is to a great degree structured by institutional norms which determine the citizen's expectations as to how he will behave, and thus his own beliefs about how he will be expected to behave, which in turn provide him with reasons for action. By virtue of the nature of his professional training, the standards in terms of which his decisions will be criticized extralegally, the grounds upon which they will be over-turned by higher courts, the sorts of arguments which are treated as relevant by litigants and their lawyers, and a host of other factors, the direction which the judicial decision will typically take can to a large degree be predetermined by the deliberate creation of the appropriate sorts of institutional and extra-institutional considerations—considerations which, as an act-utilitarian, the judge will have to take into account. Given such background considerations, the judge who is an act-utilitarian can be expected to act in that manner which he believes is likely to have the best consequences. But in speaking of his institutional role and responsibility, what is at issue is the design of the institutional framework within which he must

---

[25]As a "simplifying assumption," Wasserstrom (*Judicial Decision*, 8) considers a legal system in which legislation is absent. It should be clear from what follows that on my view such an assumption is disastrous.

decide, and which will to a considerable extent determine what the likely consequences of his decisions will be. My claim is simply that that framework is best designed which subjects him to institutional and extrainstitutional norms which bar direct appeals to utility as a basis for decision, and rather define the adjudicator's role as that of treating legal disputes as conflicting claims of right to be resolved on the basis of pre-existing judicial standards. There is no inconsistency in the notion of a judge (a) being bound as a matter of conscience as a moral agent to decide each case on direct utilitarian grounds, but (b) being bound as a matter of institutional role and responsibility to decide each case according to the law. On the one hand, there is an individualistic moral principle of right action. On the other hand, there is a social norm in the form of an institutionalized decision rule. The point is simply that the former can require support of the latter, while the latter in turn can to a considerable degree determine what is required by applications of the former. Support of a system of adjudication characterized in part by the institutional decision rule that the job of the judge is to apply the law and not to make it thus turns out to be but another instance of men deliberately acting so as to restructure the sets of considerations of utility of which they or others will predictably have to take account.

I have already argued that good reasons for avoiding the creation of nondemocratic political elites militate against judges being given the authority to modify extant legal rules on the basis of their personal perceptions of what is likely to have the best consequences in the instant case. But a second argument was promised, one having to do with the relationship between the in-court adjudication of disputes and the operation of the law so as to control behavior out of court. The point is this: Unless the standards which the adjudicator applies in court are the same standards which have been promulgated with the aim of controlling behavior out of court, there is little reason for the private citizen to conform his behavior to those standards rather than regulate it in terms of his predictions as to how the courts will decide. Assuming what was argued earlier (Chapter 4)—that there is a need for legal rules which bar direct appeals to utility—the whole point of the legislative enterprise would be lost if the courts were given the authority to subvert it. The point is especially well put by Paul Weiler:

> Why and when does judicial respect for established rules in litigation affect the efficacy of the legal system in controlling purely private activity? The answer is that there must be a real

4. *The Rule of Law*

relation between the law as enforced officially, and as promulgated for private obedience, in order that those who might disobey be deterred or encouraged by the official consequences and that those who would obey voluntarily be protected from those who would not. Only if the same rules are used to assess conduct when a dispute arises, as could reasonably have been expected at the time the decision to act was made, is there any real incentive to orient this conduct in accordance with these announced rules.[26]

Weiler goes on to note a closely related consideration which carries considerable weight under those (nearly universal) social conditions where it is desirable to discourage recourse to the expensive and often devisive process of adjudication as a means of resolving legal controversies.

Since the vast majority of tort actions, criminal prosecutions, and so on are privately negotiated and settled, and the continuance of this practice is absolutely essential to stave off the breakdown of the judicial system, we cannot afford to do anything which lessens the incidence of such private settlements. The theory is that the best way to ration the costly process of adjudication is to allow private individuals to decide rationally that the likely gains are outweighed by the likely costs. Only if there is a substantially accurate awareness of the standards the courts will use will such prediction and negotiation be rational.[27]

I conclude, then, that in a constitutional democracy where there is a commitment to adjudicating disputes rather than having them decided by judicial fiat, the rule of law requires that the institutional role and responsibility of the judge be that of applying the law rather than making it. What remains to be shown is that what I have argued *should* be the case *could* be the case, and that it indeed *is* the case within judicial systems such as our own.

---

[26]Weiler, "Legal Values," 11.
[27]Weiler, "Legal Values," 12.

10   *The Judicial Decision*

It was my argument in the previous chapter that the judicial role and responsibility in a constitutional democracy such as our own *ought* to be confined to that of applying the law rather than making it. I also believe that this *is in fact* the institutional role of the judiciary, this in the sense that it is this conception of their role which best squares with a wide variety of salient features of our legal institutions. Modes of legal argument and the manner in which judges are trained, recruited, and held accountable have already been mentioned. Among other significant aspects of the legal process which also seem to imply that the judicial role is not a legislative one are the following: the limited fact-finding apparatus available to courts; the adversary nature of judicial proceedings, participation in them being limited to the parties to a suit (as qualified by the *amicus curiae* doctrine); the judicial demand that a live case and controversy exist, accompanied by the requirement that judicial proceedings must be initiated by someone other than the deciding body; the ability of courts to get their decisions—often in a strong sense retrospective in effect—accepted by the litigants and lesser judicial organs; our conception of what sorts of pressures it is appropriate to bring to bear on judicial decision-makers; the character of legal scholarship, as engaged in by judges, lawyers, and academics.[1]

In spite of the above, it is the nearly universal view of academic lawyers and legal philosophers that the judicial role neither is nor *could* be limited to that of applying the law. For it is argued that in at least some cases judges must, and are therefore entitled to, exercise an essentially legislative discretion, and through an appeal to their own personal conceptions of the

---

[1]Much of this is noted by Weiler, "Two Models."

relative importance of various extralegal considerations, play an active role in the formulation of social policy by the creation of new legal standards. Although it would be admitted that the great majority of judicial decisions are controlled by pre-established rules, and while it would be urged that there are many important differences between judicial and statutory legislation, it would be claimed that there are many significant decisions of social policy—expecially those made by high appellate courts—which represent a necessary exercise of legislative power by the judiciary.[2]

Before turning to the arguments for it, we must be clear on what this claim comes to. It is not being claimed that judges are sometimes free to decide on the basis of whim or bias; those who maintain that judges must play a legislative role are typically careful to point out the possibility and desirability of discretionary judicial decisions reflecting "the judicial virtues" of impartiality, fairness, principled generality, and so on.[3] Neither is it being claimed that courts are ever totally free from the control of authoritative decisional standards which *limit* their discretion.[4] Rather, the claim is that there are cases in which the decisional alternatives, although limited by authoritative standards, are nonetheless not limited to only one uniquely correct decision. In such cases, where authoritative "guidance dries up,"[5] the choices which judges must make, it is concluded, are discretionary in nature. As Hart and Sacks once put it, "*discretion* means the power to choose between two or more courses of action each of which is thought of as permissible."[6]

Now I do not mean to deny that there are or have been legal systems in which judges are entitled to exercise discretion. Indeed, it is probably correct that "an exceptional exercise of discretion by the judiciary characterized the formative years of the common law."[7] My contention is rather that no such discretion exists now in legal systems such as our own and, more importantly, given the prescriptive argument of the last chapter, that judicial descretion is by no means a necessary feature of the rule of law.

---

[2]Found in journal articles far too numerous to mention; two recent book-length studies which adopt this position are Hart, *Concept of Law*, and Gottlieb, *Logic of Choice*.

[3]For example Hart, *Concept of Law*, 200; Gottlieb, *Logic of Choice*, 155.

[4]See the quotes from Freund and MacCallum on pages 190 and 195.

[5]Gottlieb, *Logic of Choice*, 154.

[6]Hart and Sacks, *Legal Process*, 162.

[7]Berman and Greiner, *Nature and Functions*, 71-75.

1. Judges as Legislators: Some Familiar Arguments

J.C. Gray once claimed that "all law is judge-made law"[8] and that particular precedents, statutes, and constitutional provisions are not really laws but only "sources of law."[9] Gray's reasons for adopting this curious position are suggested in a famous passage from Bishop Hoadly which he often repeats: "Nay whoever hath an absolute authority to interpret any written or spoken laws it is he who is the Lawgiver to all intents and purposes and not the person who first wrote or spake them."[10] This view that "the law (or the constitution) is what the judges say it is," attributed to U.S. Chief Justice Hughes,[11] still flourishes and, on the basis of my own limited experience, seems to be especially popular amongst first-year law students.

I shall not review here in detail the conclusive objections which have been raised against such simpleminded views. As Hart and Dworkin have pointed out, the finality of a decision implies absolutely nothing about its correctness, let alone that it cannot be properly spoken of as either correct or incorrect.[12] In particular, that a supreme appellate court may have the *power* to ignore the decisional standards which it ought to apply by no means implies that it has the institutional *authority* to do so. This is not to deny that the finality of the decisions of ultimate courts of appeal is a most significant feature of the judicial process. Given the rule of *stare decisis*, it implies that some mistaken judicial decisions which go uncorrected will be repeated to the point where they become the law. This institutional analogue to the doctrine of adverse possession is surely a powerful instrument for bringing about changes in the law through judicial action, but it does not imply that judges sometimes have the authority to make law.

A second familiar argument concludes that there are some cases in which there is no uniquely correct result, and that courts must therefore play a legislative role in deciding them, on the basis of what one can reasonably expect rational argument to accomplish with respect to the justification of the decisions reached. Such an argument need not rest on a simple confusion between various senses of 'discretion', as Dworkin suggests when

[8]Gray, *Nature and Sources*, 125.
[9]Gray, *Nature and Sources*, 125.
[10]Gray, *Nature and Sources*, 85.
[11]Quoted in Hart, *Concept of Law*, 250.
[12]Hart, *Concept of Law*, Chapter VII, Section 3; Ronald Dworkin, "Model of Rules."

he notes that there is a "weak" sense of 'discretion' which it is appropriate to employ when a decision is controversial and the standards in terms of which it is to be justified difficult to apply.[13] As in the case of Thomas Perry's carefully argued analysis of judicial reasoning, it may rather be based upon a supposed asymmetry between rational method in law and its analogue in the formal and empirical sciences.[14]

Perry's contention is that it is the possibility of interpersonal agreement being achieved upon the validity of conclusions reached that characterizes the rationality of method in the formal and empirical sciences, but which is notably lacking with respect to the justification of decisions in very hard cases at law. "If we are to speak of uniquely correct decisions in such cases," he writes, "the notion of a consensus of competent lawyers seems indispensable."[15]

> To sum the matter up, we could only know that a case involving conflicting or doubtfully applicable legal standards has a uniquely correct result by knowing that the experts do or would agree on some particular result for that case.
>
> Now, I think it is practically certain that there are many difficult cases on which there is no such consensus. If this is so, then it follows that there can be no way to identify the uniquely correct or best decision in such cases, and that there is very little point in even speaking of such a decision in such cases.[16]

I would agree with Perry that expert consensus is a reliable way to identify the correct decision in hard cases—perhaps even the most reliable way. Lacking such a consensus, I also agree that it may be practically impossible to *identify* the correct decision, or to *demonstrate* that what one has identified as such is uniquely correct. But it surely does not follow from this that a uniquely correct decision does not *exist* in every case, just as it does not follow that none among a number of competing empirical theories is correct because at a given time there is no consensus among scientists as to which one of them is the correct one. Indeed, with respect to the possibilities of rational justification and persuasion, it seems to me that the judicial and scientific methods, rather than being radically different, are quite on a par.

---

[13]Ronald Dworkin, "Model of Rules," 32.
[14]Perry, "Judicial Method"; I had the pleasure of commenting on an earlier version of Perry's paper and the published version reflects those comments.
[15]Perry, "Judicial Method," 5.
[16]Perry, "Judicial Method," 5-6.

I am far from clear what Perry's thesis concerning the connection between deductive method and the possibility of intersubjective agreement comes to with regard to statements having either a conjectural or formally undecidable status in mathematics, but it is clear that, in mathematics, we have learned that truth cannot be equated with provability. Perry's argument would seem to establish nothing more than this with regard to law. Noting this objection, Perry replies as follows:

> In the (formalized) deductive sciences, one can at least always check a *proof* that has been advanced and determine that it certainly is or certainly is not a good proof. In contrast, a judge's "proof" of "legal theoremhood" cannot be similarly checked in (the very hard cases).[17]

Leaving aside the difficulties that might be raised by noting such things as the existence of disagreement amongst mathematicians as to what constitute acceptable proof procedures (for instance, intuitionistic strictures with regard to nonconstructive proofs), Perry's point might be granted. But although it would constitute *an* asymmetry between judicial and mathematical method, it is not of the general sort required by his argument. For the same point might be made with respect to the limitations upon demonstration in the empirical sciences. It no more follows that a uniquely correct decision does not exist in a given case because the argument in support of the decision reached does not establish the conclusion with certainty than it follows that no true theory of matter exists because atomic physics is not a purely deductive science. In both cases, quite clearly, the conclusions of what can be cast as valid deductive arguments may be controversial and in that sense "undemonstrated" because their premises are.

Turning, then, to the empirical sciences, where is the putative disanalogy between the judicial and the scientific methods? Intersubjective agreement amongst the users of "scientific method" may be the textbook ideal, but reality falls far short of it. At any given time there may be considerable disagreement as to which among a number of competing theories is best supported by the evidence, and, indeed, even disagreement as to what constitutes "the evidence." Although scientists, unlike judges, may enjoy the relative luxury of being able to withhold judgment, it cannot be denied that the use of rational methods in science does not preclude the possibility of rational disagreement. And if it be argued that in spite of such

[17]Perry, "Judicial Method," 15.

disagreement at "the frontiers," the use of scientific method in the empirical sciences leads to eventual intersubjective agreement in the long run,[18] the analogous claim might with equal plausibility be made for the judicial method. Hindsight works wonders in law as well as in science. Rather than there being a disanalogy in these respects, it is here that judicial and scientific methods seem to me to be quite on a par; both dictate agreement in relatively simple cases, but provide room for reasoned controversy and ultimate disagreement as the issues in question grow increasingly complex. Indeed, I believe that one must explicate some of the same concepts, such as formal coherence, simplicity, relevance, and centrality of principle, to account for either method. To reply at this point, as does Perry, that in the very hard cases at law "we do not even have the goal and concept of unique, interpersonal, correctness"[19] is simply to beg the question.

A third argument for the exercise of discretionary choice by judges represents an attempt to mediate between the equally unacceptable extremes of mechanical jurisprudence, on the one hand, and total skepticism as to the existence of binding legal rules on the other hand. Well expressed in the writings of John Dickenson in the 1930's,[20] it has recently received a clear and careful defense by H.L.A. Hart in *The Concept of Law*. Basically, the view is that general standards of conduct are inherently incapable of providing authoritative guidance in all the particular cases to which they apply. Although they will have clear implications with respect to the central or core cases of their application, they will also determine a penumbral class of cases in which their implications can only be settled by the exercise of discretion on the part of those who apply them.

> Whichever device, precedent or legislation, is chosen for the communication of standards of behavior, these, however smoothly they work over the great mass of ordinary cases, will, at some point where their application is in question, prove indeterminate; they will have what has been termed an *open texture*.[21]
> . . . In these cases it is clear that the rule-making authority must exercise a discretion, and there is no possibility of treating the question raised by the various cases as if there were one uniquely correct answer to be found, as distinct from an answer which is a reasonable compromise between many conflicting interests.[22]

[18]Perry, "Judicial Method," 15.
[19]Perry, "Judicial Method," 15.
[20]Dickenson, "Legal Rules: Their Function," and "Legal Rules: Their Application."
[21]Hart, *Concept of Law*, 124.
[22]Hart, *Concept of Law*, 124.

As it stands, this argument is at best inconclusive, for it totally ignores the fact that the interpretation of precedents or statutes in the penumbral cases may be guided by broader legal policies and principles which the judge is also bound to apply. Indeed, in one sense I would go even further than Hart and argue that the rule of *stare decisis* does not directly obligate the judge to apply the members of a class of authoritative rules—the *rationes decidendi* of cases—at all. But this is quite consistent with the view that the rule of *stare decisis*, when coupled with other elements of the overarching decision rule which determines how courts are to decide, does in principle determine a uniquely correct decision in every case, and thus completely eliminates the opportunity for the exercise of judicial discretion.[23]

Dworkin has located the genesis of Hart's claim that judges must sometimes exercise discretion in the "positivistic" thesis that law is a system of authoritative *rules* identifiable by a fundamental test such as Hart's *rule of recognition.*[24] According to Dworkin, this view directly implies that standards other than rules are not binding law because they are not the sorts of things which such a fundamental test could certify as valid law.[25] On this view, according to Dworkin, an appeal to considerations of social policy and broad principle must appear as an act of essentially discretionary judgment. Specific legal rules are seen as the only relevant binding legal standards; their application in hard cases clearly demands an appeal to more general principles and policies; and since these principles and policies are not part of the law, their use is a matter for judicial discretion.

The difficulty with such a position, of course, is that it rests upon an excessively narrow and totally unwarranted view of what constitutes binding law. As Dworkin has convincingly argued, the broad principles and policies in question, although obviously different in important respects from valid rules, are treated by courts as standards which they are bound to apply, and viewed by litigants as part of a body of law which entitles them in every case to the correct decision as a matter of legal right. Law, Dworkin argues, is a system of entitlements determined by a whole constellation of public standards which incorporates binding principles and policies as well as authoritative rules. Rather than at any point being free to impose his own personal preferences in choosing among extra-legal

---

[23]See Sartorius, "Doctrine of Precedent."
[24]See Hart, *Concept of Law,* especially Chapter 6.
[25]Ronald Dworkin, "Model of Rules," 37, and "Judicial Discretion," 634.

considerations as a basis for decision, the judge must at all times do his best to determine which decision the litigants are entitled to as a matter of law. Although a decision in a hard case may be controversial, or clearly wrong but unappealable, it is nevertheless demanded that it be viewed by the judge as representing the result which the law *requires* him to reach. Once one abandons "the model of rules," and appreciates what *the law* is which judges are bound to apply, Dworkin concludes, we shall understand why there simply is no room for the exercise of judicial discretion in any strong sense.

There are surely good grounds for arguing that Hart's *The Concept of Law* represents a sophisticated version of legal positivism: Hart does adopt the view that in some cases judges must legislate social policy; and it does seem that his version of positivism lies behind his belief in the exercise of judicial discretion. For Hart claims that a legal system represents a union of what he calls "primary" and "secondary" *rules*,[26] and would apparently relegate other decisional standards to the status of what he calls "permissive sources" of law. It is to these extralegal considerations that the judge must appeal, states Hart, when "no statute or other formal source of law determines the case before him. . . . The legal system *does not require* him to use these sources, but it is accepted as perfectly proper that he should do so."[27]

Hart's view that there are cases in which "judicial decision . . . involves a choice between moral values"[28] and that in some of them "all that succeeds is success"[29] thus does appear to be liable to the very criticisms which Dworkin levels against the model of rules and the doctrine of judicial discretion.

Although certainly to the point, it seems to me that Dworkin's arguments nevertheless do not go nearly far enough, for the grounds which are most often given in support of the view that judges are legislators explicitly build upon, rather than deny, Dworkin's claim that there are binding legal standards other than authoritative rules. Once we see what these other arguments for the prevailing view are, in fact, it will become clear that Dworkin not only fails to give them adequate consideration, but, because of his rejection of the thesis that there is an ultimate test for binding law in each legal system, is really in no position to meet them.

[26]Hart, *Concept of Law*, especially Chapter 5.
[27]Hart, *Concept of Law*, 246-247 (italics mine).
[28]Hart, *Concept of Law*, 200.
[29]Hart, *Concept of Law*, 149.

2. Judges as Legislators: The Argument in Terms of the Recognition of Relevant Decisional Standards

Both Dworkin and I are in agreement that law is a system of entitlements, although, as we shall see, we differ as to what is their basis. At any rate, we share the view that a litigant before a court of law is not in the position of one begging a favor from a potential benefactor, but rather in that of one demanding a decision as a matter of right—as something to which the law entitles him. Such a demand has two aspects: (1) A claim that a right exists which the law recognizes; (2) A claim that this right takes precedence over any competing rights or obligations that the other party to the dispute may claim are involved. Let me refer to these two sorts of claims respectively as ones involving decisions as to (1) recognition, (2) weight.

Now it seems to me that many would agree that the law consists of much more than valid rules and that they would acknowledge that judges are bound to consider the authoritatively established principles and policies upon which Dworkin places so much emphasis. What they would contend, though, is that judicial discretion is called for in (1) the recognition of new principles and policies which prior to their employment were not authoritatively established, as well as in (2) the assignment of weights or priorities to established principles and policies which can come into conflict in a given case. I shall turn first to the problem of recognition, and then, in the following section, to the problem of relative weight.

There is no doubt that an established principle of law may be just as binding as a valid legal rule, it might be admitted; the problem is rather one of accounting for how certain binding standards other than rules become established in a body of law in the first place. Although the proponent of the view that judges play an active role in the formulation of social policy will admit that rules, principles, and policies can all enter the law by way of constitutional provision, legislative enactment, or the accumulation of judicial precedents, he will typically maintain that such standards often enter the law *de novo* by way of judicial legislation as well. There will be hard cases in which a decision is not dictated by established legal standards, or else where the decision which is determined by extant standards is rejected because it is no longer felt to be desirable; in such cases, it would be contended, the judge may exercise a discretionary choice amongst extralegal standards in order to justify his decision. Since it is his personal preferences among the plethora of available extralegal considerations which determine which ones he chooses to apply, the judge's decision in such a case must be recognized as an essentially legislative one. Paul Freund, who clearly does not accept the model of rules, expresses this view as follows:

> Much of the law is designed to avoid the necessity for the judge to reach what Holmes called his "Can't helps," his ultimate convictions or values. The force of precedent, the close applicability of statute law, the separation of powers, legal presumptions, statutes of limitations, rules of pleading and evidence . . . all enable the judge in most cases to stop short of a resort to his personal standards. When these prove unavailing . . . the judge necessarily resorts to his own scheme of values. It may therefore be said that the most important thing about a judge is his philosophy; and even if it be dangerous for him to have one, it is at all events less dangerous than the self-deception of having none.[30]

There are two important problems which have for the most part been neglected by those who have been content to leave the problem of the justification of the judicial decision at the point where the judge is depicted as having to reach an essentially legislative decision by exercising his discretionary choice amongst principles which are firmly rooted outside of, rather than within, the legal system.

In the first place, those who have claimed that the judge may appeal to principles which are external to the law have failed to explain how it is that only *some* of these principles, but not others, are *ever* good grounds for a judicial decision. In the second place, it does not seem that this theory can account for the fact that a principle which is an acceptable basis for decision in one sort of case may be totally unacceptable in other sorts of cases where it might be applied with equal ease.

On my view, to make a case for the relevance of some "extralegal" policy or principle, a judge must demonstrate, not that it is there, applicable, and meets with his approval, but rather that it is either an established part of the law, or is made relevant by some other rule, principle, or policy that is. On the one hand, there are broad principles and policies which are embedded in or exemplified by numerous authoritative legal enactments: constitutional provisions, statutes, and particular judicial decisions. Thus, although it has never been authoritatively enacted, one may say that it is a principle of our legal

[30]Freund, "Social Policy," 110.

system that a man shall not profit by his own wrongs— Dworkin's favorite example. On the other hand, established legal standards may implicitly or explicitly direct the court to a consideration of extralegal community standards. Thus constitutional standards of due process and constitutional prohibitions against cruel and unusual punishment clearly render relevant community standards of fair play; just as rules and principles in the law of negligence may link reasonable care to the standards of care which are in fact being observed in a given profession, industry, or within the community at large. Such extralegal considerations may, of course, change over time, and the law will change with them; not through legislation or constitutional amendment, but through judicial action.

The point remains, though, that changing extralegal considerations constitute good reasons for a judicial decision only insofar as they are directly or indirectly incorporated into the law by rules, principles, and policies which are themselves already well established legal standards. The problem or recognition evaporates, on my view, once one understands that courts are always bound in the final analysis by authoritative standards found within, rather that outside of, the law. My position does imply, though, that there is some ultimate criterion by which one can in principle determine whether or not any given standard *is* a *legal* standard; a criterion closely conforming to the spirit, if not the letter, of Hart's rule of recognition.

But we have seen that Dworkin rejects this fundamental tenet of "positivism" upon which rests my rejection of the view that judges are sometimes entitled to legislate new principles and policies into the law as well as appeal to ones already established. "If the positivists are right . . . that in each legal system there is an ultimate *test* for binding law . . .," writes Dworkin, "it follows that principles are not binding law."[31] Since almost the entire burden of Dworkin's argument is to maintain that principles *are* binding law, he must of course deny that there is such an ultimate test. In doing so, he deprives himself of what strikes me as the most persuasive argument against the claim that judges are free to exercise discretion in choosing among extralegal principles which are not yet recognized as an established part of the law.

Dworkin himself points out that "not any principle will do to justify a change, or no rule would ever by safe. There must," he thus rightly concludes, "be some principles that count and others

[31]Ronald Dworkin, "Model of Rules," 37.

that do not . . ."[32] Those that do count, I have suggested above, can be identified by something quite like Hart's ultimate rule of recognition. I see no reason, in other words, to accept Dworkin's contention that this tenet of positivism implies that standards other than rules are not binding law. Such an ultimate test, I shall argue, can provide a complex criterion by means of which it can be determined that certain principles and policies, as well as formally valid rules and judicial precedents, are binding law within a given legal system.

We may begin by loosening up a bit Hart's concept of a rule of recognition, which must include the rule of *stare decisis*, so as to take account of the fact that the doctrine of precedent gives authoritative status directly only to particular decisions, rather than to general rules.[33] As so modified, it will identify constitutional provision, legislative enactment, and judicial decision as authoritative sources of law. Certainly Dworkin is right that there is much more here than valid legal rules; already included are broad constitutional principles, statements of policy accompanying statutory legislation, and particular judicial decisions. The additional standards which both Dworkin and I wish to identify as binding upon judges—and which I wish to identify as binding *law*—may be recursively defined as those exemplified, established, or implied by these first order standards, either directly or indirectly.

We may actually have three stages here, as can be seen if we consider that the ultimate test could identify as binding laws: (1) The statutes enacted by a particular legislative body; (2) The principles and policies embedded in (1); (3) "Extralegal" principles and policies directly or indirectly incorporated into the law by either (1) or (2). Although the actual filling out of such an ultimate criterion would be a complex and demanding task for any mature legal system, if it is indeed a practical possibility at all, the only claim that need be made is that it is in principle possible, and that it is this possiblity which in theory underlies the identification of something as an authoritative *legal* standard. Although it is perhaps a good way from Hart's version of positivism, it is in accord with the fundamental positivistic tenet as described by Dworkin: "The law of a community . . . can be identified and distinguished by specific criteria, by tests having to do not with . . . content but with . . . pedigree . . ."[34] It is also quite consistent with Dworkin's penetrating comments

[32]Ronald Dworkin, "Model of Rules," 38.
[33]See Sartorius, "Doctrine of Precedent," for support of this position.
[34]Ronald Dworkin, "Model of Rules," 17.

upon the way in which one must argue for the existence or weight of a legal principle in terms of its institutional support.

> . . . [I]f we were challenged to back up our claim that some principle is a principle of law, we would mention any prior cases in which that principle was cited, or figured in the argument. We would also mention any statute that seemed to exemplify that principle. . . . Unless we could find some such institutional support, we would probably fail to make out our case, and the more support we found, the more weight we could claim for the principle.[35]

3. Judges as Legislators: The Argument in Terms of the Weighing of Relevant Decisional Standards

It might be admitted that *which* principles and policies are to be recognized as law is in theory determined in the manner discussed above, but, it might be contended, judicial discretion must be exercised in the assigning of *weights* to these principles and policies. Which decisions will be perceived as justifiable will depend upon the weights which relevant principles and policies are determined to have in those cases where, as frequently occurs, competing principles and policies point in different directions. Legal principles and policies, it might be claimed, do not come with pre-existing weights assigned to them, and there is no recognized priority rule which would permit a lexical ranking of them. Insofar as they have the dimension of weight, it would be concluded, this merely represents the weight which courts, exercising discretion, have given to them in the past and are likely to give to them in the future.

My reply to the claim that judges exercise discretion in assigning weights to various legal standards is implicitly contained in my discussion of the problem of recognition contained in the preceeding section. I there argued that a principle is relevant if and only if, *and to the degree to which*, it enjoys what Dworkin aptly calls "institutional support." Although a precise account of this notion is not presently available,[36] it seems to me to be intuitively clear enough to provide the basis for at least a partial answer to the present objection. Further considerations concerning the weight to be assigned to legal principles and policies follow below in the context of my discussion of what I think is a much more important argument for the existence of judicial discretion, one closely related to that just considered.

[35]Ronald Dworkin, "Model of Rules," 41.
[36]But see Miller, *Principles*, Chapter 6.

The strongest and, I believe, most widely held ground for the view that in at least some cases judges are not bound by authoritative standards to reach a particular result, and that they must then exercise discretion, rests neither on the claim that there are no authoritative standards other than rules, nor on a denial of the possibility of in principle identifying, and restricting the judge to a consideration of, legal standards. Rather, the claim is that the necessity for judicial discretion arises because of the possibilities of conflict among principles and policies which, because of their authoritative status, may—with the pre-existing weights which they have—all be relevant to the decision of a given case. For what is argued is that if good sense can be made out of the notion that extant principles and policies have established weights of varying degrees, then it is only reasonable to expect that principles of equal weight may come into conflict in a case where the law contains no further grounds upon which to choose between them. Since such a case could with equal legal justification be decided in more than one way, and because it can and must be decided in only one of these ways, any decision amongst the available alternatives must be recognized as an exercise of the judge's personal discretion. Although in such cases the judge's options may be *limited* by authoritative standards, in them no uniquely correct decision can be said to exist.

Grant Gilmore, for instance, observes that in cases of sellers' warranty liability, different results may be obtained by bringing a case under either the rules of contract or those of tort. And an appeal to more general legal principles, he implies, will merely move the problem on to a different level, for this kind of case "neatly sets in opposition to the principle of freedom of contract the *equally important* principle that a man may not contract out of liability for his own wrongdoing."[37]

John Dickenson put it this way:

> The broader and more fundamental principles of the law are themselves almost never capable of being applied directly as rules of decision for the settlement of controversies. On the one hand the principle may be so broad—as, e.g., that property rights should be protected—that it will embrace within its scope both the opposing interests in a particular controversy, and therefore give no clue as to which should prevail over the other. . . . On the other hand, if the principle is less broad in its scope, it is likely to express the interest of only one of the parties in the controversy, and so come into square collision with another equally valid principle expressing the interest of the opposing party.[38]

---

[37]Gilmore, "Law, Logic, and Experience," 34 (italics mine).
[38]Dickenson, "Law Behind Law," 298-299.

And this is precisely the line taken by Gerald MacCallum in his comment on Dworkin's original attack on the doctrine of judicial discretion:

> There are instances where judges cannot find *within the recognizably established accumulation* of policies, etc., guidance sufficient to lead them to one and only one decision in an instant case, either because of insufficient guidance as to the relative weights to be attached to realizing various policies or acting in accordance with various principles and rules found to be antagonistic to each other, or because clearly applicable policies, etc., do not unequivocally guide them to one and only one specific decision.[39]

Now although I believe that Dworkin is correct in claiming that litigants and lawyers *expect*, and judges typically speak *as if* there exists "the decision in every case that constitutes the best resolution of the stipulated principles and policies,"[40] this by itself does not suffice to show that they are not, as the prevailing view maintains, sadly deluding themselves.

The problem of assigning priorities among competing principles and policies is typically viewed by the proponents of the view that judges are legislators as one of weighing the substantive importance of the purposes of such standards. The position seems to be that when there are no authoritative commitments to which the judge can defer which establish an order of priorities among such purposes, he must then impose his own values, and decide that some substantive goals of the law are more important than others.[41] Now there is a particular kind of model being accepted here of the sort of guidance which could be provided by authoritative legal standards; when, in terms of this model, it is seen that "guidance dries up,"[42] it is concluded that judges must exercise discretion.

What is this underlying model of justification? It is one in which a rule or principle at any given level is validated by deriving it from some standard (in conjunction with statements of relevant fact) at a still higher level, the process terminating at the point where an ultimate substantive principle is reached which cannot be validated in the manner of subordinate standards, but whose validity lies simply in its acceptance. But the legal system within a pluralistic society such as our own does not contain any such ultimate principle; there simply is no one overriding goal or aim, but rather a plurality of policies and

---

[39]MacCallum, "Dworkin," 634 (italics mine).
[40]Ronald Dworkin, "Judicial Discretion," 633.
[41]Clearly found in Gottlieb, *Logic of Choice.*
[42]Gottlieb, *Logic of Choice*, 154.

principles which in some cases come into quite direct conflict.
The reason why on this view there can be no such thing as "the
best resolution" of such a conflict on authoritative grounds is
because it is believed that this would require the existence of a
supreme principle or priority rule which just does not exist.
Where the law runs out in this way, and the view is that it
inevitably will even when it is construed so broadly as to contain
extralegal principles having no authoritative legal grounding,
the judge, as Freund puts it, "necessarily resorts to his own
scheme of values." Indeed, it is this argument, rather than his
acceptance of "the model of rules," which I believe is at the root
of Hart's conclusion that in some hard cases "all that succeeds is
success."

> Judicial decision, especially on matters of high constitutional
> import, often involves a choice between moral values, and not
> merely the application of some single outstanding moral
> principle; for it is folly to believe that where the meaning of
> the law is in doubt, morality always has a clear answer to
> offer. . . .[43]

Legal rules, principles, and policies do, of course, have
purposes, and a corresponding aspect of importance which is to
be assessed in terms of the desirability of the aims that they
promote and the efficiency with which they promote them.
Neither is there any denying that the judicial *interpretation* of
such standards often involves a consideration of such purposes.
But this does not entail, as is typically assumed,[44] that the weight
which they are to be given in the justification of decisions
requires that the judge make his own judgment of their importance in this substantive sense. Rather, it may be argued that the
only manner in which a court is entitled to weigh a legal
standard is to determine what Dworkin has called its formal
"institutional support" in terms of other established standards.
Any judicial decision takes place against the background of an
entire legal system containing a wide variety of interrelated and
interdependent decisions, rules, principles, policies, etc. In any
case, it may be argued, the obligation of the judge is to reach
that decision which coheres best with the total body of authoritative legal standards which he is bound to apply. The correct
decision in a given case is that which achieves "the best resolution" of existing standards in terms of systematic coherence as
formally determined, not in terms of optimal desirability as
determined either by some supreme substantive principle or by

[43]Hart, *Concept of Law*, 200.
[44]As, for instance, by Gottlieb, *Logic of Choice*.

the judge's own personal scheme of values. Although the degree of weight or importance in this formal or systematic sense which will attach to a given rule or principle will typically reflect the importance in the sense of desirability which it is perceived to have extrasystematically, it is the distinctive feature of the institutionalized role of the judiciary, in contrast to the legislative, that it may not directly base its decisions on substantive considerations of the value of competing social policies.

The degree of systematic, authoritative control which exists in even the hardest of hard cases is thus on my view so great that it is incorrect to speak of judicial creativity as *at any point* becoming discretionary. Alf Ross, who some years ago drew the important analogy between the status of the statements within a scientific theory and the status of rules within a legal system, in terms of which he stresses "the system as a whole" being "used as a scheme of interpretation," saw this point clearly. In both law and empirical science, Ross concluded, "the question is whether the particular law is compatible with the hitherto accepted system. But nothing is established beyond doubt."[45]

If one is inclined to speak in terms of the traditional epistemological notions of coherence and correspondence, as is Israel Scheffler,[46] one might put the point in the following manner. That to which a maximum of *correspondence* is to be sought is the total set of judicial obligations as determined by the legal system's ultimate rule of recognition. In viewing the law as a systematic whole, there is a subset of this general class of obligations—the particular decisions which he is strictly bound to follow and the specific rules and principles which he is strictly obligated to apply—for which any particular judge must find a place within the system. As for the remainder of the members of this class of authoritative legal standards, the judge must try to fit as many of these into the system as well. Any particular judicial decision will then be justified in terms of its *coherence* with that system which at any given time achieves a maximum of correspondence in the above sense to the total set of relevant existing judicial obligations. If one views the judge as having an initial commitment—one derived from his acceptance of the office of judge—to the legal correctness of the acts represented by particular judicial decisions and to the patterns of action represented by general legal rules and principles, then one can speak of the judicial decision in terms of the judge's overriding obligation to attempt to *maximize* his adherence to these initial

[45]Alf Ross, *Law and Justice*, 36-37.
[46]Scheffler, "Justification."

commitments. It is "the systematic import of acts," writes Scheffler,

> which forms the basis of . . . legal justification. Justification is never a question of an isolated act. . . . It is the systematic rechanneling of initial commitments in such a way that each act is judged in terms of all others. We do not start from scratch, but always with initial commitments of some degree; but neither do we rest content with the latter.
>
> While rules . . . are justifiable . . . to the extent to which they maximize initial commitment, sets of acts are justified when maximal in this respect, and individual acts are justified when they belong to the maximal set. Circularity is avoided here, . . . since, while each act singly is justified by inclusion in the standard act-set, it is the totality of acts which exerts control over the choice of a standard act-set.[47]

One should not be mislead here by the emphasis upon the tying back of rules to particular cases, for Scheffler is well aware of the importance of the systematic connections which exist among rules and principles themselves, and he takes account of the fact that these connections may develop in relative independence from the cases. In a somewhat different connection, and some years later, Scheffler writes that

> [I]t is enough if *at some point* justifying principles are tied back to cases; particular rules may then be justified by *connecting* them with the principles in question. It would, indeed, be an oversimplification to suppose that each and every rule is itself adjusted with cases, independently. Rules may, alternatively, be justified through systematic connectedness with other rules or principles, which are themselves adjusted to cases. In some circumstances, indeed, a "systematic" justification of this sort seems clearly preferable to a direct justification by case-adjustment, for the relevant governing principle is much more basic than the rule being judged, and would dislodge it in a case of conflict, even if the rule were supported by direct case-adjustment. It is this case-adjustment of the whole set of principles which is in point, rather than that of any given rule that may be in question.[48]

This model of rule-justification, I believe, represents a substantially correct analysis of the justification of the judicial decision in those hard cases where an attempt must be made to achieve a satisfactory resolution of competing legal principles; for it is here that new rules, often formulated to meet new conditions, will be tested against the results to which their application would lead in both hypothetical cases and cases

[47]Scheffler, "Justification," 188.
[48]Scheffler, *Anatomy*, 318.

already decided, and it is in such cases that the interplay among these rules and those rules and principles already established will appear most conspicuous.

What Scheffler and Ross have failed to note is that the judge will be faced with a majority of initial commitments which he is not free to revise in the light of systematic considerations: formally valid legal rules he *must* apply; binding precedents he *must* follow. There is thus an asymmetry here with empirical science, where any belief may in principle be revised or withdrawn in the light of systematic considerations.[49] The reason for this asymmetry, of course, is that there is no analogue in science to the structure of power and authority which exists within a well-developed legal system. Whereas *any* scientist may in principle be free to make *any* change in *any* scientific theory on the grounds that such a change will result in a simpler and at least equally well-confirmed theory, any particular judge will be bound by some authoritative standards which he is not free to revise on any grounds. It is thus that the judge can say: "I feel obliged to uphold some laws which make me gag."[50] Although the individual scientist, like the judge, is a member of a wider community which subjects him to a variety of institutional methodological norms,[51] we would not know what to make of such a claim if it were taken to refer to empirical laws.

4. Judges as Legislators: A Final Argument

In and of themselves, the arguments of the previous section do not refute the claim that there are some cases in which the relevant principles, policies, etc., are so finely balanced that there is no one uniquely correct decision, and that the judge deciding among alternatives supported by reasons of equal weight is therefore exercising discretion. It seems that at best they merely necessitate a recasting of the prevailing view that judges are legislators in terms of the notion of equal coherence rather than that of equal importance. This recasting is significant, though, in that it demands an appropriate reformulation of the position in which the judge must be said to find himself before being forced to resort to his own scheme of values. For it is one thing to say that either of two possible decisions in a given

---

[49]I am referring here, of course, to the holistic epistemological views of Duhem and Quine.

[50]Harlan Fiske Stone, quoted in Mason, *Harlan Fiske Stone*, 556.

[51]See Kuhn, *Scientific Revolutions*.

case would have equally desirable consequences if evaluated in terms of relevant substantive purposes; it is quite a different thing to claim that they both cohere equally well with the entire background body of relevant law. Could a judge in an instant case ever really justify such a claim?

Unfortunately, there are two considerations which suggest that an unequivocal answer to this question cannot at present be given.

In the first place, no one has developed anything which even approaches a precise characterization of what it means to "maximize adherence to initial commitments" or to "maximize institutional support." What is needed is some sort of a *comparative measure* of the relative weights of particular commitments. That the construction of such a measure is bound to be a most difficult job arises from the fact that what is obviously required is some way of determining the relative weights to be assigned to individual decisions, as against general rules, as against even broader principles of varying orders of generality. Even comparing rules against other rules, principles against other principles, etc., raises difficult enough problems. One thing which is clearly of great importance here is the degree of systematic connectedness involved. But how is this degree of systematic connectedness to be measured, and how does it relate to the question of the simplicity of the total system?[52]

In the second place, even if some measure function did exist which would permit the comparison of the degrees to which alternative decisions affected the systematic resolution of conflicting legal principles, what guarantee could we possibly have that there would never be more than one decision in a particular case which was optimal in the required sense? The decision theorist generally speaks of an optimal decision as one which is as good as any other in terms of the preference function involved, and in most domains of human choice we typically assume that in a given set of circumstances the optimal decision need not be unique. Might it not be that in at least some of the hard cases the issues are so finely balanced that more than one optimal decision exists amongst the alternatives for which there are legitimate and acceptable reasons? Even if one had a measure of institutional support or coherence, then, how could it be shown even *in principle* that every correct judicial decision must be unique? And given the degree of abstraction that the construction of a satisfactory measure function of this sort would involve, could we ever be able to demonstrate *in practice* that there was no

[52]See Miller, *Principles*, Chapter 4.

conceivable alternative to an admittedly correct decision in an especially hard case?

It has already been admitted (Section 2 above) that it is unreasonable to expect that it would be possible, even in principle, to develop some form of judicial proof procedure which would permit one to demonstrate the correctness, let alone the unique correctness, of a putatively correct decision in all cases. But this, we saw, at best implies the existence of judicial discretion in a weak, rather than in the required strong, sense.

On the other hand, though, if more than one correct decision might exist in a given case, must it not be concluded after all that a judge making a choice amongst the available alternatives is exercising discretion in the strong sense? And have I not conceded, in terms of the very model of justification that I have supported, that such cases in which there is no uniquely correct decision in all likelihood exist? In such cases, although *limited* by authoritative standards, is it not true that there is a range of alternatives amongst which the judge must decide, but within which his choice is not determined by the law? The conclusion that judges must therefore sometimes act as legislators would seem, at this point, to be inescapable.

Throughout this chapter, the apparently universal assumption that judicial discretion in the strong sense must be admitted to exist if it must be admitted that there are some cases in which there is not a uniquely correct decision has not been challenged. But it is just this assumption that I mean to reject. For if it is admitted, as I believe it must be, that in the vast majority of cases there is only one correct decision, and if it is also admitted, as, again, I believe it must be, that there is no reliable criterion by means of which the exceptional cases in which there is no uniquely correct decision can be identified, it remains both possible and desirable to hold judges in all cases responsible to their role of applying the law rather than making it. The pattern of argument which I have in mind should by now be one which the reader is able to anticipate.

The issue about the existence of uniquely correct decisions is to some extent a red herring.[53] For the argument to the conclusion that judges must exercise discretion in the strong sense can just as well be made, not in terms of cases in which there does not *exist* a uniquely correct decision, but simply in terms of cases where after honest intellectual effort the judge has been unable to *identify* a uniquely correct result. The judge must decide in one way—he cannot suspend judgment—and, by

[53]As Tom Kearns has convinced me.

hypothesis, in such a case authoritative guidance is not sufficient to lead *him* to a particular decision. What else could one expect him to do but to decide amongst the alternatives which the law at least appears to make available in the way which he believes best? If he is a utilitarian, must one not expect him to render that decision which he believes will have the best consequences, and to clothe it in the best legal arguments which he can muster in its support?

These questions may be answered in the affirmative without abandoning the view that the possible and desirable role of the judiciary *in all cases* is to apply the law rather than make it. For what is at issue is the institutional role and responsibility of the judge as defined by those social norms which it is reasonable to apply in the evaluation and criticism of his decisions. In most cases, if he tries hard enough, the judge will be able to identify the uniquely correct decision to which the litigants are entitled as a matter of law. Although there are other cases where he will not be able to identify a uniquely correct decision, perhaps because none exists to be identified, there is no reliable criterion which the judge could apply which would permit him to identify those cases in which his failure could be explained in terms of the absence of that which he is institutionally obligated to seek. Were the judge to feel free to justify his decisions on extralegal grounds whenever he believed that the law did not provide sufficient guidance as to how he should decide, he would more often than not be mistaken in concluding that a uniquely correct decision did not exist. Thus it is reasonable to support social norms which will incline courts to try as hard as possible to determine in every case which decision the litigants are entitled to by the law which they are bound to apply.

It is interesting to note that Hart and Sacks, whose definition of 'discretion' was noted above, seem to acknowledge this point in spite of the fact that their general approach is in accord with the prevailing view that judges are at least sometimes entitled to exercise discretion. Speaking of a difficult case of statutory interpretation involving considerations of the weights to be given to competing social policies, they write as follows:

> In these circumstances there may be thought to be a justification for describing the act of interpretation as one of discretion, even within the definition which has been given. But this would be to obscure what seems to be the vital point— namely, the effort, and the importance of the effort, of each individual deciding officer to reach what *he* thinks is *the* right answer.[54]

[54]Hart and Sacks, *Legal Process*, 168.

Institutional norms which channel judicial decision-making behavior into lines that it would not otherwise take are means for assuring that such efforts will be maximal, and that the consequences of a failure to exert them will be minimal. I thus conclude that it is always appropriate to criticize a judicial decision which cannot be justified in terms of extant legal standards, even one reached in a case where, by hypothesis, no *one* decision could possibly be justified in this manner. Rather than being perverse or absurd, this position is merely a special, and especially important, application of my general structural account of the relationship between individual conduct and social norms. Here, what I have called "the reflection principle" in Chapter 4 breaks down because there is a sense in which the principle that "ought implies can" breaks down as well. It all hinges upon the judge being unable to reliably identify, at least at the time of decision, exceptions to the institutional decision rule that a judicial decision is to be justified solely in terms of pre-existing legal standards. It must be admitted—and this is one of the insights behind the prevailing view that judges are legislators—that not all decisions can be so justified. But if it is also admitted that attempts to identify cases for which there is no one legally correct result would more often than not be mistaken, then it makes good sense *never* to permit appeals to the exceptional case to justify overt judicial legislation. Insofar as there are cases where judges could not, or, on direct utilitarian grounds, should not, conform their behavior to their institutional role, they are, or should be, creators as well as appliers of law. But to describe them in the latter way is to describe their individual conduct as political actors, not their institutional role as members of the judiciary.

The question, in other words, is one of how judges are to view their task, not their accomplishments, and the debate has centered about the nature of the grounds to which their institutional role entitles them to explicitly appeal in support of their decisions. The view that judges are entitled to exercise legislative discretion implies that judges are sometimes entitled to base their decisions explicitly on their own perceptions of desirable social policy. The model which I have presented implies that they are not. Although the (large) grain of truth in the prevailing view is that judges do make law, in the sense of changing the law through legally unjustified decisions which, given *stare decisis*, may be binding on lower courts, this does not imply that they are legislators, even on a small scale. For the concept of a legislator is tied to a notion of the institutional role which an individual is recognized as being entitled to play, and which he himself can publicly avow without incurring justifiable criticism. A "legislator" who is not entitled to appeal to anything other that pre-established authoritative legal standards in justification of his decisions is simply not a legislator.

5. *Rules, Principles, and "The Law"*

Ronald Dworkin has recently been kind enough to reply to some of the foregoing comments on his views, and I believe that a brief concluding discussion of our differences may serve to clarify both of our positions.[55] Although similar in important respects, there are nonetheless significant differences between them.

Dworkin's distinction between rules and principles has not gone unchallenged,[56] and as it is clear that I, too, rely heavily upon such a distinction, I must say something about the sense in which I accept it. As originally drawn by Dworkin, the distinction between rules and principles revolves around two central features: (1) "Rules are applicable in an all-or-nothing fashion. If the facts which a rule stipulates are given, then either the rule is valid, in which case the answer it supplies must be accepted, or it is not, in which case it contributes nothing to the decision."[57] A principle, on the other hand, "states a reason that argues in one direction, but does not necessitate a particular decision."[58] Counter instances to a rule thus either invalidate it or show that it must be qualified in terms of exceptions; not so with principles, counter instances to which merely weaken their strength. (2) "Principles have a dimension that rules do not—the dimension of weight or importance."[59]

I reject (2), for rules, like principles, have the dimension of weight. Rules have weight in the quite unproblematic sense defined by the number of principles which they are supported by and the number of particular decisions they in turn support. A particular rule occupies a central place in our legal system especially if its abandonment would necessitate a recognition that important principles had thereby been considerably weakened. This is not to deny (1), for Dworkin's claim that (1) entails (2) is

[55]Most of my comments on Dworkin were contained in Sartorius, "Social Policy." Dworkin's reply is found in his "Social Rules."

[56]See Christie, "Model of Principles"; Raz, "Legal Principles"; and "Understanding the Model of Rules."

[57]Ronald Dworkin, "Model of Rules," 25.

[58]Ronald Dworkin, "Model of Rules," 26.

[59]Ronald Dworkin, "Model of Rules," 27.

simply false.[60] This may be seen most clearly in the case of a valid statutory rule; (1) surely holds, as Dworkin maintains, but (2) does not—consider what might be said about the consequences of the repeal of the rule, if it is an especially "important" one, by way of the erosion of certain legal principles.

Dworkin might reply here that what he had in mind was a functional distinction having to do with the way in which courts are entitled to treat different kinds of decisional standards. But this would be to say, not that rules do not have the dimension of weight, but rather that courts are not entitled to consider this dimension as a basis for choosing to apply one rule rather than another. The only questions which courts are entitled to ask about rules, he might claim, have to do with their validity, applicability, and interpretation.

But what about so-called "common law" rules? It is Dworkin's failure to distinguish their status from that of valid, authoritatively binding rules which, I suspect, has been partially responsible for the controversy which has arisen over his distinction between rules and principles. For the doctrine of precedent does not make the members of any class of judge-made rules authoritatively binding, and yet common law rules do exist. Unlike statutes, they function like Dworkin's principles in that they not only have the dimension of weight, but this dimension may be considered as a basis for the decision whether or not to apply them in a given case.

So I would seek to qualify Dworkin's distinction in the following way: When, but only when, a rule is authoritatively binding, it functions in an all-or-nothing fashion, and although it must have a weight, judges are not entitled to consider this dimension of it in deciding upon either its validity or applicability. Nonbinding rules and principles, on the other hand, do not apply in an all-or-nothing fashion, and courts are entitled to consider the weights which they clearly have in deciding whether or not to apply them.

With these qualifications, I surely agree with Dworkin that broad principles and policies which can function as reasons for decisions are established by and indirectly incorporated into the law through specific authoritative obligations. That they are "merely a brief allusion to a number of rules" unless themselves authoritatively enacted[61] is about as distorted a view as one can imagine concerning the nature of judicial reasoning. Fortunately, it is not widely shared, much more typical being Morris

---

[60]Ronald Dworkin, "Model of Rules," 27.
[61]Raz, "Legal Principles," 828.

Cohen's observation that "any decision may be criticized on the ground that it is not consistent with the principles generally recognized or embodied in specific statutes or repeated previous decisions."[62]

The most important difference between Dworkin and myself has to do with the genesis of such legal principles. I have argued that they may be recursively defined as those established in or by formally valid rules, binding decisions, and other legal materials which are authoritative because they are in accordance with the formal criteria of validity contained in something like Hart's fundamental rule of recognition. Dworkin has maintained his rejection of this tenet of "positivism," and continued to contend that the distinction between law and morals which the positivists defended, and thus the closely related notion that the job of the judge is to apply "the law," is fundamentally mistaken.

In his earlier writings, Dworkin seemed content to rest his rejection of the positivistic distinction between law and morals on the claim that judges were entitled to appeal to extralegal community moral standards as a basis for decision.[63] But which ones? As Dworkin himself has noted, not all such principles could possibly be relevant. Given his analysis of Devlin's position (see Chapter 8, Section 3), one might have expected Dworkin to reply that it is only a community's *principled* moral convictions that count. But in a pluralistic community such as our own, is not this notion of shared community moral standards a myth, as Raz has suggested?[64] Dworkin's reply is instructive:

> Raz is right in supposing that very few large communities share a consistent code of moral beliefs, but he misunderstands those judges who appeal to community morality. . . . He fails to distinguish between concepts of the moral standards of a community. That phrase may refer to a consensus of belief about a particular issue, as may be elicited by a Gallup poll. Or it may refer to moral principles that underlie the community's institutions and laws, in the sense that these principles would figure in a sound theory of law. . . . Whether a principle is a principle of the community in this sense would be a matter for argument, not report, though typically the weight of the principle, not its standing, would be at issue.[65]

Dworkin has written elsewhere of "recognized examples of explicit and implicit reference to moral standards in statutory and constitutional law,"[66] and he admits that his denial of

[62]Cohen, *Reason and Law*, 89.
[63]Ronald Dworkin, "Judicial Discretion," 635.
[64]Raz, "Legal Principles," 850.
[65]Ronald Dworkin, "Social Rules," 890.
[66]Ronald Dworkin, "Philosophy, Morality, and Law," 690.

judicial discretion is based upon the possibility of viewing the judge as bound by the law as determined by a "sound theory of law."[67] Why, then, does he reject the claim that such a theory *is* a theory *of law* which identifies what the law is directly or indirectly in terms of its formal origin rather than in terms of its substantive moral content? The answer, in brief, seems to be that Dworkin believes that the construction of such a theory necessitates the intrusion of the moral views of the individual constructing it. His argument, as I understand it, runs as follows:

A *social rule* like Hart's rule of recognition is defined in terms of concordant social practice. Where there is no uniform practice, in particular, where there is disagreement as to what is implied by "the rule" in specific circumstances, there simply is no social rule governing the case in question.[68] But there can be, for any given individual, a *normative rule* reflecting his view of what the social rule *ought* to be in such cases. Although any given person's acceptance of such a normative rule might have to do with the expectations, etc., created by an ongoing practice of the sort reported in the associated social rule, his acceptance of it represents *his* conception of the morally right.[69] Now a fundamental test for law defined in terms of such notions as coherence and institutional support obviously goes well beyond reporting concordant judicial practice, and indeed is tantamount to the construction of a theory of law. It must, Dworkin concludes, thus represent a *normative* theory based upon such practice, seeking not to provide an *historical explanation*, but rather a *moral justification*, for it. Hart's thesis fails, according to Dworkin, because there is no *social* rule which constitutes a rule of recognition;[70] my emendation of it fails, he claims, because the test in terms of institutional support to which both of us would appeal involves a commitment to a substantive moral position.[71]

Dworkin captures my position quite well when he writes that

> Sartorius must say, not that any particular lawyer's theory of law supplies a social rule of recognition, but rather that the test of institutional support *itself* is such a social rule. . . . [t]hat is, that the social rule of recognition is just the rule that a principle is to be applied as law if it is part of the soundest theory of law, and must be applied with the weight it is given by that theory.[72]

[67]Ronald Dworkin, "Social Rules," 878.
[68]Ronald Dworkin, "Social Rules," 864.
[69]Ronald Dworkin, "Social Rules," 867.
[70]Ronald Dworkin, "Social Rules," 870.
[71]Ronald Dworkin, "Social Rules," 876-878.
[72]Ronald Dworkin, "Social Rules," 877.

That this fundamental test for law must be in terms of content rather than "pedigree" is argued for as follows:

> If a thoery of law is to provide a basis for judicial duty, then the principles it sets out must try to justify the settled rules by identifying the political or moral concerns and traditions of the community which, in the opinion of the lawyer whose theory it is, do in fact support the rules. This process of justification must carry the lawyer very deep into political and moral theory, and well past the point where it would be accurate to say that any "test" of "pedigree" exists for deciding which of two different justifications of our political institutions is superior. . . .
> I do not mean to say that no basis can be found for choosing one theory of law over another. On the contrary, since I reject the doctrine of discretion . . ., I assume that persuasive arguments can be made to distinguish one theory as superior to another. But these arguments must include arguments on normative political theory . . . that go beyond the positivist's conception of the limits of the considerations relevant to deciding what the law is. The test of institutional support provides no mechanical or historical or morally neutral basis for establishing one theory of law as the soundest. Indeed, it does not allow even a *single* lawyer to distinguish a set of legal principles from his broader moral or political principles. His theory of law will usually include almost the full set of political and moral principles to which he subscribes; indeed it is hard to think of a single principle of social or political morality that has currency in his community and that he personally accepts, except those excluded by constitutional considerations, that would not find some place and have some weight in the elaborate scheme of justification required to justify the body of laws.[73]

It is clear that the difference between Dworkin and me goes well beyond any questions concerning the conditions under which it is or is not misleading to speak of a "test" of "pedigree." Indeed, it seems to me that Dworkin has virtually conceded the case to those who have argued for the existence of judicial discretion in the strong sense. For if it is his own personal moral and political views which must enter into any theory of law upon which his decision in a hard case must be based, has not the judge been freed from authoritative *legal* guidance? Is not this the very notion of judicial discretion which Freund and others have had in mind?

Dworkin is surely correct that the sort of theory of law which is in question would be "complex" and, as he repeats time and

[73]Ronald Dworkin, "Social Rules," 877-878.

again in his recent article, "controversial." But it is Dworkin himself who has taught us to be careful in drawing any strong implications from the fact that judgments might be of such a nature. Just as judicial decisions may be difficult and controversial without implying the existence of discretion on the part of those who make them, so may theories of law be complex and controversial without implying that those who propose them are appealing to their own personal moral views as the ultimate basis for their justification. Dworkin's argument, it seems to me, rests upon a series of not-so-subtle confusions and false dichotomies.

In the first place, the distinction between social and normative rules is anything but exhaustive for the purposes at hand, and does little justice to my position. In the second place, neither explanation nor justification as Dworkin understands them are appropriate as ways of characterizing the sort of theory of law which I have in mind, and which I hope that Dworkin does, too. The spurious nature of both of these distinctions are but two sides of the same coin, and I shall thus deal with them together.

A rule may be imputed to the members of a community on the grounds that it provides the best systematic rationale for certain aspects of that community's normative practice. As such, although it must be based upon concordant practice, it may go beyond it to settle controversial cases in a manner which need not coincide with the judgments of any member of that community. One who proposes the rule may be claiming neither to be providing an historical explanation of the underlying practice nor a moral justification of it. He might know nothing about its historical origins, and be personally convinced that the practice is immoral. All of this, though, has nothing to do with the question of whether or not the practice can be provided with a consistent rationale in the sense of a systematic representation in terms of a network of interconnected rules and principles which may go well beyond the ground-level facts of concordant behavior, patterns of criticism and justification, etc., which are manifested within the community in question. That moral and political principles may be involved implies nothing; the point is simply that they need not be the principles of the individual constructing the theory in question. Such was Kelsen's view of the *"grundnorm"* as the central "juristic hypothesis"[74] of a "pure theory of law," and it is a view which I believe Hart at least

[74]Kelsen, *General Theory*, and "Basic Norm," 108-109.

could follow with respect to the status of the rule of recognition.[75] Dworkin is correct that one can not claim that such a rule *must* exist within any legal system;[76] but, at least in his more careful moments, Hart does not make that claim,[77] and I certainly never have.

Dworkin's claim that "the test of institutional support . . . does not allow even a *single* lawyer to distinguish a set of legal principles from his broader moral or political principles" is, I conclude, simply without foundation. A fundamental test for law of the sort which both Dworkin and I wish to construct is to be understood as identifying the law (directly or indirectly) in terms of its formal origin rather than its substantive moral content. Although I have admitted that "extralegal" considerations may be rendered relevant by extant legal rules and principles, my argument has been that they are relevant only because they are made so in this way; not, as Dworkin claims, that they are bound to be so given the nature of a theory of law unless they are "excluded by constitutional considerations."

The institutional role of the judiciary as defined by a decision rule incorporating the notion of a theory of law in the sense at issue is surely difficult, and even more often controversial, but it remains one of applying the law rather than making it, either on the basis of the judge's own personal moral convictions, or on the basis of extralegal community moral standards.

That there may be sound utilitarian reasons for a judge to depart from his institutional role as so defined is a point that at this stage of my overall account of individual conduct and social norms should not require further elaboration.

---

[75]I criticized Hart's treatment of the status of the rule of recognition along lines very similar to Dworkin's some years ago in Sartorius, "Concept of Law," Section XI. But I believe that the modifications in his views which such criticisms suggest could quite easily be made without changing any other essential aspects of his general position.

[76]Ronald Dworkin, "Social Rules," 870.

[77]See Sartorius, "Concept of Law," 173.

11   *Concluding Remarks*

This essay began with a quotation from Jeffrie Murphy:

> [I]f one is going to decide each case solely upon its merits as one sees them, then there is no sense to the notion of social rule or the rule of law as a social decision procedure. And it is this realization, I think, which is at the heart of the belief that there is such a thing as political obligation—a prima facie obligation to obey the law as such.

Act-utilitarianism is a normative theory which does permit each case to be decided on its merits, and the autonomy of judgment which it allows the individual agent to retain is surely one of the chief sources of its persistent appeal. As against the prevailing view that for the act-utilitarian social rules can function only as rules of thumb, I have sought to demonstrate how and why they can function as much more than this. In particular, I have attempted to show that they can in a quite strong sense serve as reasons for action, and by barring direct appeals to utility play the central social role of directing human behavior into channels that it would otherwise not take. It is for this reason that act-utilitarians would support them, thus manifesting that aspect of human rationality which lies in man's ability to control his environment in significant ways—in this case the environment of considerations of consequences within which choice and deliberation take place.

I have explored and sought to develop the implications of this theme in a variety of directions, specifically with respect to those legal and moral rules which structure the most important of a society's social obligations. I have reviewed the general notion of social obligation, and discussed the status of a number of moral norms which play a key role in our social lives, including those having to do with promissory obligation and the obligation of obedience to law. Majority rule, the rule of law, and the institutional role of the judiciary have been examined as procedural forms, while principles of justice and liberty have been dealt with as matters of substance. My conclusion, in general, is that there is no difficulty whatsoever in the act-utilitarian supporting these central elements of a social morality. In so doing, he helps to create the basis for the shared expectations upon which a viable social order depends. In addition to more or less strong ties of mutual benevolence, the bonds of reciprocity within a community of morally like minded act-utilitarians would consist primarily of such structures of shared expectations. For a member of such a community to recognize his social obligations is not for him to acknowledge the existence of binding reasons for action the status of which is independent of the consequences of his acts, but rather for him to take into account the kinds of expectations, which themselves serve as reasons for action, which are associated with the various social roles in which he is cast.

The application of moral norms, I suggested in Chapter 4, is generally diffuse, although some, such as parents, may be expected to play the primary role in their enforcement in some cases. By and large, though, it is self-application that is relied upon, or at least what would be relied upon within a community of rational and benevolent adult moral agents.

The legal case is, in this respect, quite different. Courts have binding obligations to apply the law, obligations which represent not only expectations as to how they are likely to behave, but social norms which provide them with second order reasons to fulfill these obligations. What relationship, if any, is there between the judge's obligation to apply, and the citizen's obligation to obey, the law? There is, I believe, a significant one.

As Fuller suggests, it is one of reciprocity. The obligations in both cases represent structures of mutual expectations; under appropriate conditions, the sorts of expectations which society should seek to foster. On the one hand, the integrity of the judicial role is supported by voluntary compliance to specific judicial decisions, even those which are legally and morally controversial. On the other hand, the citizen's reasons to obey the law, either in the form of general laws or particular decisions, are strengthened by the belief that it is *the law* which the courts are applying. Where the order of a court is successfully resisted, there is a good chance that the rule of law has to some extent been undermined. Where courts are suspected of lacking a firm legal ground for their decisions, both private citizens and other courts are likely to base their decisions on extralegal grounds as well. Courts wavering in their role as adjudicators, and individuals engaging in unjustified forms of resistance to law, is the inevitable product of a sustained failure on the part of either judges or citizens to fulfill their respective obligations under the rule of law. The tragic history of judicial and public resistance to school desegregation orders in the (not only Southern) United States remains a current example some twenty years after the 1954 Supreme Court decision in *Brown* v. *Board of Education.*

None of this is to say, of course, that specific legal orders ought never to be resisted, nor that courts ought never to depart from their role of adjudicators. Social norms which demand that the law be obeyed and applied are, under conditions which are surely widespread, worthy of the act-utilitarian's support. But, like other social norms, they only create reasons for action of a sort that are to be accorded no more and no less a weight than other relevant consequentialist considerations. Although society, reasonably and deliberately, may structure many of the considerations of which the conscientious moral agent can and should take account, an autonomous act is an act of an individual for which that individual, and he alone, remains responsible. For a consistently benevolent man, the act-utilitarian principle must remain the ultimate criterion of the morality of individual conduct; not in spite of, but rather in light of, the demands made by an enlightened morality of social norms in the support of which an act-utilitarian can and should in good faith participate.

Appendix:
From J.S. Mill, Principles of Political Economy, Book IV, Part XI, Section 12

To a fourth case of exception (to the laisser-faire principle) I must request particular attention; it being one to which as it appears to me, the attention of political economists has not yet been sufficiently drawn. There are matters in which the inter-ference of law is required, not to overrule the judgement of individuals respecting their own interest, but to give effect to that judgement: they being unable to give effect to it except by concert, which concert again can not be effectual unless it re-ceives validity and sanction from the law. For illustration, and without prejudging the particular point, I may advert to the question of diminishing the hours of labour. Let us suppose, what is at least supposable, whether it be the fact or not—that a general reduction of the hours of factory labour, say from ten to nine, would be for the advantage of the workpeople: that they would receive as high wages, or nearly as high, for nine hours labour as they receive for ten. If this would be the result, and if the operatives generally are convinced that it would, the limi-tation, some may say, will be adopted simultaneously. I answer, that it will not be adopted unless the body of operatives bind themselves to one another to abide by it. A workman who re-fused to work more than nine hours while there were others who worked ten, would either not be employed at all, or if employed, must submit to lose one-tenth of his wages. However convinced, therefore, he may be that it is the interest of the class to work short time, it is contrary to his own interest to set the example, unless he is well assured that all or most others will follow it. But suppose a general agreement of the whole class: might not this be effectual without the sanction of law? Not unless enforced by opinion with a rigour practically equal to that of law. For however beneficial the observance of the regulation might be to the class collectively, the immediate interest of every individual would lie in violating it: and the more numerous those were who adhered to the rule, the more would individuals gain by departing from it. If nearly all restricted themselves to nine hours, those who chose to work for ten would gain all the advantages of the restriction, together with the profit from infringing it; they would get ten hours' wages for nine hours' work, and an hour's wages besides. I grant that if a large majority adhered to the nine hours, there would be no harm done; the benefit would be, in the main, secured to the class, while those individuals who preferred to work harder and earn more, would have an opportunity of doing so. This certainly would be the state of things to be wished for; and assuming that a reduction of hours without any diminution of wages could take place without expelling the commodity from some of its markets—which is in every particular instance a question of fact, not of principle—the manner in which it would be most desirable that this effect should be brought about would be by a quiet change in the general custom of the trade; short hours becoming, by spontaneous choice, the general practice, but those who chose to deviate from it having the fullest liberty to do so. Probably, however, so many would prefer the ten hours' work on the improved terms, that the limitation could not be maintained as a general practice: what some did from choice, others would soon be obliged to do from necessity, and those who had chosen long hours for the sake of increased wages, would be forced in the end to work long hours for no greater wages than before. Assuming then that it really would be the interest of each to work only nine hours if he could be assured that all others would do the same, there might be no means for attaining this object but by converting their supposed mutual agreement into an engagement under penalty, by consenting to have it enforced by law. I am not expressing any opinion in favour of such an enactment, which has never in this country been demanded, and which I certainly should not, in present circumstances, recommend: but it serves to exemplify the manner in which these classes of persons may need the assistance of law, to give effect to their deliberate collective opinion of their own interest, by affording to every individual a guarantee that his competitors will pursue the same course, without which he can not safely adopt it himself.

Another exemplification of the same principle is afforded by what is known as the Wakefield system of colonialization. This system is grounded on the important principle, that the degree of productiveness of land and labour depends on their being in a due proportion to one another; that if a few persons in a newly settled country attempt to occupy and appropriate a large district, or if each labourer becomes too soon an occupier and cultivator of land, there is a loss of productive power, and a great retardation of the progress of the colony in wealth and civilization: that nevertheless the instinct (as it may almost be called) of appropriation, and the feelings associated in old countries with landed proprietorship, induce almost every emigrant to take possession of as much land as he has the means of acquiring, and every labourer to become at once a proprietor, cultivating his own land with no other aid than that of his family. If this propensity to the immediate possession of land could be in some degree restrained, and each labourer induced to work a certain number of years on hire before he becomes a landed proprietor, a perpetual stock of hired labourers could be maintained, available for roads, canals, works of irrigation, etc., and for establishment and carrying on of the different branches of town industry; whereby the labourer, when he did at last become a landed proprietor, would find his land much more valuable, through access to markets, and facility of obtaining hired labour. Mr. Wakefield therefore proposed to check the premature occupation of land, and dispersion of the people, by putting upon all unappropriated lands a rather high price, the proceeds of which were to be expended in conveying emigrant labourers from the mother country.

This salutary provision, however, has been objected to, in the name and on the authority of what was represented as the great principle of political economy, that individuals are the best judge of their own interest. It was said, that when things are left to themselves, land is appropriated and occupied by the spontaneous choice of individuals, in the quantities and at the times most advantageous to each person, and therefore to the community generally; and that to interpose artificial obstacles to their obtaining land, is to prevent them from adopting the course which in their own judgement is most beneficial to them, from a self-conceited notion of the legislator, that he knows what is most for their interest, better than they do themselves. Now this is a complete misunderstanding, either of the system itself, or of the principle with which it is alleged to conflict. The oversight is similar to that which we have just seen exemplified on the subject of hours of labour. However beneficial it might be to the colony in the aggregate, and to each individual composing it, that no one should occupy more land than he can properly cultivate, nor become a proprietor until there are other labourers ready to take his place in working for hire; it can never be the interest of an individual to exercise this forbearance, unless he is assured that others will do so too. Surrounded by settlers who have each their thousand acres, how is he benefited by restricting himself to fifty? or what does a labourer gain by deferring the acquisition altogether for a few years, if all other labourers rush to convert their first earnings into estates in the wilderness, several miles apart from one another? If they, by seizing on land, prevent the formation of a class of labourers for wages, he will not, by postponing the time of his becoming a proprietor, be enabled to employ the land with any greater advantage when he does obtain it; to what end therefore should he place himself in what will appear to him and others a position of inferiority, by remaining a hired labourer, when all around him are proprietors? It is the interest of each to do what is good for all, but only if others will do likewise.

The principle that each is the best judge of his own interest, understood as these objectors understand it, would prove that governments ought not to fulfill any of their acknowledged duties—ought not, in fact, to exist at all. It is greatly the interest of the community, collectively and individually, not to rob or defraud one another: but there is not the less necessity for laws to punish robbery and fraud; because, though it is in the interest of each that nobody should rob or cheat, it is not any one's interest to refrain from robbing and cheating others when all others are permitted to rob and cheat him. Penal laws exist at all, chiefly for this reason—because even an unanimous opinion that a certain line of conduct is for the general interest, does not always make it people's individual interest to adhere to that line of conduct.

Reference Bibliography

Armstrong, W.E., "Utility and the Theory of Welfare." *Oxford Economic Papers, New Series,* Vol. 3, 1951.

Arrow, Kenneth J., *Social Choice and Individual Values,* 2d Ed. New York: John Wiley and Sons, Inc., 1963.

————, "Some Ordinalist-Utilitarian Notes on Rawls's Theory of Justice." *Journal of Philosophy,* Vol. LXX, No. 9, 1973.

Austin, John, *The Province of Jurisprudence Determined.* New York: The Noonday Press, 1954.

Austin, J.L., "Performative Utterances," in Austin, *Philosophical Papers.* Oxford: Oxford University Press, 1961.

Baier, Kurt, *The Moral Point of View.* Ithaca, New York: Cornell University Press, 1958.

Bambrough, Renford, "Universals and Family Resemblances." *Proceedings of the Aristotelian Society,* Vol. LXI, 1960-1961.

Barry, Brian, *The Liberal Theory of Justice.* Oxford: Oxford University Press, 1973.

————, "The Public Interest." *Proceedings of the Aristotelian Society,* Supplementary Vol. 38, 1964.

Baumol, William J., *Welfare Economics and the Theory of the State,* 2d Ed. Cambridge, Massachusetts: Harvard University Press, 1965.

Berman, Harold J., and William R. Greiner, *The Nature and Functions of Law.* Brooklyn, New York: The Foundation Press, Inc., 1966.

Black, Duncan, *The Theory of Committees and Elections.* Cambridge: Cambridge University Press, 1963.

Brandt, Richard, "The Concepts of Obligation and Duty." *Mind,* Vol. 73, No. 291, 1964.

————, "Rational Desires." *Proceedings of the American Philosophical Association,* Vol. XLIII, 1969-1970.

————, "Some Merits of One Form of Rule Utilitarianism." *University of Colorado Studies Series in Philosophy,* No. 3. Boulder, Colorado: University of Colorado Press, 1967.

————, "A Utilitarian Theory of Excuses." *Philosophical Review,* Vol. 78, No. 3, 1969.

Buchanan, James, *The Demand and Supply of Public Goods.* Chicago: Rand McNally & Company, 1968.

———, "Ethical Rules, Expected Values, and Large Numbers. *Ethics,* Vol. LXXVI, No. 1, October, 1965.

Buchanan, James, and Gordon Tullock, *The Calculus of Consent.* Ann Arbor, Michigan: University of Michigan Press, 1963.

Carnap, Rudolf, *The Logical Foundations of Probability,* 2d Ed. Chicago: University of Chicago Press, 1962.

Christie, George, "The Model of Principles." *Duke Law Journal,* 1968.

Cohen, Morris R., *Reason and Law.* New York: Collier Books, 1961.

Dahl, Norman, "Is Mill's Hedonism Inconsistent?," in N. Rescher (ed.), *Studies in Ethics.* American Philosophical Quarterly Monograph Series, No. 7. Oxford: Basil Blackwell, 1973.

Devlin, Lord Patrick, *The Enforcement of Morals.* Oxford: Oxford University Press, 1965.

———, "Mill On Liberty In Morals," in Devlin, *The Enforcement of Morals.* Oxford: Oxford University Press, 1965.

———, "Morals and Contemporary Social Reality," in Devlin, *The Enforcement of Morals.* Oxford: Oxford University Press, 1965.

———, "Morals and the Criminal Law," in Devlin, *The Enforcement of Morals.* Oxford: Oxford University Press, 1965.

Dickenson, John, "The Law Behind Law." *Columbia Law Review,* Vol. 29, 1929.

———, "Legal Rules: Their Application and Formulation." *University of Pennsylvania Law Review,* Vol. 79, 1931.

———, "Legal Rules: Their Function in the Process of Decision," *University of Pennsylvania Law Review,* Vol. 79, 1931.

Downie, R.S., "Social Roles and Moral Responsibility." *Philosophy,* Vol. 39, No. 147, 1964.

Dworkin, Gerald, "Paternalism," in Richard Wasserstrom (ed.), *Morality and the Law.* (See also Wasserstrom.)

Dworkin, Ronald, "Judicial Discretion." *Journal of Philosophy,* Vol. LX, No. 21, 1963.

———, "Lord Devlin and the Enforcement of Morals." *Yale Law Journal,* Vol. 75, 1966.

———, "The Model of Rules." *University of Chicago Law Review,* Vol. 35, 1967.

———, "On Not Prosecuting Civil Disobedience." *New York Review of Books,* 1968.

———, "Philosophy, Morality, and Law—Observations Prompted By Professor Fuller's Novel Claim." *University of Pennsylvania Law Review,* Vol. 113, 1965.

———, "Social Rules and Legal Theory." *Yale Law Journal,* Vol. 81, No. 5, 1972.

Falk, David, "Morality, Self, and Others," in H. Castenada and George Nakhnikian (eds.), *Morality and the Language of Conduct.* Detroit, Michigan: Wayne State University Press, 1963.

Feeley, Malcolm, "Coercion and Compliance: A New Look at an Old Problem." *Law and Society Review,* Vol. 4, No. 4, 1970.

———, "A Solution to the 'Voting Dilemma' in Modern Democratic Theory." *Ethics*, Vol. 84, No. 3, April, 1974.

Feinberg, Joel, "Forms and Limits of Utilitarianism." *Philosophical Review*, Vol. 76, No. 3, 1967.

———, "Supererogation and Rules." *Ethics*, Vol. 71, No. 4, 1961.

Freund, Paul, "Social Policy and the Law," in Richard Brandt (ed.), *Social Justice*. Englewood Cliffs, New Jersey: Prentice-Hall, Inc., 1962.

Fried, Charles, *An Anatomy of Values*. Cambridge, Massachusetts: Harvard, University Press, 1970.

Frolich, Norman, and Joe A. Oppenheimer, "I Get By With a Little Help From My Friends." *World Politics*, Vol. 23, 1970-71.

Fuller, Lon, "Collective Bargaining and the Arbitrator." *Wisconsin Law Review*, Vol. 1963, No. 1, 1963.

———, "The Forms and Limits of Adjudication," unpublished mimeo.

———, *The Law In Quest of Itself*. Evanston, Illinois: Northwestern University Press, 1940.

———, *The Morality of Law*, 2d Ed. New Haven, Connecticut: Yale University Press, 1969.

———, "Positivism and Fidelity to Law." *Harvard Law Review*, Vol. 71, 1958.

Galanter, Eugene, "An Axiomatic and Experimental Study of Sensory Order and Measure." *Psychological Review*, Vol. 63, 1956.

Gellner, Ernest, "Contemporary Thought and Politics." *Philosophy*, Vol. 32, No. 123, 1957.

Gilmore, Grant, "Law, Logic, and Experience." *Howard Law Journal*, Vol. 3, 1957.

Goodhart, A.L., "An Apology for Jurisprudence," in Paul Sayre (ed.), *Interpretations of Modern Legal Philosophies*. New York: Oxford University Press, 1957.

Goodman, Nelson, *The Structure of Appearance*, 2d Ed. Indianapolis, Indiana: The Bobbs-Merrill Company, Inc., 1966.

Gorovitz, S. (ed.), *Mill: Utilitarianism, With Critical Essays*. Indianapolis, Indiana: The Bobbs-Merrill Company, Inc., 1971.

Gottlieb, Gidon, *The Logic of Choice*. New York: The Macmillan Company, 1968.

Gray, J.C., *The Nature and Sources of the Law*, 2d Ed. New York: The Macmillan Company, 1927.

Harrison, Jonathan, "Utilitarianism, Universalization, and Our Duty to be Just." *Proceedings of the Aristotelian Society*, Vol. 53, 1952-1953.

Harrod, R.F., "Utilitarianism Revised." *Mind*, Vol. 45, No. 2, 1936.

Harsanyi, John, "Cardinal Welfare, Individualistic Ethics, and Interpersonal Comparisons of Utility." *Journal of Political Economy*, Vol. 63, 1955.

Hart, Henry M., Jr., and Albert M. Sacks, *The Legal Process: Basic Problems in the Making and Application of Law*. Cambridge, Massachusetts: mimeo, 1958.

Hart. H.L.A. "Are There Any Natural Rights?" *Philosophical Review*, Vol. 64, 1955.

———, *The Concept of Law*. Oxford: Oxford University Press, 1961.

———, "Definition and Theory in Jurisprudence." *Law Quarterly Review*, Vol. 70, 1954.

———, "Immorality and Treason." *The Listener*, Vol. 62, 1959.

———, *Law, Liberty, and Morality*. Stanford, California: Stanford University Press, 1963.

———, "Legal and Moral Obligation," in A.I. Melden (ed.), *Essays in Moral Philosophy*. Seattle, Washington: University of Washington Press, 1958.

———, "Positivism and the Separation of Law and Morals." *Harvard Law Review*, Vol. 71, 1958.

———, *Punishment and Responsibility*. Oxford: Oxford University Press, 1968.

———, "Social Solidarity and the Enforcement of Morality." *Chicago Law Review*, Vol. 35, 1967.

———, "Theory and Definition in Jurisprudence." *Proceedings of the Aristotelian Society*, Supplementary Vol. 29, 1955.

Hempel, Carl G., "A Logical Appraisal of Operationism," in Philipp G. Frank (ed.), *The Validation of Scientific Theories*. New York: Collier Books, 1961.

Hobbes, Thomas, *Leviathan*. Oxford: Basil Blackwell, 1957.

Hodgson, D.H., *Consequences of Utilitarianism*. Oxford: Oxford University Press, 1967.

Hoebel, E.A., and Karl Llewelyn, *The Cheyenne Way: Conflict and Case Law in Primitive Jurisprudence*. Norman, Oklahoma: University of Oklahoma Press, 1941.

Hume, David, "Of the Original Contract," in Henry D. Aiken (ed.), *Hume's Moral and Political Philosophy*. New York: Hafner Publishing Company, 1948.

———, *A Treatise of Human Nature*. Oxford: The Clarendon Press, 1888.

Kadish, M.R., and S.H. Kadish, *Discretion to Disobey*. Stanford, California: Stanford University Press, 1973.

———, "On Justified Rule Departures By Officials." *California Law Review*, Vol. 59, No. 4, 1971.

Kadish, S., "The Crisis of Overcriminalization." *Annals of the American Academy of Political and Social Science*, 1967.

Kelsen, Hans, *General Theory of Law and State*, Anders Wedberg (trans.). New York: Russell and Russell, 1961.

———, "On the Basic Norm." *California Law Review*, Vol. 47, 1959.

Krislov, Samuel, *The Supreme Court and Political Freedom*. New York: The Free Press, 1968.

Kuhn, Thomas, *The Structure of Scientific Revolutions*. Chicago: University of Chicago Press, 1962.

Lemmon, E.J., "Moral Dilemmas." *The Philosophical Review*, Vol. 81, No. 2, 1962.

Lewis, David, *Convention*. Cambridge, Massachusetts: Harvard University Press, 1969.

———, "Utilitarianism and Truthfulness." *Australasian Journal of Philosophy*, Vol. 50, No. 1, May, 1972.

Little, I.M.D., *A Critique of Welfare Economics*, 2d Ed. Oxford: Oxford University Press, 1967.

Locke, John, *Second Treatise of Government*. New York: The Liberal Arts Press, 1952.

Louch, A.R., "Sins and Crimes." *Philosophy*, Vol. 43, 1968.

Luce, R. Duncan, and Howard Raiffa, *Games and Decisions*. New York: John Wiley and Sons, Inc., 1957.

Lyons, David, *Forms and Limits of Utilitarianism*. Oxford: Oxford University Press, 1965.

———, *In the Interest of the Governed*. Oxford: Oxford University Press, 1973.

———, "On Sanctioning Excuses." *Journal of Philosophy*, Vol. LXVI, No. 19, 1969.

MacCallum, Gerald, "Dworkin on Judicial Discretion." *Journal of Philosophy*, Vol. LX, No. 21, 1963.

McCloskey, H.J., "Ross and the Concept of a Prima Facie Duty." *Australasian Journal of Philosophy*, Vol. 41, No. 3, 1963.

McNaughton, Robert, "A Metrical Concept of Happiness." *Philosophy and Phenomenological Research*, Vol. 41, 1953-1954.

Malinowski, Bronislaw, *Crime and Custom in Savage Society*. Paterson, New Jersey: Littlefield Adams and Co., 1962.

Marshall, Geoffrey, "Justiciability," in A.G. Guest (ed.), *Oxford Essays in Jurisprudence*. Oxford: Oxford University Press, 1961.

Mason, A.T., *Harlan Fiske Stone: Pillar of the Law*. New York: Viking Press, 1956.

Mill, John Stuart, *On Liberty*. Indianapolis, Indiana: The Bobbs-Merrill Company, Inc., 1956.

———, *Principles of Political Economy*, Donald Winch (ed.). Harmondsworth, England: Penguin Books, 1970.

———, *Utilitarianism*. Indianapolis, Indiana: The Bobbs-Merrill Company, Inc., 1957.

Miller, Bruce L., *Principles, Rules, and Cases: The Logic of Judicial Decisions*, Ph.D. dissertation. Cleveland, Ohio: Case Western Reserve University, 1970.

Moore, G.E., *Principia Ethica*. Cambridge: Cambridge University Press, 1903.

Morris, Herbert, "Persons and Punishment." *The Monist*, Vol. 52, No. 4, 1968.

Murphy, Jeffrie, "In Defense of Obligation," in J. Roland Pennock and John Chapman (eds.), *Nomos XII: Political and Legal Obligation*. New York: Atherton Press, 1970.

Nagel, Thomas, "Rawls on Justice." *Philosophical Review*, Vol. 82, No. 2, 1973.

Narveson, Jan, *Morality and Utility*. Baltimore, Maryland: The Johns Hopkins Press, 1967.

———, "Utilitarianism and New Generations." *Mind*, Vol. 76, No. 1, 1967.

———, "Promising, Expecting, and Utility." *Canadian Journal of Philosophy*, Vol. 1, No. 2, 1971.

———, "Utilitarianism and New Generations." *Mind*, Vol. 76, No. 1, 1967.

Nozick, Robert, "Moral Complications and Moral Structures." *Natural Law Forum*, Vol. 13, 1968.

Olson, Mancur, *The Logic of Collective Action*. Cambridge, Massachusetts: Harvard University Press, 1971.

Perry, Thomas D., "Judicial Method and the Concept of Reasoning." *Ethics*, Vol. 80, No. 1, 1969.

Pitcher, George, *The Philosophy of Wittgenstein*. Englewood Cliffs, New Jersey: Prentice-Hall, Inc., 1964.

Putnam, Hilary, "The Analytic and the Synthetic," in Herbert Feigl and Grover Maxwell (eds.), *Minnesota Studies in the Philosophy of Science*, Vol. III. Minneapolis, Minnesota: University of Minnesota Press, 1962.

Quine, W.V.O., "Two Dogmas of Empiricism," in Quine, *From a Logical Point of View*. Cambridge, Massachusetts: Harvard University Press, 1953.

———, "Ontological Reduction and the World of Numbers." *Journal of Philosophy*, Vol. LXI, No. 7, 1964.

Radcliff, P. (ed.), *Limits of Liberty*. Belmont, California:Wadsworth Publishing Company, 1966.

Rawls, John, *A Theory of Justice*. Cambridge, Massachusetts: Harvard University Press, 1971.

———, "Justice as Fairness." *Philosophical Review*, Vol. 67, No. 2, 1958.

———, "Two Concepts of Rules." *Philosophical Review*, Vol. 64, No. 1, 1955.

Raz, Joseph, "Legal Principles and the Limits of Law." *Yale Law Journal*, Vol. 81, No. 5, 1972.

Riker, William H., and Peter C. Ordeshook, *An Introduction to Positive Political Theory*. Englewood Cliffs, New Jersey: Prentice-Hall, Inc., 1973.

Robbins, Lionel, *An Essay on the Nature and Significance of Economic Science*. London: Macmillan and Company, 1932.

Ross, Alf, *On Law and Justice*. Los Angeles, California: University of California Press, 1959.

Ross, W.D., *The Right and the Good*. Oxford: Oxford University Press, 1930.

Rostow, E., "The Enforcement of Morals." *Cambridge Law Journal*, 1960.

Rousseau, J.J., *The Social Contract*, H.J. Tozer (trans.). London: 1895.

Runciman, W.G., and A.K. Sen, "Games, Justice, and the General Will," *Mind*, Vol. 74, 1965.

St. John-Stevas, Norman, *Life, Death, and the Law.* New York: World Publishing Company, 1964. Reprinted in part in Radcliff (ed.), *Limits of Liberty.*

Sartorius, Rolf, "Book Review: *In the Interest of the Governed.*" *Journal of Philosophy,* Vol. LXXI, No. 17, October, 1974.

———, "Book Review: *The Logic of Choice.*" *Harvard Law Review,* Vol. 82, No. 8, 1969.

———, "The Concept of Law." *Archives for Philosophy of Law and Social Philosophy,* Vol. LII, No. 2, 1966.

———, "The Doctrine of Precedent and the Problem of Relevance." *Archives for Philosophy of Law and Social Philosophy,* Vol. LIII, No. 3, 1967.

———, "The Enforcement of Morality." *Yale Law Journal,* Vol. 81, No. 5, 1972.

———, "Individual Conduct and Social Norms." *Ethics,* Vol. 82, No. 3, 1972.

———, "The Justification of the Judicial Decision." *Ethics,* Vol. 78, No. 3, 1968.

———, "Social Policy and Judicial Legislation." *American Philosophical Quarterly,* Vol. 8, No. 2, 1971.

———, "Utilitarianism and Obligation." *Journal of Philosophy,* Vol. LXVI, No. 3, 1969.

Scheffler, L., *The Anatomy of Inquiry.* New York: Alfred A. Knopf, Inc., 1963.

———, "On Justification and Commitment." *Journal of Philosophy,* Vol. LI, 1954.

Schelling, Thomas C., *The Strategy of Conflict.* Cambridge, Massachusetts: Harvard University Press, 1960.

Scriven, M., "Definitions, Explanations, and Theories," in H. Feigl, M. Scriven, and G. Maxwell (eds.), *Minnesota Studies in the Philosophy of Science,* Vol. II. Minneapolis, Minnesota: University of Minnesota Press, 1958.

Searle, John, "How to Derive 'Ought' From 'Is.'" *Philosophical Review,* Vol. 73, No. 1, 1964.

———, *Speech Acts.* Cambridge: Cambridge University Press, 1970.

Sen, A.K., *Collective Choice and Social Welfare.* San Francisco, California: Holden-Day, Inc., 1970.

Shklar, Judith, *Legalism.* Cambridge, Massachusetts: Harvard University Press, 1964.

Shwayder, David, *The Stratification of Behavior.* London: Routledge and Kegan Paul, 1965.

Sidgwick, Henry, *The Methods of Ethics,* 7th Ed. New York: Dover Publications, Inc., 1966.

Simon, Herbert, *Models of Man.* New York: John Wiley and Sons, Inc., 1957.

Slote, M.A., "The Theory of Important Criteria." *Journal of Philosophy,* Vol. LXIII, No. 8, 1966.

Smart, J.J.C., *An Outline of a System of Utilitarian Ethics.* Melbourne, Australia: Melbourne University Press, 1961.

Smart, J.J.C., and B. Williams, *Utilitarianism: For and Against.* Cambridge: Cambridge University Press, 1973.

Stephen, James Fitzjames, *Liberty, Equality, Fraternity.* London, 1873.

Stevenson, C.L., "Persuasive Definitions." *Mind,* Vol. 47, 1938.

Strang, Colin, "What If Everyone Did That?" *Durham University Journal,* Vol. 53, 1960.

Thurstone, L.L., and Lyle V. Jones, "The Rational Origin for Measuring Subjective Values." *Journal of the American Statistical Association,* Vol. 52, December, 1957.

Toulmin, Stephen, *An Examination of the Place of Reason in Ethics.* Cambridge: Cambridge University Press, 1950.

"Understanding the Model of Rules." Note, *Yale Law Journal,* Vol. 81, No. 5, 1972.

Urmson, J.O., "The Interpretation of the Moral Philosophy of J.S. Mill." *The Philosophical Quarterly,* Vol. 3, No. 1, 1953.

Waismann, F., "Verifiability," in Anthony Flew (ed.), *Essays on Logic and Language,* First Series. Oxford: Basil Blackwell, 1960.

Waldner, Ilmar, "The Empirical Meaningfulness of Interpersonal Utility Comparisons." *Journal of Philosophy,* Vol. LXIX, No. 4, 1972.

Waltzer, M., *Obligations.* Cambridge, Massachusetts: Harvard University Press, 1970.

Wasserstrom, Richard, *The Judicial Decision.* Stanford, California: Stanford University Press, 1961.

———— (ed.), *Morality and the Law.* Belmont, California: Wadsworth Publishing Co., 1971.

————, "The Obligation to Obey the Law." *UCLA Law Review,* Vol. 10, May, 1963.

————, "Strict Liability in the Criminal Law." *Stanford Law Review,* Vol. 12, 1960.

Weiler, Paul, "Legal Values and Judicial Decision Making." *The Canadian Bar Review,* Vol. 1970, 1970.

————, "Two Models of Judicial Decision Making." *The Canadian Bar Review,* Vol. 1968, 1968.

Whiteley, C.H., "On Duties." *Proceedings of the Aristotelian Society,* Vol. 53, 1952-1953.

Wittgenstein, L., *Philosophical Investigations.* New York: The Macmillan Company, 1953.

Wolfenden Committee, *Report of the Committee on Homosexual Offenses and Prostitution.* London: Stern and Day, 1963.

Wolff, Robert Paul, "Beyond Tolerance," in H. Marcuse, B. Jones, and R. Wolff (eds.), *A Critique of Pure Tolerance.* Boston: Beacon Press, 1965.

————, *In Defense of Anarchism.* New York: Harper and Row, 1970.

————, "On Violence." *Journal of Philosophy,* Vol. LXVI, No. 19, 1969.